Adonis & Abbey Studies in African Cultures and the Diaspora

***Series Editor*: Osita Okagbue**

Resistance and Politics in Contemporary East African Theatre

Trends in Ugandan Theatre Since 1960

Published by

Adonis & Abbey Publishers Ltd

United Kingdom
Southbank House
Black Prince Road
London
SE1 7SJ
United Kingdom
Emails: editor@adonis-abbey.com,
Tel: 0845 388 7248

Nigeria
No.3 Akanu Ibiam Street,
Aso-villa, Asokoro.
P.O. Box 10546
Abuja
Tel: +234 (0) 8165970458, 07066997765

Year of Publication 2013

British Library Cataloguing-in-Publication Data
A catalogue record for this book is available from the British Library

ISBN: 9781909112384

Resistance and Politics in Contemporary East African Theatre

Trends in Ugandan Theatre Since 1960

Samuel Kasule

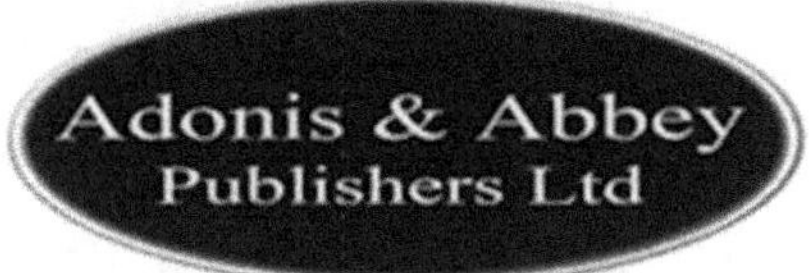

Dedication

I dedicate this book to my father, Michael W. Kalule, one of the thousands of victims of armed violence.

Table of Contents

ACKNOWLEDGEMENTS

The publication of this book is an appropriate time to acknowledge the people who have helped in the process of its writing. I would like to begin by thanking Professor Martin Banham, Emeritus Professor of African Theatre at Leeds University, for his generous support, patience and advice when I was starting the most of this research. I would also like to thank friends and scholars in the field of theatre and performing arts who I met at Makerere and Leeds Universities and in the African Theatre Association: Peter Cooke, Edward Kasolo Kimuli, Patrick Mangeni, Slyvia Nannyonga-Tamusuza, Olu Obafemi, Jumai Ewu, Ssalongo Justinian Tamusuza, Victor Ukaegbu, and and many others who helped me but wish to remain anonymous. I must also thank Osita Okagbue who supported and encouraged me to undertake this project. I need to thank S.S. Busulwa, Flavia Nalwanga, Edward Kasolo Kimuli and Joseph Walugembe, who assisted me when I visited Uganda to research into theatre and *KinaUganda.*

For financial help to write this book and to travel to Uganda, I am most grateful to the Arts and Humanities Research Council and the University of Derby research awards scheme. Finally, I owe a debt of gratitude to my wife, Claire, and my children, Michael, Alice and Jill-Charlotte for their tolerance and love. Without all of you, it would have been difficult to complete this work.

The author and publishers would like to thank the following for permission to reproduce copyrighted material:

Previously published version or portions of chapter 3 appeared in 'More than just Musical Plays: Intersections of Politics and Folklore in Byron Kawadwa's Theatre', *African Performance Review*, Vol. 3, No., 1, 2009.

PREFACE

In June 1894, Britain colonised and declared a protectorate over an area made up of different indigenous political states and systems, ranging from kingdoms of Buganda, Bunyoro, Tooro and Ankole, with hereditary kings while the others such as Acholi, Bugisu, Lango and Teso, among other smaller states, had republican political organisation.[1] These republican states elected their leaders and could remove them if they did not fulfil what they had been elected to do. The whole area was named Uganda. Nevertheless, traditional enmity and hostility existed among and between communities such as Buganda and Bunyoro or Acholi and Lango. Baganda (Muganda for individuals) are people from the Buganda region. The concept Kiganda denotes that which belongs to the Baganda, for example culture, dance, music and dress. Ganda, another concept, is used synonymously with Kiganda. Banyoro (Munyolo for individuals) are people from Bunyoro. The concept Kinyoro denotes that which belongs to the Banyoro. Because of the traditional rivalry between the Baganda and the Banyoro, the former label all non-Baganda (strangers) Banyolo. Finally, Banyankole (Munyankole for individuals) means people from Ankole.

At the turn of the nineteenth century, European travelers and colonial administrators give conflicting reports about these people's theatrical expressions. Writing in *Uganda*, early European travelers, Thomas and Robert Scott, describe the protectorate as a 'collection of *mutually hostile tribes*, each adhering to its traditional ways' that have 'been fitted into an organized state which conforms to certain rules of conduct generally related to the framework of British civilization' (1935: 272) (emphasis added). Similar to other Europeans, they write simplistic interpretations of Ugandan performance: 'There is little evidence of any genius for the plastic arts among the local tribes' and '[t]he only means by which the very great majority of natives are able to give expression to their artistic sensibilities is through dancing' (1935: 294). While we cannot know what these dances signified to the travelers, later European missionaries to the country introduced the literary form of expression, which they sought to substitute the indigenous orality with. They were less inclined to encourage activities related to storytelling and recitations, perhaps since they found them neither entertaining nor equivalent to performances in some of their folk cultures. Specifically, they attempted to '[turn] the indigenous theatrical activities ... into instruments of their own power' (Diana Taylor, 1991: 27). The European missionaries and colonial administrators, however, considered festivals/rituals, indigenous religious worship/spectacles, and musical instruments, as *taboo* or pagan. Today theatrical elements, including role-playing, mimicry, dance and song, embedded within these forms, play a significant role in contemporary theatre.[2] Indigenous theatre expressions offer more unique possibilities such as aspects of style that have been inserted into performance scripts to capture the dialogue between audience and performers including repetition. In a way, theatre's popularity over the period covered by this book has been enhanced by music and dance, which overlap with a Ugandan conception of performance and resistance.

My central premise in this book is that indigenous theatrical expressions, colonization and the culture of violence were fundamental in influencing contemporary theatre in Uganda. The book will demonstrate how performance and politics have been interconnected. Performances of power unfolded in Uganda beginning with 1894 when Uganda was colonised. When Apollo Milton Obote, leader of Uganda People's Congress (UPC), became the Prime Minister at independence in 1962, his reign, generally referred to as Obote I, was overshadowed by problems. Two years after independence in 1962, the 1964 referendum on the disputed 'lost counties'[3] rekindled the traditional conflicts between Buganda and Bunyoro. The Baganda did not accept the legitimacy of such a referendum and agitated for Buganda's secession from Uganda. This climaxed in the Nakulabye Massacre[4] when members of the armed forces killed twelve civilians. It was the 'first major application of political violence in independent Uganda and the first time that civilians in Uganda perceived that the violence was politically motivated, aimed at a specific section of society' (Abdu Kasozi, 1994: 80). Kasozi writes, 'Nakulabye inaugurated the use of the gun by government agents, who have been pointing it at civilians ever since' (Kasozi, 1994: 80). The political standoff resulted in the 1966 May Revolt that was crushed by the army and special force. Whereas Obote, Uganda's first Prime Minister, regarded the 1966 crisis as an attack on religious discrimination, 'Bugandaism'[5] and indigenous differences, the Baganda viewed this as a crucial betrayal of their trust. In attempting to explore viable solutions to these problems, the educated elite responded by writing and performing plays about the shared communal experiences.

A consequence of this violence was the removal of the Independence Constitution, the imposition of a Republican Constitution in 1967 as well as a state of emergency in Buganda that lasted until 1971. According to Edward Khiddu Makubuya, 'the period 1966-71 saw the emergence and active operation of a paramilitary organisation called the General Service Department'. This security organ was 'instrumental in the torture, harassment, and persecution of real and imaginary opponents of the government of the time' (1979: 149). Obote, ambitious to detribalise Uganda and propagate a nationalistic system, argued that his move was to enhance nationalism and address religious discrimination, Bugandaism and tribalism. As a result, the Baganda, concerned that the government was denying them their cultural identity and curtailing the individual freedom mobilized themselves into cells of resistance. On one side was the government, the army, indigenous states conquered by the Baganda in pre-colonial times, and people who subscribed to the UPC republican ideologies. While on the other side were the conservative pro-federal Baganda elites and peasants. On 25 January 1971, however, Amin, the army, and a cross-section of Ugandans staged the performance of power to mark the deposition of Obote and his sympathizers. This time, not only the Baganda, but also most indigenous communities who had been terrorized by the UPC government's General Service Unit, and the paramilitary police, staged celebrations. People gathered at Kololo airstrip, a space used by the British to hand over the instruments of independence to Uganda in 1962, to celebrate the *coup d'état*. Elsewhere in village compounds, trading centres and towns, people wearing traditional dress played and sung indigenous music, previously banned by the defunct government, purporting that they were sectarian songs that celebrated their indigenous identity.

General Idi Amin's regime was murderous, rapacious and tyrannical. Amin's move to Africanise businesses and all aspects of Ugandan society was underlined by his declaration of the 'Economic War' in 1972. His years of terror were characterised by military tribunals, which exercised summary executions and suppressed communal resistance, disappearances, persecution of non-indigenous Ugandans, torture, imprisonment, mass murders and violence. On 11 April, liberation forces supported by the Tanzanian Army overthrew Amin and appointed Yusuf Lule to lead the government. The Military

Commission, composed of representatives of different fighting groups, threw out Yusufu Lule on 20 June 1979. When general elections were held on 10 and 11 December 1980, Obote was elected back into office. Between 1980 and 1985, a period generally referred to as Obote II, the second UPC government faced an armed resistance and a civil war located in Buganda or what came to be known as the 'Luwero Triangle'. Once again, on July 27 1985, a combined force of the army and a coalition of fighting groups led by General Tito Okello overthrew Obote. Throughout the brief period of military rule between July and December 1985, the army killed people with impunity. However, Yoweri Museveni's National Resistance Movement army forced them out of power on 25 January 1986.

The social madness euphemistically referred to as Oboteism and Aminism transformed theatre into a space where, particularly after Amin, stage presentations focused on shared communal and personal experience. As a post-colonial phenomenon that merged socialism and nationalism, Oboteism *falsely* conflated Obote (the individual) and national liberation. Although the UPC Party song, 'The congress of the people', chanted by his party followers and some members of the armed forces, alluded to his love for the nation, it disguised the reality that the majority of the Baganda did not favour his return. This was in spite of the fact that there was a national general election. These sentiments were reflected in newspaper reports, which alerted people to the return of Akena Adoko, the previous Head of the General Service Unit under the first Obote government, also referred to as Obote I. Consequently, for the people, the spectacle of the second UPC government became a theatre of disappearances, horror, and silence. This is underlined by the failed *mayumba kkumi* (ten house cells) system, a project by which the state reduced the public space and placed ordinary people under surveillance. The struggle between Tito Okello Lutwa's forces, who overthrew the UPC government, and various warlords and fighting groups (1985 - 1986),[6] resulted in increased acts of murder, disappearances, looting, oppression and surveillance. There were abortive attempts to reach a peaceful agreement between the fighting groups and Yoweri Museveni's National Liberation Movement but the conflicting agendas made it difficult to enforce the agreements. Therefore, the NRA attacked and expelled the soldiers who had pillaged, raped and murdered ordinary people.

Taylor's influential book, *Disappearing Acts: Spectacles of Gender and Nationalism in Argentina's "Dirty War"* (1997), which looks at the way artists used theatre and performance to resist and subvert the oppressive institutions during the "Dirty War" (1976-1983), gives a focus to the discussion about terror and resistance. In ways that echo the Argentinean people's experience under military rule, Ugandans 'were assigned to spectatorship - watching themselves looking up to (or out for) the military, scrutinizing others' (Taylor, 1997: 94). The military police, paramilitary, and intelligence service sirens and gunshots as well as 'screams of victims broke the imposed quiet' of the government (Taylor, 1997: 94). The use of cultural performances as a counterpoint to the disappearances, murders and violence that was important to the ordinary people, attracted Amin's attention; hence, soon after the 1977 Festival of African Arts and Culture (FESTAC) he 'disappeared' and murdered artists including Byron Kawadwa and Galabuzi Mukasa.

The aim of this book is not to show that the culture of violence made it possible for theatre to exist but where it is evident, political violence would be shown to have influenced the performances. Various performances are not overtly political, therefore, requiring political details to help contextualize how the artists made them relevant to the audience. However, there are moments when the relation between performance and politics is vivid, for example, in Chapters 2, 3 and 4.

Resistance and Politics in Contemporary East African Theatre illustrates the richness of Ugandan theatre, introduces selected artists, plays and performances that have challenged various Ugandan oppressive political systems. It seeks to focus on a variety of plays and performances that reflect a range of ideas relating to the function of theatre in contesting authority. Thus, each chapter is informed by the interplay of politics, theatre and performance.

The case studies selected represent dramas and performances of the period covered in the book. Undeniably, it is impossible to do justice to the rich and varied output of theatre and performances staged since 1962 as well as the socio-political situation entailed. While highlighting these aspects, the book continually engages with individual playwrights and groups that present different experiences and forms of performance - hence the use of interviews in Chapters 3 and 4.

The first chapter introduces the book and reflects on the character and nature of post-colonial Ugandan theatre. It explores ideas of theatre revolving around the notion of *katemba* or performance. Concentrating on debates on the concept of performance and its function in society and the experience of political oppression, the discussion introduces resistance, theatre, performance, audience and the performance contexts. The term performance is used here as a concept that consists of various practices, such as dance, song and ritual, which do not assume the idea of a specific stage (see Taylor and Townsend, 2008: 2). As a broader concept, performance provides us with the opportunity to include distinctive pre-colonial practices such as *okukuba ebivuga* (playing instrumental music), *okuzannya emizannyo* (staging plays), *okunnyumya engero* (storytelling), *okwevuga* or *okutontoma* (recitations), *okuzina* (dance and dance-dramas), and *okukola emikolo* (performing rituals). Today acts of performances are not referred to as theatre but, *nnyimba* (folksongs), *mazina* (dances), *bitontome* (recitation), *mikolo* (festivals/rituals), *mizannyo* (games or plays) and, beginning with colonial times, *katemba*, theatre/drama.

Using different critical approaches, it examines the interrelations of politics and performance as they apply to Uganda's post-colonial theatre since 1962. This period is not arbitrary for, it includes moments where resistance occupied a central place in theatre. Through their works and critical essays Pio Zirimu, Okot p'Bitek and Robert Serumaga demonstrate that this was undertaken using indigenous theatrical expressions. Chapter 3 examines the resistance context but from a different perspective, exploring the work and role of Byron Kawadwa. Music is significant in the construction of oppositional performance and instrumental in the development of the plot and enjoyment of the plays. The fourth chapter examines the theatre of Wycliff Kiyingi who pioneered radio, television and stage drama. Framed by an in-depth interview with the playwright, this chapter examines the relationship between politics and theatre using a selection of plays centred on authoritarianism. The fifth chapter provides a detailed examination of the work of Cliff Lubwa p'Chong. Concerned with the contestation of authority it explores how theatre functions as a syncretic and intra-cultural performance. It reveals how the state is a contested space where varied indigenous cultures co-exist. Chapter 6 explores the drama of Eli Kyeyune, John Ruganda,

Nuwa Sentongo and Elvania Namukwaya Zirimu. While Elvania Zirimu's immersion in cultural politics makes her a good model for political resistance, Eli Kyeyune, Ruganda and Sentongo's writing with the emphasis on indigenous theatrical expressions as well as post-colonial politics provides a significant image of Ugandan theatre. Collectively, their work demonstrates that while it is not possible to translate the world of folklore tradition into performance, playwrights should be able to reimagine and re-express it. Chapter 7 looks at music theatre as the most dynamic and most subversive in which Ugandan artists significantly challenge authority and the parameters of performance. Finally, Chapter 8 explores the role of new media in transforming the performance landscape in Uganda. Framed by interviews with Mariam Ndagire and Ashraf Simwogerere, two leading directors of *KinaUganda*, it examines the view that the genre has threatened the role of theatre.

A Note on Translation

In order to make it accessible to a wider community, I have translated from Luganda, Runyoro, and Runyankore and Swahili originals into English when translations have not been available. What I have valued most, in my attempt to bring it to a new audience, are the intellectual, practical and social connections that have shaped my understanding of this area as well as the people who have supported me on this journey.

Chapter 1: Introduction

THE CHANGING FACE OF THEATRE AND PERFORMANCE IN UGANDA

This book draws together different forms of performances-indigenous theatre, dramas, musical theatre, home movies - to signify ways in which these practices have contested authority. The discussion revolves around theatre and performance - with the aim of showing how these practices have contributed to the struggle against political oppression in Uganda. One of the assumptions often made by scholars is that theatre, which is linear and representational, is closely associated with the arrival of missionaries and colonial administrators and the construction of the Uganda National Cultural Centre (UNCC) in 1962. On the other hand, performance, which is more presentational, is identified with non-scripted practices including indigenous theatrical expressions such as dance, song, music, and ritual, and did not require a specified space. During the colonial period, new hybrid forms of performance developed that drew from both European and indigenous roots despite the missionaries' and government's attempts to ban most forms of native performances. Indeed, missionaries introduced church sponsored theatre but local writers, such as Wycliff Kiyingi, exploited it to their advantage. Various ethnic groups appropriated and altered Christian traditions and principles, as well as religious stories, using them to make defiant statements that presented 'other' worldviews aimed to subvert Christianity and colonialism. Whereas, after independence in 1962, there was no strictly Ugandan formal theatre, there was performance with indigenous theatrical elements and in indigenous languages. Nonetheless, as Taylor suggests, theatre's 'power in maintaining an indigenous consciousness and sense of identity is hard to measure' (1991: 29). Notably, the 1940s and 1950s audio recordings by Columbia records of various performers, while not staged theatre, have significant 'strong elements that are indicative of the future developments of popular music theatre. The 1950s provide interesting examples of public performances 'playing a somewhat more prominent role in the wider drama of oppression and provoking "real" and devastating political results', which in the context of this book, provide some of the examples of 'passive resistance to authority, in both theme and style, in the indigenous theatre within this period' (Taylor, 1991: 29). Various plays discussed in this book demonstrate a theatre in transition from romanticizing the past, to exploiting myths and legend. This was evidenced in newspaper reviews, interviews, and journal articles that, with the exception of those by Elvania Namukwaya Zirimu, were written by male theatre activists such as Robert Serumaga, and Byron Kawadwa, who aimed to engender a new consciousness.[1] Thus, Western theatre that had dominated the stage for nearly a century gradually moved to multi-indigenous performances and with Ugandan voices. This changed the theatre landscape. It allowed the translation of indigenous people's experience into performance, which energised both the Western educated artists and indigenous community leaders who aspired to show a new communal awareness. Serumaga argued that if a national theatre was 'to be meaningful to' the people 'it must reflect the totality of [their] experience and sensibility' (Serumaga and Janet Johnson, 1970: 53). Not surprisingly, a few years later, specifically under Amin's military regime (1971-1979) and the Obote's second Uganda People's Congress (UPC) government (1980-1986), theatre became a political tool and had a significant effect on the community. Thus, 1970s and 1980s witnessed the beginning of a political performance space in which Ugandans, disenfranchised by the colonial and post-colonial leaders, voiced their concerns.

Throughout Amin's military regime, playwrights and theatre groups had to struggle to survive the armed forces and special service agents' murderous acts. Kawadwa, who directed *Oluyimba lwa Wankoko*, was tortured and murdered while playwrights such as John Ruganda, Lubwa p'Chong, and Serumaga went into exile. Under the military rule of Amin, people were 'disappeared', abducted, and taken away by special services agents to be tortured or murdered in police cells, army barracks, and the State Research Headquarters in Nakasero or Nile Mansions. Bodies were thrown into lakes, dumped in forests, or buried in shallow graves as illustrated in *The Floods* (1980) or Serumaga's *Amayirikiti* (1974) and *Majangwa* (1974). Yet, most theatre groups managed to continue staging plays, utilising allegory to avoid government informants. Other playwrights, such as Lubwa p'Chong and Ruganda, disguised their criticism of political traditions by returning to indigenous theatrical expressions such as folktales, founding myths, ritual, dance, and music performance. In this way, utilising different processes artists staged contemporary shared communal experiences on stage. For example, *Amayirikiti*, *The Floods*, and Nuwa Sentongo's *The Invisible Bond* (1976) were staged between 1974 and 1977, when the government was still violating people's human rights in its attempt to stay in power. Throughout this period, oppressive governments violated bodies, as well as boundaries between politics and performance. For instance, in *The Invisible Bond*, Ddamulira, the protagonist speaks to us from the dead, an act that reminds the audience that the country is still plagued by death squads. Ruganda's *The Floods* and *The Burdens* (1972) are a 'bitter portrait of the despair suffered by countless [Ugandans] who were impoverished and marginalized by [Obote's] economic reforms' (Taylor and Townsend, 2008: 21), while Serumaga's *Renga Moi*, on the other hand, uses dark humour to challenge Amin's tyrannical political system. After Amin's military regime was overthrown, civilian rule was temporarily restored; therefore, playwrights returned to Uganda 'from exile eager to stage works they had written abroad, along with new ones written for the tentative transition to democracy' (Taylor and Townsend, 2008: 21).

Under the successive governments of Paulo Muwanga, Obote and Okello Lutwa, between 1979 and 1986, the security forces were out of control and it was difficult to distinguish between these and Amin's tyrannical system. For instance, although Obote was democratically elected in 1980, his government (1980 - 85) was strikingly similar to the previous military regime. The government agents and para-militaries murdered and tortured political opponents as well as innocent civilians. Cultural festivals and funerals were often transformed into politicised events.

Although people had perceived theatre as a space where anti-people political practices could be challenged, its role became irrelevant in the post-Obote II period. Instead, in the context of recent communal experiences of bloodshed, musical theatre and farcical dramas were used to revise ethnic and national myths. In 1986, the National Resistance Army (NRA), the armed wing of the National Resistance Movement (NRM), won the war against factions of military groups who had overthrown the Obote's UPC government and ended the brutal years of post-colonial rule. Various theatrical expressions associated with this war include folksongs, dances and guerrilla fighters' war songs, which collectively carried a powerful rhetoric of resistance. As Sylvia Tamale has noted, the National Resistance Movement (NRM) government's 'political rhetoric' defied 'conventional wisdom' and 'cut through deep-seated ideologies that stemmed from strong patriarchal forces', thus increasing women's participation in 'all spheres of society' (Tamale, 1999: 2). A significant difference between this struggle and past campaigns for independence was that, for the first time, women were on the frontline as combatants, political commissars and cadres. Nonetheless, gender inequality has always been problematic in Uganda.

Ugandan theatre achieves its distinctive character not only by resistance to oppressive political institutions, but also by maintaining a dynamic relationship with its 'rebellious, iconoclastic, and inventive impulses' (Mary Washington, 1998: 4). What makes indigenous festivals, rituals, and other popular performances remarkable, are the embedded theatrical elements, such as role-playing, spectacle and mimicry, which allow the performance space to be transgressed, fractured and reconfigured according to the specific aesthetic requirements of performances. Performances and dramas discussed in this book try to capture the orality, ritual, aesthetic, and rhetorical qualities of indigenous performance traditions; specifically those qualities that highlight Ugandan theatre's capacity to accommodate the pluralism of performance forms and styles. As playwrights in this book demonstrate, the articulation of resistance and transgression is a central concern in Ugandan drama. Improvised and scripted drama, musical plays and musical theatre, which draw on indigenous performance forms and styles, are some of the ways in which artists critique dispossession, ethnic and gender discrimination, and the politics of intimidation, silencing and violence.

Memory as Resistance

One of the most significant features of post-colonial Ugandan theatre is that since 1962, cultural aspects like dance, music, ritual and song, from indigenous groups including Acholi, Langi, Baganda, Bagisu, Banyankore, Basoga, and Batooro intersect, and impact on one another. In this context, the Baganda, from central Uganda, are perhaps the most exploited culturally. In addition, other Ugandan indigenous groups, Acholi and Langi in the north; Basoga and Bagisu from the East; Bakiga and Banyakole, from the West; Banyoro and Batooro from the North West continue to generate performance practices and forms, which influence Ugandan artistic practices, particularly at the level of theatre performance. Thus, to examine performance in Uganda today is to think of it as encompassing theatre, dance and music, always crossing (institutionalised and ethnicised) boundaries. These crossovers are acts of defiance, challenging the disenfranchisement of the people and celebrations, offering compelling examples of resistance to indigenous discrimination and intimidation as well as an affirmation of the community's existence. Indeed, accurately translating the people's experience in words and performance was the aim of post-colonial theatre. The plays, which embody the character of post-colonial performance, suggest ways in which theatre, using indigenous forms, can incorporate and accommodate resistance to political tyranny. To this end, artists such as Elvania Zirimu and Ruganda use multi-linguistic expressions to show the multi-vocalities of a post-colonial society and ancestral myths to explore present realities. Further, their dramas show the connection between society and the individual, and performance and the metaphysical world. Their work blends aspects of dance, recitations, rituals, festivals, folk songs, oral stories, myths and legends, which are converted into improvised or written dramas to comment on the status quo and to express society's dissatisfaction with political institutions. Inevitably, since they are translated into new performing forms and spaces, these dramas do not entirely capture the aesthetics, humour, satire or all the nuances of the original stories. Nevertheless, drawing energy from the simultaneous activities of civil disobedience, armed rebellion and political liberation, indigenous forms and styles, music, song, dance and ritual, are used to express dissent.

In a way, Ana Elena Puga's critical perspective in *Carlos Manuel Varela and the Role of Memory in Covert Resistance,* which adopts the concept, 'memory-as-resistance' (2003: 42), is significant to this discussion. Her aim is to present how the exploration of 'memory-as-resistance must eventually involve revelation [and] communication among those who would build a movement or even stage a single resistant performance' (2003: 43). Further, she suggests that memory is one of the 'devious types of resistance to which the disenfranchised must resort, "an art of the weak"'. Rejecting Joseph Roach's (1996) view that theatre cannot 'function as [a zone] of transgression', Puga argues that theatre presents a new kind of 'memory-as-resistance', which is 'a site of memory, in which communal history may be formed by the interplay between performers and spectators' (2003:42). Her paradigm of revelation, communication and building of a resistant movement, goes beyond its concern for Latino theatre, toward theatre (performance) practices in comparable socio-political environments. Thus, in the context of this book, Ugandan theatre engages with questions of oppression, resistance and identity, focusing on the possibility of freedom. This expresses a multiplicity of complex issues that relate to the understanding of performance as a concept, part of the 'hidden script'.[2] Transgressive performances by such artists as Ruganda, Sentongo, Lubwa p'Chong or Kawadwa, which use indigenous forms, become events for the manifestation of hidden scripts that can only be interpreted by the indigenous audiences. These performances are open to challenge by the audience, through call and response, activities that allow them to participate in the interpretation and construction of meaning.

Post-colonial theatre, like all other forms of popular performance, is inherently political and, indeed, some of the most popular performances are extremely transgressive. In this context, artists discussed in this book manage to use particular generic qualities to present a political message. Thus, the critical discourse articulated by playwrights such as Serumaga, Elvania Zirimu, Pio Zirimu, Ruganda and Kawadwa,[3] has been central to the disruption of oppressive conservative traditions, and totalitarian regimes and their narratives in Uganda theatre. Their works use a shared performance memory to subvert and transgress political authority. Performance memory, therefore, forms 'part of a broader oppositional discourse' (Puga, 2003: 42) in this theatre. Notably, while indigenous performance forms and styles form the foundation of contemporary Ugandan popular theatre, the genre uses a juxtaposition of indigenous paradigms and transgressive themes, which allow the audience to interpret and question the issues presented. Moreover, its intra-cultural and inter-indigenous character allows it to cross the boundaries that were laid down during the colonial period.

Performance, Scenography and Space

All the forms by which performances can be staged are no longer related to verbal otherness, since these are easily discernible by oppression; however, creating new forms/styles that speak to the audience, enables *the participants* to understand who they are, where they are, where they have been, and where they are going. Not all the plays and performances discussed in this book are still performed in their original form. Nor, arguably, are they tied to a specific indigenous group, since every song, dance and ritual performance allows transgression to some extent, however minimally, creating a shift that affects the form, content, aesthetics and message. Watching a ritual, dance, song, or folktale, as individualised performances or embedded in a staged play, reminds us that these cultural expression, which construct people's creative sensibilities, are a continuation of the pre-colonial indigenous performance forms and processes. In a way, they encapsulate their cultural identity, as demonstrated in Serumaga's *Majangwa*, or more recently, Stephen Rwangyezi's *Lawino and Ocol* (2000).

While reminding us that as a concept, performance 'implies a sense of agency' (Taylor and Townsend, 2008: 2) which the Europeans, at the time of the encounter, denied the indigenous people, Taylor and Townsend assert that performance was 'fundamental to indigenous and European colonial epistemologies' since it was 'a primary means through which both cultures maintained or contested social authority' (Taylor and Townsend 2008: 4). Simon Gikandi's assertion that 'forms of cultural expression that were the most likely to be dismissed as [a]meaningless spectacle' by slave masters in America, 'were most valued by the slaves' (2011: 262-3) echoes the development of performance in colonial (and post-colonial) Uganda. For, performances that were undervalued by Uganda's colonial rulers gained 'value' as people 'sought to produce a counterculture, including one that went against the grain of sense and sensibility' (Gikandi, 2011: 263). Europeans could categorise rituals and other modern artistic forms as *taboo* since, although they 'could discern the significance of what they saw', they 'were not sure what it meant and were then left pondering the meaning of a spectacle that was disharmonious and at odds with European aesthetic practices' (Gikandi, 2011: 263). Therefore, Gikandi's comments have a pertinent meaning to theatre and performance in Uganda. Pius Ngandu Nkashama, the Congolese critic, in his seminal essay, 'Theatricality and Social Mimodrama', focuses debate on transgressive performances and offers a critical framework for Ugandan theatre. He examines, among other things, two indigenous ritual performances in Congo, which present 'a socially sanctioned "site of transgression"' of shared cultural values and in the process, create thematic and semiotic transgression in popular theatre (Nkashama, 2004: 7). His theoretical discussion is useful to this book in various ways: first, because Nkashama is writing about theatre and performance in the Congo, a Central African country whose cultures of colonial and post-colonial experiences closely relate to Uganda and their Bantu languages are mutually intelligible. Second, his delineation of the concept of "transgression" and its application to Congolese indigenous and contemporary performances relate to my interests in transgression as a central paradigm.[4] He demonstrates that no performance form can be static or 'in-ward looking', for it has to recognise the forces within and without its society. This is further enhanced as the ritual, dance, song or play is performed outside its original community, mutating literary and metaphorically within different spaces or utterances. In his discussion of Congolese performance, Nkashama identifies the 'transgression' (Nkashama, 2004: 239) as one of the main characteristic of African aesthetics, arguing that rituals are a good example of sites where 'aesthetic acts of social transgression' (2004: 239) are staged. His reading of ritual, popular performances, and audience reception, maps a web of knowledge, alternative sensibilities, mythologies and conflicts, which are integral to theatre. In this way, he offers a model that is applicable to the examination of Ugandan theatre.

Interestingly for Nkashama, applying '"performance"' as a concept to African theatre is too delimiting because it excludes 'the implications of "scenography"' (Nkashama, 2004: 238). In applying the concept, we might also consider 'the relationship that must be established between the actors … and the audience … through the intermediary of the scenic space', since Nkashama is concerned with the dialogical relationship between the 'median character', the 'scenography' and the audience (2004: 238). His intention here is to investigate significant dominant discourses of transgression in performance through exploring the symbols, language, song and dance, ritual and popular performances that deliberately incorporate and accommodate oppositional discourses. Hence, his discussion demonstrates that in Congolese and other African societies, there is no 'art for art's sake', only art with 'aesthetic acts of social [and political] transgression' (2004: 239). Like Gilles DeLeuze, Nkashama considers how performances might use scenography to transgress and explore ethnically specific theatrical languages, making 'the [theatrical] language itself scream, stutter, stammer, or murmur' (Deleuze, 1998: 109-10),[5] thus, opening up alternative ways of challenging repressive systems. This intersection between scenography, the performer, and audience offers a more definitive framework within which the practice of resistance operates. Indigenous theatre, with its 'dramatic space', is an 'ethical and aesthetic no-man's-land' in which performers 'cease to behave according to their social attributes' and in moments of defiance 'perform extravagant and outrageous acts'. Therefore, as 'a space of total inviolability and integrity, it has power of impunity to criticise, malign, and contradict confirmed truths' (Nkashama, 2004: 243). Nkashama develops this further and claims that 'theatre confers upon itself the authority to attack social hierarchies, challenge established rules, and contest political power without anyone else being able to intervene or condemn its pertinence' (2004: 243).

For the purpose of this book then, contemporary Ugandan theatre provides the lens through which to reflect upon the conflicts, intersections and resistance through performance, which transgress perceived meanings of performance and theatre. Kenyan writer Ngugi wa Thiong'o' s influential essay, 'Enactments of Power: The Politics of Performance Space'(1997), is concerned with exploring the 'battle over performance space' which includes 'spaces for prayers, funeral dirges, marriage ceremonies, naming tea parties, family gatherings, sports and theatre' that exists 'between the arts and the state' (Ngugi, 1997: 11). Ngugi talks about the tension between the performance spaces of the artist, and the director's 'utilization' of the performance space 'to [maximize the] effect on both the actors and the audience', and the state, particularly the latter's 'consistent efforts to control the space' (1997: 12). Ngugi links the multifaceted nature of performance space to other ideas discussed in this book:

> The main ingredients of performance are place, content, audience, time, and the goal. The state has its areas of performance, as does the artist. While the state performs power, the power of the artist is solely in the performance.

> Both the state and the artist may have a different conception of time, place, content, and goals, either of their own performance or of the other; but they have the audience as their common target (1997: 12).

Ngugi asserts that the 'main arena of struggle is the performance space: its definition, delimitation, and regulation'. In this way, the 'real politics of the performance space' is located in its 'potential conflictual engagement with all the other shrines of power' (Ngugi, 1997: 16). The contention is not about 'what happens or could happen on the stage at any one time but rather the control of continuous access and contact' (Ngugi, 1997: 16). Nevertheless, this is likely to happen in Uganda where 'the population is divided' along fissures such as, ethnic origin, 'the urban and the rural' and 'the poor and the rich' (Ngugi, 1997: 13). Ngugi's aim, however, is to find a critical perspective on the contest between the artist's 'performance space' and the 'state's own areas of performance' (Ngugi, 1997: 13). His approach is tied to the point that 'the struggle for performance space is integral to the struggle for democratic space and social justice' (Ngugi, 1997: 19) where the space is 'always the site of physical, social, and psychic forces in society' (Ngugi, 1997: 13). Hence, 'the performance space is defined by the presence or absence of people', not the state legislature.

According to Ngugi's argument, the colonial 'creation' of physical performance spaces into what constitutes a National Theatre in the Western sense, with 'clear-cut boundaries that defined the dominated space with controlled points of exits and entrances', was not practical in post-colonial countries. This exercise led to the restriction of the access and exit of the performers and the audience. Inevitably, it resulted in the suppression and censorship of artistic expression and performance forms as evidenced in Kenya, Uganda and South Africa (Ngugi, 1997:27). In these countries, Ngugi explains, the 'open space among the people [was] perceived by the state to be the most dangerous area' since 'it [was] most vital' (p. 28). His preferred model is for theatre to 'define its space [in relation to] both' its 'physical location and language' (p. 20), open 'access and contact' (p 13), free interaction between 'internal and external forces', and performers and audience. Further, he explains that his preference is for 'a theatre that scraped the bottom of the historical space of the people's experience in order to speak to their immediate presence as they faced their tomorrow' (Ngugi, 1997: 20).

Ngugi's work is relevant to this book because it focuses attention on the relationship between performance space, the performer, the audience, and the state. His work offers a model applicable to the examination of Ugandan theatre. In addition, his critical position allows a rethinking of the uses of performance space for political resistance by artists such as Kadongo Kamu singers and *abadongo* (travelling musicians). Ngugi's notion of the 'open space' (p 26) suggests all the elements implicit within performance (in Uganda), but which were 'suppressed' by *gavumenti enkuumi* (the protectorate/colonial government), and post-colonial tyrannical regimes. When examined, these performances revealed the conditions of people's existence. The transgressive aspects articulated by Nkashama when he presents a post-colonial vision of an independent contemporary theatre reveal ways in which specific socio-political (and cultural) conditions reconstitute theatre in diverse ways that engender the reconceptualization of performance. Using Michel Foucault, as Ngugi does, to criticise the state's creation of confined spaces to 'act out its power', allows him to show how the state 'organizes the space as a huge enclosure, with definite places of entrance and exit' (Ngugi wa Thiong'o, 1997: 21). Theatre (the open performance space), therefore, must be rethought not in terms of individual actors but as a collective community of performers and the audience whose experience and understanding of the socio-political issues is their own truth.[6]

Traditionally, ritual is identified as the original space where Ugandan 'authentic' performance was 'formed' with music, dance and song. For instance, in one indigenous folk solo, the performer tells the audience, *Nze bwemba nnyimba saagala ayogera* (don't talk into my song) which echoes the Luganda phrase, *bwemba njogera saagala ayogera* (don't talk into my talk), which suggests a strategic method of resistance, or a refusal to be silenced, that is evident in the daily individual experience of repressive systems. However, implicit in this caution is the recognition of moral and political transgression in the performer's (or artist's) voice. They articulate the concerns of the community, and the appropriated open (public) space that offers resistance to dominant ideologies and structures. Therefore, they activate various transgressive strategies to deal with their lived conditions. Through examining the rupture within the performing arts in a post-independence/post-liberation society, the idea of culture as fractured and unstable is revealed. Importantly, the Ugandan context reveals identities that have become blurred by post-colonial intra-national and international migratory experiences; people move from country to urban areas, overseas, or to other areas for education, work and security. Hence, cultural values and performance forms have become more porous and are exposed to internal and external influences. To playwrights discussed in this book, performance, whether staged in urban or rural spaces, is always being remade. It is always travelling as a site of intersections of multiple indigenous forms, styles and aesthetics, where artists project indigenous identities as national identities. The performance space, therefore, is no longer a fixed located memory, but is the 'meeting place' or intersecting location of performance activities from which the artist starts to recreate forms and styles of local and other communities. In this state of constant human and artistic migration, as Nkashama (2003) suggests, the idea of any sense of a 'true' or 'original' performance is essentialist, and its 'authenticity [is] constantly interrogated' by the artists. This derives from the traditional style where, as opposed to Western derived theatre, no two performances of the same song are the same; or otherwise, the artist stands to be accused of lacking professional skills. In contrast with Eurocentric performances, a performer who extemporizes and expands his *oeuvre*, even within the context of a specific staging, is a true professional. Performance, therefore, can be conceived as transgressive, a space of 'intersections where different texts and styles crisscross from within and beyond its borders' (Neil Campbell, 2008: 26).

The 'theatricality' of post-independence politics 'allows countless iterations' (Taylor, 1988: 3) of performance that creates resistant statements, as evidenced in Kawadwa's *Wankoko*. Here, similar to Taylor, 'theatricality' is used to refer to the 'aesthetic, political, and perspectival structures within which the characters are positioned and perform their prescribed roles' (Taylor, 1988: 161). Thus, the underpinning idea of transgression within these performances allows a new viewpoint on theatre as a space that is inevitably located at the intersection between the indigenous and the national, and the national and the global, which challenges our notion of cultural authenticity. This theatre challenges colonial concepts of indigenous performances, rooted in a colonial world, when policies of divide and rule were practised. For instance, attributing behavioural patterns to specific indigenous groups - Nilotics, Baganda or Bagishu - to define and label the people, their cultural practices and identities as either noble or savage[7] (Mamdani, 2001). That performance is dynamic is suggested by the mixing of several indigenous forms of scripted and oral genres.

Gender and the Performance of Transgression

The Ugandan human rights activist, Tamale's, *When Hens Begin to Crow* (1999) is concerned with examining the transgressive responses by women to cultural norms and gender roles, recognising the critical role of women in challenging conservative patriarchal behaviour in contemporary politics. The metaphor, 'when chicken [hens] begin to crow', which derives from the Luganda (African) saying, '*wali owulidde enseera ekkookolima*? challenges the tradition of the social and political marginalization of women. As Abbas Kiyimba explains, in spite of fervent efforts to break the mould, Kiganda cultural norms exclude women from participating in male-gendered activities, for: '*Enseera ne bw'eyiga okukokolima, esigala nga y'erina okubiika amagi n'okugaalula*, - "*Even when the hen learns to crow, it still has to lay the eggs and to hatch them*"' (Kiyimba, 2008: 219, footnote 1). Tamale's thesis, embedded in the metaphor of a crowing hen, concerns itself with the politics of gender and transgression in performance. Her theoretical approach aims to disrupt the model of normative oppressive systems where 'women are not supposed to speak up or express their opinions in public. A view deeply embedded in African patriarchal values which relegates women to the domestic arena of home and family' (Tamale, 1999: 1). Significantly, this is where her work fits with performance; this social perception allows space for transgression. Indeed, it is from this counter-interpretation of the saying that Tamale is able to conclude that 'women are increasingly negating the metaphor of the crowing hen' and 'are defying custom, culture, discrimination and marginalisation' (1999:1).

Tamale's attempt to counter traditions points toward new transgressive acts that are significantly located in the space where, in the post-colonial and post-liberation context, indigenous performances intersect with new performance forms, thus creating new spaces for the destruction of normative perceptions of character, gender, and indigenous identity; and the construction of a dynamic critical theatre relevant to society. For instance, when we read the 1960s and 1970s plays of the first Ugandan published female playwright, director and actress, Elvania Zirimu, the key features are hidden sexuality and transgression. Her work presents images of oppression and a blend of diffidence and assertiveness. Thus, Zirimu's strategy is to underline women's transgression of boundaries that in pre- and colonial times had forced them to live in oppressive environments. Interestingly, Taylor's views in an essay entitled, 'Staging Traumatic Memory: Yuyachkani', on the critical role of women in challenging repressive institutions through performance, resonates with Tamale's argument encouraging women to initiate changes in their position through exploring (recreating) folklore and cultural beliefs to their advantage. Taylor argues that 'multiple forms of embodied acts are always present, reconstituting themselves -transmitting communal memories, histories, [and] values' from each generation offering a significant rethinking of 'embodied knowledge as that which disappears' (2008: 193). In the essay, she argues for an understanding of theatre as a space, specifically for women, for social and political intervention. For Taylor, the interconnection between 'atrocity', 'embodied knowledge' and 'subjectivity' in the work of the Yuyachkani performing company, and oppositional performing groups elsewhere, suggests a blending of 'dance', song, speech, 'historical memory', 'literary and historical texts' and 'archival documents' (2008: 193). The work of early Ugandan male playwrights, for example, Ruganda, Serumaga, Kiyingi and Kawadwa, evidence this rupture in the traditional writing of female parts that challenge the normative woman behaviour, specifically women who actively challenge oppressive patriarchal behaviour.[8] As discussed later, critics such as Helen Nabasuta Mugambi and Sylvia Nannyonga-Tamusuza have explored women's transgression of normative behaviour, evident in Kadongo Kamu performances.

Katemba: A New Perception of Performance?

Post-colonial Ugandan society expresses itself through *katemba,*[9] a multi-generic dialogic and hybridized performance form, with all the possibilities it suggests, that exists alongside other folk forms and discourses whose 'authority' it disrupts (to borrow concepts from Homi Bhabha (1994: 88-89). As a post-colonial form, *katemba* works within the frame of oral performance (dance, instrumental music, the folk song and solo) to provide 'new possibilities and connections' that take the audience beyond its respective (individual) indigenous cultures into the present reality. In this way, it signals embodied performance practices and memory, blurring the boundaries between sacred and secular spaces, subjects and rulers, performance, memory and lived experiences.[10] Much as artists projected it as a respectable field with a positive role in society, on the streets and in market places, *katemba* acquired a different meaning relating to a trickster or joker, someone who projects utopian ideals. This may also allude to a lack of seriousness and professionalism among the popular actors, therefore, presenting them as *bakazanyirizi* (comedians). Nevertheless, popular performers such as Benoni Kibuuka and Charles Senkubuge[11] who, in the contemporary context, have become critical of the popular construction of dramatic stage performers as cheap comedians argue that this concept was no longer the definitive representation of actors.

A number of significant factors led to the emergence of *katemba* and its irruption throughout the country. First, the spread of indigenous performances (dance, song and instrumental music) throughout the schools; second, was the celebration of the Roman Catholic and Church of Uganda centenaries (1977); third, was the victimisation of various indigenous groups such as the Acholis and the Baganda that later led the people to join the opposition against tyranny; and lastly, the search by the younger generations for performance forms that related to international contemporary popular styles. A key concern of the artists was the development of a set of artistic practices informed by folk and Western forms that would enable people to sustain their identity and sanity in a period of social and political upheavals. Through shared laughter, *katemba*, it was assumed, would serve as a medium of discourse about the lived experiences and a (comic) relief for the audience. Thus, once again, artists transformed *katemba* to shape society's discourse on oppression, immorality and excessive consumption. The embedding of hybrid theatrical expressions and farce into this theatre alludes to the transformation that permeated many areas of Ugandan society during this period. By 1989, for example, neither folk performance forms and ritual, nor dramas derived from Western theatre, were viewed as standard performances; however, a cross section of audiences determined the quality of a popular show by its farcical, musical and dance content.

Given its 'sense of deviance' (Gikandi, 2011: 264), *katemba* (performance) can be the focal point of expressing resistance among the oppressed communities. Dramas, as noted earlier, may comprise 'an assemblage of values', including cultural expressions and forms, which are 'inaccessible' or incomprehensible to the oppressive institutions (Gikandi, 2011: 263). In this way, while music helps to 'spread the language of insurgency', ritual festivals and cultural practices, for instance, funerals and final funeral rites ceremonies, give people opportunities to congregate. Not surprisingly, the use of cultural performances as a counterpoint to the disappearances, murders, and violence, was important to the ordinary people and attracted Amin's attention.[12] Through *katemba*, artists staged farce to resist oppressive practices. However, sometimes the process of merging such types of folk theatrical expressions and modern Western styles and form created concerns. These concerns that transformed performance styles were brought about by the use of electronic equipment such as electric guitars, synthesisers and video technology, as well as amplifiers and modernised stage performances. *Katemba* is as much concerned with the use of farce, amidst times of political crisis, as with the radical transformation of performance to develop hybrid theatrical expressions and a stage *lingua franca* that mixes Ugandan languages with Swahili and English. Despite the inherent aesthetic quality of these developments, some people felt this theatre disrespected cultural traditions and disrupted conventional theatre styles. It is for this reason that two streams of theatre (occupying two performance spaces) developed.

Katemba presents an interesting convergence, bringing together transgression, spectacle and verbal discourse, memory, politics and performance, and overlapping them with related forms elsewhere in Africa and its diaspora. It underlines contemporary performance practices, which can be examined through Nkashama's essay, 'Theatricality and Social Mimodrama' (2004). Nkashama links Soyinka's '*transe maitrisee* (controlled state)' and his own '*panique orientee* (directed state of panic)' to the indigenous ritual performances that simultaneously construct conflicting theatrical discourses through which the gods are 'called in question' (Nkashama, 2004: 240). In Nkashama's view, this is a subversive practice, which transgresses social and political boundaries, allowing the community to present oppositional and alternative points of view.[13] The invocation of the metaphysical spaces of ritual and the stage, traversing either the internal or external open space, is why we are reminded of the significance of indigenous performance theories and conventions in our consideration of contemporary theatre. (Ngugi wa Thiong'o, 1998)

Performance and Transformation

Similar to Nkashama and Taylor, another critic, Esiaba Irobi (2009), underscores the significance of Africa's '*embodied but unwritten performance theory*'. He postulates that theatre in Africa 'is primarily an act of community by which a given group ritualizes and perpetuates its sense of identity, its values, history, performance aesthetics and sense of spirituality as a basis for community' (Irobi, 2010: 16). He presents an elaborate articulation of the theory of '*ase*', a 'transformative force' (2010: 18), which he claims to be 'a performative construct driven by the phenomenological episteme of [African] theatre' (2010: 17). A 'subversive episteme' (2010: 18) that is 'intrinsically revolutionary', enables the people to 'challenge and change the cultural/political destiny' imposed by colonialists and contemporary tyrannical rulers. The essence of 'power' to 'change reality' and to 'transform the given existential circumstances of the playwrights, the participants and the audience' (2010: 18) is what underlines the dynamics of transgression in the Ugandan practice of *katemba.* In her essay, 'Transformational Discourses, Afro-Diasporic Culture, and the Literary Imagination' (1996), Carol Boyce Davies concentrates on the notion of 'transformation' evident in the Brazilian *candomble.* Similar to Irobi's articulation of the theory of *ase*, she offers another conceptualization of how spirit possession is a metaphor for resistance and a site of transformation. *Candomble* performance, Boyce explains, is 'a movement from the daily circle of life, work, and struggle to one [level] of emotional and spiritual possibilities' (1996: 200). Further, in a statement that links her analysis with Irobi, Nkashama, Wole Soyinka and Taylor's 'embodied knowledge', she asserts that in *candomble*, when the ancestral spirits are 'recalled to practical existence they are also given space to move outward, from the past, into a realm of present and future existence' (Davies, 1996: 200). Even more indicative in the context of my discussion, since it highlights the notion of transgressive performance, is the transformation Davies describes which relates to the sense of performance visualised in *katemba*. This is where '[t]he individual physically becomes something else, somebody else, momentarily escapes the mundane, the "real," the normal, and, with the sanction of the community, exists in different space and time and history' (1996: 200/201). As discussed later in this book, *katemba* offers a performance of resistance and transgression since it embodies the 'deliberate journeying outside the boundaries of restriction and oppression' (1996: 203). This is because it has the same performative qualities and transformative powers as evidenced in spirit possession rituals. What the playwrights discussed in this book 'try to achieve for their [audience] through their plays/productions is exactly what the collective of [indigenous] choreographers, poets, dancers and musicians, attempt to achieve through the 'complex polyvalent, performance texts of festival dramas and rituals' (Irobi, 2010: 19).

Urbanisation, Buganda and Performance

After colonisation, several new urban areas, in particular Kampala, the capital of Uganda, were created where urbanisation influenced the development of new theatre/performance forms. Kampala is not only the capital of the country but also the seat of government, including civil service and parliament. The movement of various indigenous groups and foreign workers, for instance Indians, Europeans, Rwandans and Burundians, to the capital led to a breakdown of traditional family and other social structures (David Coplan, 2008; Elizabeth Ramirez, 2000). Urbanisation, therefore, is a significant influence on the experiences of gender, indigenous identity, discrimination and economic deprivation on stage, particularly in relationship to new gender roles, marital relationship, and socio-economic settings. New communities were forged in Kampala by immigrants and local inhabitants who shared local languages and/or English, and cultural values. Christine Obbo examines the 'status of strangers in Buganda', as a model that offers a view on the experience and impact of rural-rural/rural-urban migration since colonisation (Obbo, 1971: 281). She points out that apart from the 'rural-rural migration' that was 'stimulated from different parts of Uganda and Ruanda-Urundi, and Luo from Kenya, the rural-rural urbanisation also involved foreigners of Arabic and Indian descent who started small shops, coffee and cotton buying businesses' (Obbo, 1971: 227). She goes on to explain that 'most popular plays on the radio in the late 1960s and early 1970s featured people speaking Luganda with foreign accents. ... families ... used to listen to the radio broadcasts after dinner [and] hysterical laughter from young and old always followed the Ruandese and Gisu accents, in particular' (Obbo, 1971: 236 note 9). Foreigners such as Indians (*abagwiira*) and strangers or people from other indigenous groups (*banamawanga*) provided the best stereotypes for the Baganda in their attempts to discipline children and instill cultural values: 'mothers would tell their children not to have a Soga's stubbornness (*emputtu yomusoga*). Peer group members would discipline an obnoxious individual by saying his head was like that of a Nyoro (*omutwe gw'omunyolo*)' and 'Children who dressed in a slovenly fashion were asked, "Where has this *munyarwanda* come from?"'; girls who walked in ways that were thought to be ungraceful were called Luo (*bajaluo*)' (Obbo, 1971: 236, note 9). In addition, Obbo notes the Baganda viewed other people's food as '"tasteless and liable to cause constipation"; their languages were "difficult" to speak and understand, besides sounding "loud" and "ungraceful"' (Obbo, 1971: 232). On the other hand, the foreigners complained of the Baganda's inability to learn other cultures and their habit of '[giving] foreign names a Ganda version' (Obbo, 1971: 233). All this could be interpreted as instilling prejudice. In the context of this book, theatre is seen to provide a way of articulating these ethnic tensions through performances such as Kiyingi's *Muduuma Kwe Kwaffe* (1977) *Wokulira* (1962 - 2000), *Olugendo lwe Gologoosa* (1982) or *The Minister's Wife* (1983) by Lubwa p'Chong, which attempt to show how cultural values and the ambitions of people were affected by colonialism and urbanisation.

Chapter 2

FROM INDIGENOUS PERFORMANCE TO SCRIPTED THEATRE

A key feature of post-colonial Uganda theatre is that in its development process, since 1960, theatrical elements from multiple indigenous groups intersect and impact on one another. This chapter examines indigenous performance 'in its salient features and as a fundamental reference [to] the experience' (Irele, 2001: 30) of theatre in Uganda. In her critical article, 'Your Experience is Your Own Truth', (1976:1) Elvania Zirimu significantly outlines the vision of a Ugandan post-colonial theatre. Referring to the aims of the founders of Ngoma Players, she states:

> The founders of this group [aimed at] realising the great need in this country for more meaningful drama for the people, and the need to develop our traditional art forms into dramatic expression as well as adapting the best of foreign drama to the local context.

Elvania Zirimu's awareness of the significance of an organic relationship between indigenous and Western forms informed both her work and that of her contemporaries. In their search for 'a grounded authenticity of expression and vision', the artists undertook 'a resourcing of their material and their modes of expression in the traditional culture' (Irele, 2001: 29), as Serumaga noted in his conversation with Janet Johnson (1970: 54):

> [T]he practice of people getting together to watch the story-teller act out his story, or to hear a musician like the famous Sekinoomu of Uganda relate a tale of *trenchant social criticism*, dramatised in voice, movement and the music of his *Ndingidi* (a one-stringed Lyre), has been with [Ugandans] for centuries. And this is the true theatre of East Africa. (Emphasis added)

However, although even today, indigenous oral performances and cultural expressions continue to function as a primary reference of Ugandan expression these are still underlined by differences that were emphasized and promoted by colonialism. These inform Uganda theatre and performances. For example, as Obbo suggests, Buganda has always housed strangers; in pre-colonial times, they raided and 'acquired' women and slaves from neighbouring states. After colonisation, they employed people from neighbouring indigenous groups and national states, for instance, Burundi, Rwanda and Kenya, to work on their *shambas* (farms). According to Obbo, since the Baganda 'absorbed the European stereotyping that they were superior to their neighbours', they used the derogatory terms, *munamawanga/munyolo*, stranger, or, *munagwanga*, foreigner, to categorise non-Baganda. She further argues that, although after colonisation in Buganda, strangers or foreigners 'could either assimilate or remain strangers', in some instances, 'total assimilation was often difficult - particularly if the individual failed to master the linguistic skills that were felt to be key to social skills' (Obbo, 1979: 241).

While Obbo never directly discusses the performance of power, its relationship to language and the tension within the post-colonial state can be perceived from her examination of 'the cognitive skills [the Baganda] employed to deal with the presence of foreigners' (Obbo, 1979: 228). Thus, this resulted in stereotypes that have been appropriated by theatre. The migration of people marginalised by colonialism and ethnocentric politics led to the formation of new classes and presented ideal opportunities that allowed the translation of people's experience into a pluralism of performance styles. The previous statements emphasise how Ugandan theatre underlines its deliberate Lugandanisation because the artists, in their attempts to preserve Baganda distinctiveness under oppression, wanted to make performances inaccessible to 'non-initiate' Ugandans, may be relevant here.[1] This practice enhances the notion of an overt exploitation of Kiganda indigenous performance forms. Yet, as noted earlier other Ugandan indigenous groups from the north, East the West and North West, Uganda continue to produce performance practices and forms, which influence Ugandan artistic practices, particularly in theatre.

Theatre, energised by both the Western educated artists and indigenous community leaders who aspired to show a new communal awareness, became a multi-vocal space that questioned paradigms of power and pre-conceived identities (Teresa Requena Pelegri, 2008). In this sense, theatre in Uganda achieves its distinctive character not only by resistance to oppressive political institutions, but also by maintaining a dynamic relationship with its 'rebellious, iconoclastic, and inventive impulses' (Mary Helen Washington, 1997: 4). Yet, such performance constructions and processes can produce both a skewed narrow and indigenous theatre, and a subversive resistant reaction to political crisis. For, as Taylor has noted, 'crisis in the more general sense of a "turning point" between death and regeneration, tak[es] into account both the objective systemic shifts or ruptures [...] that affect the nature of the society as a whole and the subjective, personal experience of disorientation and loss of identity' (Taylor, 1991: 6). Thus, the need to construct and translate the Ugandan identity in words and performance, that became an objective of post-colonial theatre in the 1960s, marked the advent of public political performance spaces in which Ugandans, formerly restricted by the colonial government and disillusioned by new political leaders, made their voices heard. If, as Taylor has observed, 'the concerns with oppression [and] colonization' are at the foundation of the Latin American playwrights' 'theatre of crisis' (1991: 6), in the Ugandan context, one could argue that this practice illustrates the transformation of indigenous performance to a contemporary theatre of resistance within which the dialectics of oral performance co-exist with Western forms and styles. Notably, the resurgence of music, dramatic performances and literary works, evidencing influences of African performance forms and styles, and the emergence of post-colonial studies, contributed to the research interests in the intersection between African/Ugandan indigenous and Western performance forms.

During the critical period after independence, between 1962 and 1966, oral tradition, narratives, songs, poetry, dances, dance-dramas, and mimetic representations enabled people to sustain the pre-colonial consciousness of their past and develop forms of resistance. Performance was important to people and their rulers and, after colonization, to the colonized and the imperial rulers as a process through which they addressed their grievances or challenged political and social authority.

Myth and Performance

The Baganda creation myth, which has several iterations, has a patriarchal bias. It blames Nambi for disobeying her father's orders when she returns to Ggulu, therefore, allowing Walumbe (Death), her biological brother, to accompany her to the new world, Buganda. John Sekamwa in his book illustrates how ritual performances embedded in this myth allow people to maintain a social balance in society and its beliefs, when he recounts the origin of traditional religious beliefs and worship linking the practice to the Baganda founding myth (Sekamwa, 1990). He cites the specific occasion when Kintu, Nambi, Lubaale and the rest of the community went to Ggulu Mountain to ask Ggulu (the Baganda Supreme God and Nambi's father) to send Kayiikuzi to come and take back the recalcitrant Walumbe, who was killing off her children. The retelling or re-staging of aspects of this myth engenders a community that is willing to challenge authoritarianism. Sekamwa's account that identifies Kintu's son, Lubaale, with possession and god Ggulu with the mountain, highlights the indigenous Baganda practice of conflating behaviour, performance or place with identity. His iteration of the myth reveals the complex interconnections between ritual(s) festivals, and the contemporary understanding of a theatrical performance, especially the idea of space and the role of dance, movement, music and possession in theatre. A variety of concepts - *kutemba* in Bunyoro and *kulinnya* in Buganda and Busoga - are used to describe the possession and trance. Additionally, terms such as: -*linnya*, *-temba*, *-yimba*, and *-zina* (climb upon, climb upon/possess, sing, and dance) incorporate ideas of performance. The etymology of *katemba,* performance or theatre, which, in this context, refers to a concept of possession and to the body (of the medium/performer) as its primary site, originates from indigenous worship. In this instance, it refers to the mixed indigenous and Western performance forms and styles. In the colonial period, however, *katemba* signified the shifting indigenous world of the people whose protected religious and social spaces, as Ngugi (1998) notes, were being replaced by new spaces.

Orature and Performance

Pio Zirimu's and Austin Bukenya's paper, 'Oracy as a Skill and as a Tool for African Development',[2] offers us a critical perspective through which we can understand the post-colonial Ugandan artists' ideas on the uses of oral traditions in the context of decolonisation (1986). This paper, first read at the 1977 Festival of African Arts and Culture, succeeds in defining Pio Zirimu's concept of oral literature and performance, 'orature' that signifies indigenous oral and plastic performance, which he uses to describe the 'best manifestation of oracy in action' (Pio Zirimu, 1971: 92). Orature is specific to a genre, while *katemba*, originally used to describe all forms of theatrical performance throughout the post-colonial era from the 1970s to the 1980s, is now restricted to stage dramatic performances. It explores the possibilities of converting oral literatures, aesthetics, style and form, into dynamic literary/performance texts. Examples of this are the works that belong to the 'song school', such as p'Bitek's *Song of Lawino* (1966), or, in this context, Serumaga's *Renga Moi* and *Majangwa*. They guide us to the important features of orature - 'immediacy', 'flexibility', 'adaptability and communality', as well as 'vividness and structure' (readily apparent in the works of Serumaga and other post-colonial artists), that make understanding orature critical to all artists who aim to address the changing socio-political conditions (Pio Zirimu, 1971: 92).

In a 1969 interview with Heinz Friedberger, Pio Zirimu stated that the collection and documentation of indigenous oral performances (recitations, folktales, dances, and folksongs) were important 'because the words themselves and the other African art forms have a message. There is a message, a performative message, and the movements in dance … which you cannot tape' (Pio Zirimu, 1969). Pio Zirimu's project aims to break down the dichotomy between/separating orature and literature. His notion of a 'performative message' (Pio Zirimu, 1969:5) indicates the depth and breadth of indigenous oral performances, which informs the critical role they play in order to maintain order in society. Serumaga, and the other artists discussed in this book, allow the Ugandan indigenous performance/oral traditions to speak and comment on its nature and multiple functions. This offers tools and the language needed for performances relevant to the post-colonial community. Isidore Okpewho, Ngugi, Pio Zirimu, and

Serumaga acknowledge the performance space as a site where 'traditions of the past can inspire the present'. Nevertheless, Serumaga is keen to emphasise that these forms and spaces 'cannot satisfy the creative urge of our generation' (Serumaga, 1970: 53). The challenge for him is to make them relevant to the present since, '[b]etween the theatrical technique of the foreign play, the symbolism of tradition, and the controversy of contemporary issues, a synthesis of body and spirit [should] be achieved' (Serumaga, 1970: 53). Seen from two or more perspectives, this gives a clear signal of the direction of Serumaga and other artists' work, intersecting or cross-fertilising indigenous theatrical elements and Western theatre forms to address contemporary concerns. As products of conjectural cultural practices, his theatre performances, and dramatic and literary texts, present us with significant levels of intertextuality and transtextuality. Orality penetrates this (new) theatre on literary, performance and similar to what Pulitano has noted about Native American theatre, 'structural level[s], in the attempt to inscribe its own theories about its nature and various functions' (Pulitano, 2003: 80); hence, entering into conversation with Western performance practices.

To a certain extent, Serumaga is echoing Abiola Irele's views, adapting indigenous theatrical elements, myths and legends but assigning them new meanings. According to Irele's argument, 'an oral text is almost never fully determined beforehand, given once and for all, as in the case of written literature', but it is 'actualized in oral performance and is thus open and mobile' (Irele, 2001: 34). Fundamentally, Irele is concerned that 'what can be abstracted as the verbal content of a given work is perpetually recreated, modified as the occasion demands', so this means giving a text 'new accents from one instance of its realization to another' (Irele, 2001: 34). Significantly, during performances, the 'principle of improvisation' allows ample scope for the free play of creative inventiveness around a cluster of motifs which are 'furnished by the culture' and operate 'within a structure of formal functions' which is often 'at work, in greater or lesser measure' in a cross section of contemporary Uganda theatre (Irele, 2001: 34). Irele's chapter, 'Orality, Literacy and African Literature', contains an important articulation of ways of appropriating and using folk and cultural tradition in contemporary literary and performance work. In addition to the 'living voice' of the performer, Irele states, 'a wider range of resources [are] brought into play in the aesthetic and imaginative framework of that experience as a function of the whole sensibility'. These 'paralinguistic features of language' as well as 'the extra-linguistic devices of movement and gesture, often accented into dance' are 'devices by which language enters into active association with the expressive possibilities of the human body' (Irele, 2001: 36). So, when, in Amin's military government and the second UPC government, theatre became a political tool that could have had a significant effect on the community, artists used it to transmit messages of freedom and the people's 'real' liberation during the National Resistance Army grassroots war, between 1980 and 1986. Serumaga and Ruganda, among others, realised the vitality of orature and movement and aimed to take the audience beyond the delimiting boundaries of the written word. If, as Taylor has observed, 'the concerns with oppression, colonization [and] self-hatred' are at the foundation of the theatre of crisis (Taylor, 1991: 22), then it could be said this practice illustrates the transformation of indigenous performance to a theatre of resistance.

Okpewho (2003), in 'Oral Tradition: Do Storytellers Lie?', observes how storytellers transform realms of reality from the past to comment on the present. While he specifically refers to the narrator's practice of intervention in oral narratives, in various forms of post-colonial performances, the playwright covertly takes on the role of the indigenous storyteller who inserts himself in the story. These 'acts of self-insertion', as Okpewho explains, 'are devices that facilitate the narrators' imaginative infiltration of, and exit from, the extraordinary worlds of the events they narrate' (Okpewho, 2003: 225). In this way, when he incorporates himself as a participant or an eyewitness of an incident/event he recreates, or when he manipulates time, embellishes his background and identifies himself with the main characters, the playwright or performer is in reality evaluating the socio-political experiences of his audience. As Okpewho suggests, by doing this, he is 'putting a signature, his seal of approval, on an experience he sees as bearing some relevance for himself or a community of interests he identifies with' (2003: 226). Invariably, '[p]erformance becomes the right setting for such an act because it facilitates the transfer of ordinary experience to a larger metaphorical level of signification, within the canons of representation recognised by the culture' (Okpewho, 2003: 226). Thus, when Serumaga resituates the travelling musician in a contemporary urban context, the performance becomes a dialogue between the playwright and the audience's post-colonial experiences, and shared memories. His retelling of Majangwa's story on stage, within which the protagonist personifies this transformation, resonates with the storytelling practices whereby, in various societies, the re-enactment of the story is used as a strategy to signify the people's resistance. Notably, his dramatic intervention aimed to articulate society's concerns with the events in Obote's turbulent post-colonial period (1962-1971),[3] and to warn Amin against repeating similar mistakes. Its staging coincided with the first of the many acts of disappearances and murder of the latter's regime.

'Speaking in Song': Helen Nabasuta Mugambi

The song (folk, solo or dance song) exists in various texts and it allows performers and writers to use and interpret it in different ways that challenge any simplistic understanding of orature and subvert oppressive discourses. In fact, Ngugi notes that in Kenya this was 'the only tradition against which the colonial state often took firm measures, banning many of the songs and performances, and gaoling the artists involved'[4] (Ngugi, 1998:105). In an essay entitled 'Speaking in Song: Power, Subversion and the Postcolonial Text', Helen Nabasuta Mugambi (2005) explores the use of song in subverting the authoritative discourse of oppressive leaders. She suggests that the 'most obvious subversive re-placement or relocation strategy that transforms the post-colonial text into a song-text is *saturation with song*' (Mugambi, 2005: 423). At the heart of Mugambi's essay, is the notion of 're-*placement*' borrowed from Bill Ashcroft *et al The Empire Writes Back*[5] (1989: 39), which she uses to theorize her ideas on the use of song in contemporary post-colonial fiction and performance. To position her argument, Mugambi suggests that since 'song is one of the most pervasive oral forms in Africa, it is possible that postcolonial writers' frequent recourse to this genre constitutes a mode of *re-placement*', or, what she describes as 'an idiomatic relocation signifying [re]placement' (Mugambi, 2005: 420). In order for narratives or performances to address the present, Mugambi and p'Bitek seem to say, artists must 're-idiomize language', theatrical or spoken (Mugambi, 2005: 426). p'Bitek chose (Acholi) Bwola dance songs whose lyrics reflected the artist's criticism of authority and society. In fact, most of his writing and concerns were underlining criticism of how things had changed both politically and culturally. As Mugambi writes, '[t]extual saturation with song contributes to the "seizure" of the language of the colonizer and to relocating it by boldly introducing song as the idiom of the colonized' (Mugambi, 2005: 427). In resonance with Mugambi's theorisation, Serumaga's work employs a critical 're-placement' of the song and other indigenous forms: 'Authors creat[e] song-texts and strategically and systematically employ song in their content, structure, themes, and style, leading to an ideological [transgressive] statement' (Mugambi, 2005: 423). In their version of performance that embeds 'elements of integrated theatre' (Pio Zirimu, 1971: 60), other artists are aware of the pervasive use of song as a '*re-placement* strategy' (Mugambi, 2005: 421): a medium of transgressive political discourse, whether royal music, *abadongo* ensemble, *Kadongo Kamu*, or even staged dramas such as *Majangwa*, *Renga Moi* and *Oluyimba lwa Wankoko* (1971). To a certain extent, Mugambi's views on the strategic role of song as theatrical shorthand resonate with the interpretation suggested by Irele concerning the proverb. Irele's view on the use of the proverb in song and other oral performances is a lot closer to writers such as Okpewho, Pio Zirimu and Bukenya, and Chinua Achebe. He further maintains that the use of song is 'the consciousness of the role that the proverb fulfils in speech' since it 'reflects experience and functions as a kind of minimalism of thought' (Irele, 2001: 32). In this way, theatre as a concept, may be literary, staged performances or vice versa. Therefore, successful theatrical experiences are those which 'incorporate such elements of integrated theatre as song, music (instrumental), dance, ritual and even audience participation'; all 'elements of black aesthetic appreciation' (Irele, 2001: 60).

'Poetic Chaos'?

Pio Zirimu and Bukenya acknowledge the significance of audience participation because, contrary to the 'othering' of African performers by Europeans, they assert that in oral performances, 'the rhythm of the chief performer(s) communicates itself to the audience…who in turn, as they are gripped by the beat, participate' (Pio Zirimu and Bukenya, 1986: 60). Like Pio Zirimu and Bukenya, p'Bitek wrote of 'the *chaotic poetical situation* that obtains during the love dance'. Consequently, 'there are not two persons who will be using identical descriptions in praising their lovers' but when '[t]he soloist calls the tune of a song that is well known…he will be thinking about his own girl'. Likewise, p'Bitek explains, 'In the so-called chorus, each male has in his mind his own girl' (p'Bitek, 1986: 31 emphasis added). In his view, therefore, there is not one but 'many soloists' in oral performances; in addition, '[at] the end of one song, and to begin another, there is much competition among soloists each one desiring to sing his other's praise' (1986: 33). Therefore, the '*chaotic poetical situation*' significantly demonstrates the type of audience participation that Pio Zirimu's essay also highlights. 'Participation', Pio Zirimu writes, 'is not professional' because 'the standards of achievement in performance vary a great deal.' He concludes: 'Such talent is discovered [spotted] in performance in group, that is, one's virtuosity, one's style, is given free range and when it strikes the pinnacles of aesthetic pleasure the not-so-good performers leave the arena for the accomplished, publicly acclaimed' (1971: 61). p'Bitek, on the other hand, applies his concept of 'poetic chaos' to dance songs when he suggests that although people sing the same tune, 'there is not one song but many songs' (p'Bitek, 1986: 35). Because a variety of artistic activities take place, 'some are humming, some shouting their praise names, some blowing their horns, [and] some making ululations'. The metaphor, 'poetic chaos' best explains the indigenous creative practice that informs the people's theorization of performance where individual participants are encouraged to display their creativity through improvising song verses and dance movements. As p'Bitek explains that there is no set text for the songs, 'myth or chant', however a group of skilled musicians provides both the 'drum measure' and 'the rhythmic beating of the half-gourds' (p'Bitek, 1986: 35). The consequence of this practice is not to construct a fixed performance text that, for instance, typifies Acholi Bwola dance, but rather something similar to indigenous theatrical expression and critical discourse that is discussed throughout this book. From within the 'poetic chaos' the songs (dance songs) articulate alternative discourses which may be aimed at disrupting social codes, subverting unpopular laws, re-inscribing new forms and styles or asserting the performers' rights to artistic license. By creating a flexible song text, in which alternative discourses and messages are embedded to signify the performers' individual experiences and identity, it is significant that there is 'no audience' but, '[f]or each poem there is one participating audience' (p'Bitek, 1986: 33). In this sense, '[t]he accomplished performer is not the one and only [performer] who simply excels in the extra flair, extra ease, integrated body expression, [or] extra inventiveness.' In this way, '[e]ffortless grace, but not static grace,' p'Bitek asserts, 'is dynamic, [and] full of emotional intensity' (p'Bitek, 1986: 33). p'Bitek's critical tone forces us to rethink how folk performance aesthetics, forms and styles which are perceived and used in contemporary theatre, in the sense suggested above, underlines the real and significant ways in which the world of performance (in Uganda) is organised.

Serumaga's *Renga Moi* (1972), *Majangwa* (1974) and *Amayirikiti* (1974)

The problem of state reception of theatre is a problem embedded in the dialectics of colonization and post-colonialism, in which critical voices are perceived to be signs of dissent and resistance. Thus, in his critical work, Serumaga began to construct, through the aesthetics of the oral performance, ritual, dance, music (instrumental) and song, a semiotics of performance that subverted Western forms as it responded to colonial cultural influence and post-colonial socio-political conditions. Among his plays, that mark him out as one of the first artists to express dissent on stage, are: *A Play* (1968); *The Elephants* (1971); *Renga Moi* (1972), *Majangwa* (1974) and *Amayirikiti* (1974). The earlier plays, *A Play* and *The Elephants*, were influenced by his concept of integration and the social/cultural experience where the writer's output is a synthesis of cultural conditioning and contemporary reality. (Serumaga, 1969) These dramas demonstrate the beginning of the transmutation of sacred beliefs, spirit possession, ghostly apparitions and communal reality in Ugandan theatre. Most notably, the unscripted plays, *Renga Moi* and *Amayirikiti*, evidence the sense of the fragmented existence that envelopes his scripted theatre.[6] Instead of dialogue, Serumaga developed non-verbal forms - cultural motifs such as ritual and taboos - through which he could enhance the sub-text and express himself more articulately. Both productions were multi-indigenous, using Western forms, Japanese Kabuki, and as many Ugandan languages, songs and dances as there were members in the cast. *Renga Moi* is about a young man who is in a dilemma, whether to serve his family or his village.[7] *Amayirikiti* (Luganda name for flame trees), graphically demonstrated the activities of Amin and his henchmen. Despite the allegorical title of the play - the flame tree is the traditional burial place for dogs in Buganda - and the mimed actions of people being carried away in car boots. Amin, who apparently watched most of Serumaga's productions, remarked that it was good 'gymnastics' (Mbowa, 1996b: 202). The theme of disappearance is underlined by the graphic stage representation of 'dangling bodies in black tunics spread over the vertical scaffold, on the floor of the stage, with a coffin in their midst'. These were 'a clear depiction of the countless Amin murders and dumping grounds - in dungeons, forests, rivers [and] lakes' (Mbowa, 1994a: 130). Serumaga's interest in performance and signification reflected his feelings on the capacity of language (in a wider form) to disseminate values that are other than purely textual and formal. In extending the indigenous performative and imaginative expression to the contemporary stage, Serumaga recognised that the use of 'drum language' and other 'non-linguistic symbolic schemes' are important to performance, since they 'give spatial resonance to human speech' and 'extend the expressive potential of language' (Gikandi, 2007: 18). Indeed, 'in the absence of spoken language', as Gikandi has explained, 'Serumaga's works relied on his audience's ability to decipher such floating movements and connect them to Ugandan politics' (Gikandi, 2007: 18). His practice echoes Irele's view that 'oral cultures have developed various strategies within the complex framework of their semiotic systems for overcoming limitations of oral communication' (Irele, 2001: 27). Hence, Serumaga's 'use of language for imaginative purposes represents a fundamental component of the symbolic structures by which the individual relates to society and by which society itself relates to its universe of existence' (2001: 27-28).

Writing about political subversion in Latin American theatre Taylor argues that theatre 'can more effectively undermine oppressive forces than other art forms' because it 'is live' and 'live actors affect live audiences in unforeseeable ways' (Taylor, 1991: 5). Moreover, if a repressive government wanted to shut them down 'each performance would have to be policed in order to ensure that the actors did not deliver a line or make a gesture that would communicate a politically prohibited message to its audience'[8] (Taylor, 1991: 5). In relation to

Taylor's view of a theatre that blends traditional and Western forms to construct subversive statements, during the period covered by this book, artists took and blended indigenous and Western performance models. By this blending, the artists transformed them into theatrical idioms and multiple signals that voiced resistance to the *status quo*. Here I underline the changing function of indigenous performances, for instance, dance, (vocal) music and storytelling, in 'a context of oppression and conflict' (Taylor, 1991: 23). Serumaga's style puts into practice his political and theoretical agenda; that of developing the language of dancing and acting, 'aesthetic resources capable of representing' (Taylor, 1991: 65) the reality of defiance and maintaining a critical attitude towards the past and the present political crisis. Interviewed following the performance of *Renga Moi* at the Belgrade International Theatre Festival (1968), Serumaga said:

> We believe in the body as the supreme instrument of theatre and then the voice, and when I say voice, I simply mean sound. Even words to us are sounds first and meaning second. Then we believe that in as much as words are communication through sound that silence is even more important than words, and in many cases, we consider this as a breach of silence (Serumaga, 1973: 3).

In *Renga Moi*, where, similar to the reality of Uganda, 'celebration and sacrifice are continuously replacing each other', Serumaga demonstrates how the 'poetic meanings and choreographic signs are skilfully combined' (Serumaga, 1969: 3) to enhance the message. Indeed, speaking to Barbara Kimenye, he stated, 'We don't use straight line stories. We use a juxtaposition of images to trigger off emotions in the audience, which we hope will carry out a process of self-examination and arrive at some truths. Each person might get a different truth, but nevertheless it is his own truth' (Serumaga, 1973: 3).

From Serumaga's dramatic collection, I will use *Majangwa* as an example of a play committed to artistic resistance to political oppression. In *Majangwa*, the practice of blending orature and other indigenous performance forms with artistic resistance to political oppression achieve significance as they make a transition into (Western) formal theatre. In employing popular performance forms, Serumaga involves his audience in the process of thinking about the political/social crisis, thereby, creating a new way of resisting tyranny.

Mbowa observes that the play was 'a criticism of the first part of Obote's unproductive reign, and a comment on society's plight'[9] during 'Amin's era [which turned] out to be replete with wanton murder and further insecurities' (Mbowa, 1994a: 128). Elsewhere, George Bwanika Seremba comments that by staging *Majangwa*, Serumaga, 'however oblique and masqueraded his signification, had knowingly put his personal survival at tremendous risk, every single night of the play's run' (Seremba, 2008: 177). In this way, Serumaga demonstrated his role as a guardian of the community's conscience; a role that resonates with indigenous artists, especially the travelling musicians who, in order to alleviate communal suffering commit themselves to exposing deviant behaviour through satire.

Majangwa had its premiere at the National Theatre, in Kampala on 13 November 1971. While the play received international acclaim when it was presented in Nairobi, Kenya, and Manila, The Philippines, local audiences found themselves alienated from the performances. This raises a question of how effective Serumaga's work was in challenging autocratic rulers if his local audiences were alienated by the play. Mbowa states, 'Ugandans who could not understand him blamed him for always talking to an alien audience' (Mbowa, 1994a: 127). How does Serumaga's criticism effectively challenge the socio-political status quo if it does not relate to the ordinary person? What, if not an academic exercise, is Serumaga's reliance on non-indigenous forms and styles? Whether the unscripted *Renga Moi* and *Amayirikiti* or *Majangwa* and *The Elephants* were effective in re-igniting the spirit of resistance is open to debate. But undoubtedly, however inaccessible, in the minds of various post-colonial theatre critics Serumaga's performance practices effectively transmitted shared experiences, memories and values. For instance, *Majangwa*'s 'telling local symbolism [and] its beautiful poetry enhanced the social and political criticism in the subtext' (Mbowa, 1994a: 126). Thus, it is possible to appreciate Serumaga's works partly because of their orality, but also because of the personal and political context in which they were written and produced. His hope was that drama framed in this way might reawaken a sense of connectedness, critical awareness and communal resistance that had always been part of the Ugandan experience but had been lost in the euphoria of independence.

In this way, Serumaga's main protagonist is based on Majangwa, who was a real life travelling musician and part of the life of the people in the city of Kampala, and Nakulabye trading centre, in the city's suburbs, between 1940 and 1975. The real Majangwa, unshaven and with long grizzled hair, as Margaret Macpherson (1976) explains, carried *engalabi* (a long drum) and was accompanied by his wife, Nakirijja, and their two dogs. He was part of Kampala's history; throughout his lifetime he drummed and sang from trading centre to trading centre, and open market to open market. As he had no permanent home, Majangwa was out of the reach of the state machinery; he had no permanent job, no house and no garden, therefore, he did not plant the mandatory coffee and cotton crops. He paid neither hut tax nor poll tax; but colonial/ post-colonial tax enforcers or paramilitary forces could not apprehend him. Majangwa, similar to other travelling musicians, often performed mimed actions to verses of songs that, sometimes, were records of the history of his community or satires of Ugandan society. By employing strategies that mirror travelling musicians and storytellers, and a performance framework in which movement, mime, music and dance, and oral narratives, Serumaga gives new meaning to shared performance forms. Thus, apparently inspired by an active and popular living performer who spent his life on the road, the play may have been an attempt to present *abadongo*[10] or *abagoma*,[11] travelling musicians who performed as an ensemble, but with one or two dancers in their troupe, perhaps the most dynamic form of traditional entertainment to be taken into formal theatre.[12] While his counterparts the court musicians had hereditary roles in the palace, similar to Majangwa, these other ordinary musicians sometimes moved alone, often playing at beer parties. Their life style, always travelling from village to village, made them conscious of the happenings in the community, giving them insight into individual characters.

The function of songs as 'the outline of a verbal structure and as reference points for the development of ideas and images' (Irele, 2001: 34) is manifest in Serumaga, Ruganda and Elvania Zirimu's works as they continuously draw on them for theme, symbol and structure and inspiration that make their works lively. Similarly, they aim to find paths to push back the boundaries of other indigenous performances, while destabilizing Western forms and resisting political oppression. For instance, Serumaga, aware of the tradition linking performers with resistance, and equally aware of royal flutist' song, '*Omusango Gw'abalere*', within which they state, '"Let me follow the fluteplayerman, let me follow the fluteplayerman, back to the big forest where I was born'" (*Majangwa*, 1974:26), weave these aspects into *Majangwa*. The song, which is very poignant and interrelates with the past glory of Buganda Kingdom, becomes a commentary on Ugandan contemporary experiences. In another sense, since flutists composed it to demonstrate their displeasure at the Buganda king's oppressive administration, as Muzeeyi Serwanga, one of the king's musicians, informed me it reminds the 'initiate' audience of the role of artists in transgressing/challenging authority. Considering more specifically the context of oral performance, Majangwa's own critical tradition derives from his experience in the *abadongo* oral traditions.[13] In one scene, to make a political statement, Majangwa highlights the charm and importance of *baakisimba* with nostalgia through a narrative of their experience at festivals.

Majangwa: It is a good road. It can't stay empty for too long. I've been on it. Travelling. A young man and his drum playing weddings across the country, at chiefs' parties. A good drum, and fingers to go with it. (*gets his drum*) Mellowed over the years.

Nakirijja: Years of nothing.

Majangwa: It wasn't always like this. You forget. I wasn't always like this.

Nakirijja: Nothing. With a future we can't see and a past we would soon forget.

Majangwa: Forget? How can I forget the road? Majangwa, yes, that's me. (*pause*) I remember them, admirers; lovers of the drum and the lyre and the fiddle. There was honour at the chief's court. We gathered to make songs and meanings and connect our souls to the earth. You could hear the dead whisper above the sound of drums and in the voice of the man with the fiddle, Sekinoomu, Temuteewo Mukasa, Namale. Honour at the chief's court. And the weddings - beneath the song, sounds of ecstasy from within. Beyond the song, another song.

(*Majangwa*, pp. 25-26)

This dialogue establishes the primary connection between *abadongo*/folkloric performance and contemporary theatre. Serumaga appropriates characteristics of oral performance, idioms, proverbs, music and snippets from myths and song archives aiming not only to transmit the Baganda worldview, which is mainly oral and musical, but also to reflect the indiscreet tradition of transmitting morals, cloaking indigenous resistance to colonialism, and in a sense, post-colonial oppression in performance. A key characteristic feature of the *abadongo* (travelling musicians) genre is the 'immediacy' of performance or 'closeness of the performer to his environment; closeness to his material; and, closeness to his audience' (Pio Zirimu and Bukenya, 1986: 92). In this way, from the perspective of the Baganda oral performance traditions, one can see that in Serumaga's *Majangwa*, Majangwa's role, as an entertainer and storyteller, derives from his profession. It should be noted that in the colonial period performances such as songs and instrumental music predominated in playing the critical role to unpopular rule. Accordingly, when Pio Zirimu and Bukenya talk about 'immediacy of derivation' (Pio Zirimu and Bukenya, 1986: 92), when the performer intimately speaks of the past, the present and the future, since he is using material drawn from his lived experience, repertoire and embodied knowledge they imply a notion of continuance of the function of artists as the conscience of society. Of course, not having much wealth or reputation to lose, they were easily dismissed - at least openly - as of no consequence. This traditional attitude to musicians, as lazy irresponsible individuals, has always, directly or indirectly, influenced the status of theatre practitioners and consequently the role of theatre in influencing change in Uganda. Whereas, during Obote's first tenure in office, theatre was regarded as pure entertainment and artists' criticisms were dismissed as inconsequential, and the artist as a person incapable of harming their political positions, Amin took offence when his security agents unfavourably interpreted *Oluyimba lwa Wankoko* to be a subversive statement on his regime.

While mindful of his responsibilities, commitment and the dangers of transgression that threatened him, Serumaga draws us in, inviting us not only to appreciate the aesthetics of the musicality of the language, the beauty of Kiganda song and music, but to participate, critique and reflect on the post-colonial condition. He 'is not revealing unheard-of marvels'; however, at the right moments, helped by gestures, music, and movement, and 'sounding the depths of *his* experience of what everyone knows' (Pio Zirimu and Bukenya, 1986: 93) he invites us to participate in the performance. Arguably, the play, named after a travelling musician and drawing from folkloric archives, is a literal and metaphorical site of inter-textualities. In addition, it is a testimony to how *katemba* can be seen as a space that allows the development of forms of discourse, and performance practices, that cross boundaries between the oral and the written, or, oral, musical and staged performances, which subvert and defy tyrannical systems.

In *Majangwa*, the couple comment on their frustration with society's problems (its immorality, poverty and increasing violence) and with people too impotent to act. Majangwa tells of how he has been tempted to turn to traditional ways of healing and spiritual worship, seeking help from medicine men. Ironically, he reveals how they, the rejects of society, have become society's talismen who might save it from its predicament. Through this presentation, Serumaga, similar to Elvania Zirimu in *The Family Spear* (1973) and *When the Hunchback Made Rain* (1975), articulates the community's post-colonial in-between location in two worlds (traditional and modern), or what Mbowa describes as the '"dualism"' in post-colonial dramas (Mbowa, 1996a: 87), struggling to find a way in which the old ways and modernity might exist together. To the audience, Majangwa's near-schizophrenic state where, in spite of his fragmented self, he seeks to find a balance between tradition and modernity, is a reflection on contemporary society. One of the preoccupations of the play is the entanglement of Majangwa and Nakirijja's lives, and Nakirijja's mourning about her predicament: it is a mourning for the damage inflicted on them by society, and the state of the country.[14]

Serumaga, as previously stated, does not appropriate the absurdist play arbitrarily, but borrows selected techniques - from Samuel Beckett, Bertolt Brecht, and Jerzy Grotowiski, for example - that mirror the sense of disillusionment in a post-colonial society. Nevertheless, he creates a fluid mixed-genre text, in which different discourses are woven together to give significance to his own post-colonial experiences. In this way, he demonstrates 'how the syncretic and adaptive nature of the oral tradition finds its way onto the written page' and the stage, 'creating a shifting, hybridized space in which [ethnically] based ideas can be creatively and effectively incorporated into a new original creation' (Elvira Pulitano, 2003: 133). Serumaga's and Ruganda's works owe much to Pio Zirimu's idea of orature and to the movement in theatre, which aimed to offer critical intervention in performance, against what he saw as the decline into authoritarianism and moral decay, through merging indigenous and Western forms. While the play self-consciously allows the actors to examine their lived reality in what Majangwa describes as '[a] cruel, mean, envious, malicious world' (*Majangwa*, p. 31) from within Majangwa and Nakirijja's world, these anxieties provoke anger, bitterness and frustration. Thus, to make sense of the abject conditions, they turn to the language of metaphors and negativity, articulating their feelings to the audience. For example, in the following extract, comedy (incorporated in many scenes) is contrived through their bitterness:

Majangwa: Your tongue is a snake; you shouldn't open your mouth too often.
Nakirijja: Talking as one snake to another.

(*Majangwa*, p.17)

Their arguments achieve counterpoint with each individual wriggling out of a trap to set another trap, like Wakayima (Hare), the trickster in Baganda and other Ugandan folklore. Their emotive visual language, which invokes the poetics of *abadongo*, is intriguing; for instance, in response to Nakirijja's comment that they 'were the puss of a very diseased society',[15] Majangwa states, 'On the contrary, we were the wound; the opening through which society got rid of its excess pus' (Serumaga, 1974: 12). This self-consciousness represents Serumaga's critical theatre with its ability to force the audience, not only to question their being, but also that of the emerging authoritarian institutions.

In *Majangwa*, Serumaga constructs a play-in-play in which he draws on the ancestral, mythical and historical aspects of Kintu and Nambi's story, specifically, Kayiikuzi descending to the bowls of the earth to seek out Walumbe, a narrative that identifies the significance of context and place. Tanda, the setting of the play, is where, in the Kiganda worldview, Walumbe (Death) resides. It signifies a mythical and real space and within it, there are traces of history and betrayal, but it also marks a kind of closure allowing other forms of performance to emerge.[16]

(*He draws her away and takes her to the crack in the road. He lights a match.*)
Majangwa: See that?
Nakirijja: A crack in the crack in the tarmac.
Majangwa: A crack in the crust of the earth.
Nakirijja: What's the difference?

Majangwa: Thirty-five miles on the road to Mityana, a crack....
Nakirijja: ...in the tarmac...
Majangwa: ...in the crust of earth.
Nakirijja: Oh, for god's sake I am going back to sleep.
Majangwa: Sleep? Are you crazy? This is the village of Tanda!
Nakirijja: (*not really scared*) What?
Majangwa: Tanda, the village of death. This is where Death went underground.
Nakirijja: (*in ridicule*) And this, I suppose, is the crack through which he went. (*sharply*) Let me go back to sleep.
Majangwa: Kayikuuzi! (*She turns and looks at him.*)
Nakirijja: What did you call me?
Majangwa: Not you, Kayikuuzi. He chased Death down into the earth, beneath the crust. Right here. We must leave immediately.

(*Majangwa*, pp. 46 - 47)

In this context, the road and the space are both real and mythic, providing the metaphor that signifies the different journeys that people have travelled, and Tanda, the space and the point of intersection and encounter between the past and the present; colonial and native, as well as urban and rural cultures.

Significantly, Majangwa's multi-layered references are similar to the style of paralleling in Kiganda musical composition and performance: he piles the symbolism of the place, the iconic anthill, and the activities of the colonial (and post-colonial) construction companies. Stirling Astaldi (Italy), Mowlem (Britain) and Solel Boneh (Israel).[17]

Nakirijja: [...] Who burnt our house?
Majangwa: How should I know? Somebody who wished destruction. (*Silence. A car passes. They wait till its sound dies in the distance. Silence.*)
Majangwa: And when he reached the village of Tanda he came face to face with an anthill.
Nakirijja: Who?
Majangwa: Stirling Astaldi... (*They laugh.*)

In the middle of the projected road, stood an anthill. There it was, a termite mountain painfully raised out of the red earth, nurturing in its maze of cavities, white ants, big driver ants, small driver ants and the queen ant - sedate, proliferous, fat; a world concealed beneath a piece of rising ground.

But the road had to go on. Another act of murder. So they started the big yellow machine. (*He starts it.*) Big

white man and his yellow machine set against an anthill. (*Tractor noise made by Majangwa*) And the people gathered to witness the adventure of metal against earth. (*He makes tractor noise and assumes the role of Stirling Astaldi.*)
"Get out of my way people! Get out! Bloody Africans!"
Then a big iron axe rose and fell upon the palace of the queen and the people shouted.

Majangwa and Nakirijja: Heh!!!

Majangwa: And in the cloud of dust as the machine wreaked destruction upon the anthill, white ants like petals riding the wind, flew away, away, away from the earth, away from the red cloud, away from the destruction and into the hands of the waiting people who caught them and ate them alive.

Nakirijja: Carry on Stirling As-taldi!

Majangwa: Oye!

Nakirijja: Carry on Mowlem!!

Majangwa: Oye!

Nakirijja: Carry on Solel Boneh!!!
(*silence*)

(*Majangwa*, p. 33)

Serumaga extends the political and communal nuance of Kintu's legend by linking the present, the desecration of the Buganda kingdom by Obote, the murders and disappearances during Amin's regime, the past, and the colonisation of Uganda. He underlines his message by implicating the community as collaborators in the destruction of their culture. Buganda's history is intertwined with the colonial conquest of Uganda, therefore, in *Majangwa* Serumaga speaks for the whole of Uganda. This is further extended by the use of the road, an 'image, usually applied to the struggle for independence' and, as Seremba explains, 'the key to the world of Serumaga's symbolic terrain, and indeed, the post-colonial prerogatives, including…the pathology/pathologies that he diagnoses and exposes' (Seremba, 2008: 178-179). The road is a way of exploring the tensions between different worlds and spaces, at the same time suggesting mythic and contemporary journeys. Hence, the roadside scene, in this sense, suggests an opening into the Ugandans' pre-independence world. The graphic scene in which the body of a man is dumped at Tanda can be attributed to a complex set of events. For example, the transgression of indigenous codes of morality is a significant comment on the contemporary experiences of torture, disappearances and murder. Furthermore, as previously discussed, the story of the woman and the last scene of the play in which a body is dumped, invokes the ritual that resonates with the story about the place, Tanda. (Seremba, 2009) The play becomes a dialogue shifting between the personal experiences of the couple caught between tradition, cross-culture, and socio-political conflicts. The quality of the play may be dependent on the music and dance elements for, as Okpewho (1983:92) suggests, 'as physical movement goes' in indigenous oral performance, 'one of the devices necessary for the basic poetic transport of the myth is the dance, with which the narrator executes many of the dramatic moments in the career of the hero'.[18]

Majangwa incorporates several moments that show the intersection of folkloric and modern performances, while it self-consciously allows the actors to examine their lived reality in what Majangwa describes as, 'A cruel, mean, envious, malicious world' (Serumaga, 1974: 31). Folklore and the specific exhibitionism of folk musicians, emphasizing solo performance, are drawn upon by Serumaga to emphasize his theme; for example, although he is a specialist drum player, Majangwa compares himself to the legendary musicians in Buganda, such as Ssekinoomu and Temuteewo Mukasa, the harpists.[19] Serumaga structurally uses 'Sekitulegge', a children's music game with sexual overtones, to illustrate Majangwa's sexual exhibitionism. It shows Serumaga's pessimism for society, drawing parallels between sexual exhibitionism and politics, which results in disillusion. Indeed, when Serumaga's Majangwa and Nakirijja contemplate their wasted life in the city, Majangwa states that while he can accept his personal failings, 'What I can't look back at without puking my guts out is the society which paid to watch us' (Serumaga, 1974: 14). For him, the commercialization of performances and the emergence of audiences titillated by sexually suggestive dance performances is a sign of a demented society. Here, Serumaga explores this couple's narrative not only to demonstrate the urbanization of performance, but the changing role of dance and music in contemporary society. Hence, if we have to engage in a dialogue with Uganda's past, we need to pay attention to musical plays and musical performances that locate people's experiences within a larger performative space.

The audience as collaborators

The relationship between orature and contemporary performance - in this context referring to performance space, place, gesture, and dance - allows the artists to engage with narratives that draw on the audience's shared experiences, while encouraging them to focus on the alternative lines of inquiry within the text (Pio Zirimu and Bukenya, 1986). The projection of fantasy is mostly evident in stories, which are epic in style, such as the tales of 'The Madman' or 'The Leper' dramatised by Lubwa p'Chong and Ruganda, respectively. In re-telling the story, the narrator intercuts the narration with personal statements about the main characters, which makes the story relevant for the contemporary audience. The repertoire of traditional folk tales is relatively well known; therefore, performers have to be very creative in re-telling a story, if they want to captivate their audience. This is achievable through spontaneity. The use of song, dance, mime, props and costume becomes inevitable in the attempt to give the tale a fresh touch and transform it into a contemporary experience. The audience, as observed by Bukenya and Pio Zirimu, and Okpewho (1983), is 'an integral part of the performance'; nevertheless, in contemporary settings, the 'literary artist' cannot rely on the function of this 'critical audience' (Okpewho, 1983: 77). Okpewho observes that in the traditional setting of the theatre in the round, 'there is no safety in distance and darkness. Everyone is known: the artist emerges from the audience and, her narrative completed, is again swallowed up by the audience.' Further, he asserts that '[t]he separate emotions and experience of individual members of an audience are interwoven into the narrative being revoked' (Okpewho, 1983: 77). Hence, the 'artistic experience is a complex one. The members of the audience know the images; they have experienced them scores of times. They know the performer intimately and she knows them. The artist seeks in a variety of ways to involve the audience wholly in her/his production' (Harold Scheub quoted in Okpewho, 1983: 77). What Okpewho describes as the audience's immediate and critical response, or call and response, can be seen in drama and musical theatre performances of the Amin period.

As Serumaga's performances engage with issues of transformation, transgression and identity in a new post-colonial society, they respond to a series of questions concerning the foregoing indigenous (oral) performance practices and theories, which are important for an understanding of the interrelationship between *katemba*, and various contemporary theatre performances. Even today the transgression of spaces in orature, whereby the piece is composed (and performed) neither by the audience nor the orator (performer), makes indigenous performance a significant force and explains why the concepts of immediacy, structure and collaboration have become bound up with the criticism of African performance. Audience participation implies the potential to transgress and subvert political and performance spaces, creating zones where new aesthetics, forms, multiple voices, and identities emerge. Most notably, similar to other playwrights' works, Serumaga's *Majangwa* explores this aesthetic and concept of the people's voice to defy the political status quo; hence, challenging definitions of performance (indigenous and Western).

Audience participation or 'communal creativity' that is 'discernible in oral performance' is dissimilar to 'gimmicky theatre productions which keep yelling provocatively at an audience until it has to hit back in self-defense', but rather 'communality in genuine oral performance' which springs from the triangular 'intimacy' that exists 'between orator, audience and material' (Pio Zirimu and Bukenya, 1986: 93). Since the performer is 'one of them', the audience has a deep concern for him and an involvement with his undertaking; moreover, because he is talking of *their* material, they have a direct stake in his performance. So, 'often, the performance becomes a collective endeavour, so much so that sometimes the role of the orator is minimal'; thus, Pio Zirimu and Bukenya conclude, to 'get it right', he 'must be helped, where necessary, to make his communication effective, complete' (1986: 93). The performance texts are syncretic, showing how various indigenous theatrical forms and texts are reworked and reimagined as they are performed for different audiences or by different artists. Serumaga achieves his goals by relying on oral indigenous and contemporary Western performance practices since these two, for him, meet in important ways. For instance, in exploring the multiple-voices, he challenges, similar to Ngugi, the 'romantic illusion' by European travellers and missionaries, of the 'free natives, yelling in delighted chaos at their tales and songs, each doing his own thing' (Pio Zirimu and Bukenya, 1986: 93). As Bukenya and Pio Zirimu may argue concerning the question of structure, if a performance "is going to 'survive' and work over the scores of voices (and temperaments) which may participate in its performance, its scope, intention, line of orientation, its structure must be firmly established by its initiator (the orator [performer]) and fully understood by his collaborators." For, '[t]he principles of composition and performance are intimately known and professionally respected by any performer or would-be performer (including the 'collaborators' or spectator - participants)". Therefore, '[s]trength of *structure* and vividness of expression are necessary also for the sheer mechanics of communication.' A performance, helped by 'supra-linguistic resources - gestures, facial expression, melodic and rhythmic aids, movement, occasion and situation of performance,' and 'mnemonics and discreet reiteration' available to the performer, 'must *strike* the recipient forcefully' (Pio Zirimu and Bukenya, 1986: 93). In a critical context, this imagined disruptive audience, the critical collaborator, is significant to the construction of a meaningful text/performance.

Chapter 3

INTERSECTIONS OF POLITICS AND FOLKLORE IN BYRON KAWADWA'S THEATRE[1]

This chapter looks at the dynamics of politics and theatre as is demonstrated in Byron Kawadwa's work. As with other discussions involving contemporary performance and theatre, the present examination of Kawadwa's theatre cannot escape the overarching issues of the nature and function of his work in times of conflict. As a politically minded playwright, Kawadwa was focused on writing plays concerning social and political issues. Mbowa, for instance, describes Kawadwa (1937 - 1977) as a dramatist who was 'so outspoken' that 'he was bound to become the first martyr of theatre under Idi Amin - just as Lwanga became [King] Mwanga II's first [Christian] martyr'[2] (Mbowa, 1999: 227-47). This view which examines the relationship between performance and resistance, mirrors overarching issues of the nature and function of theatre in times of conflict, and how his theatre resisted oppression by the state. Kawadwa worked for the then Uganda Broadcasting House, until, following the 1964 Nakulabye Massacre, he was detained at Luzira Government Maximum Prison. These, and his father's death during the Nakulabye Massacre, were instrumental in his development as a social critic. Between 1966 and 1973, when he became the first Uganda Artistic Director of the National Cultural Centre, Kawadwa worked with Wycliff Kiyingi in Kiyingi Productions.[3]

Following the arrival of the Anglican and Roman Catholic missionaries in Buganda in 1877, religious wars broke out forcing changes of power in the royal palace. Kabaka Mwanga II of Buganda violently killed Christian converts opposed to his reign. Although the victims were originally 'Baganda Martyrs', with time they have come to be perceived as Uganda Martyrs and, as Ronald Kassimir notes in 'Complex Martyrs: Symbols of Catholic Church Transformation and Political Differentiation in Uganda' (1991), the only tangible national symbol. At Independence in 1962, Obote became the first Prime Minister of Uganda, specifically because of the role he played in the independence struggle and the fragile alliance between Uganda

Peoples Congress and Kabaka Yekka (KY), the King Only Party headed by the Kabaka of Buganda. Unfortunately, the alliance would soon fall prey to religious and ethnic differences, which climaxed in the crises of 1964, 1966, and subsequently the Battle of Mengo. Collectively, these signified the end of political freedom and cultural leaders' powers and privileges.

In the intervening period between 1966 and Amin's military *coup d'état* in 1971, Kawadwa, similar to other theatre artists such as Serumaga and Kiyingi, expressed his anguish at the repressive republican UPC government through staging political and cultural performances. Serumaga and Kawadwa experimented with traditional folk forms using them as symbols to signify the discontent in society. Amin's barrage against imperialism and promotion of a false sense of 'state adulthood' blindly affected Ugandans through his declaration of the 'Economic War', indirectly affected theatre and church institutions. The 'Economic War' Ugandanised and '*magendonised* (commercialised)' theatre placing it alongside other equally profitable enterprises; it was popularised and became more important than cinema or possibly football.[4] In the religious context, both the Anglican (1977) and Roman Catholic Church's (1979) centenary celebrations of the Baganda Martyrs, killed by the Buganda King Mwanga II, were largely sponsored by Amin. This cultural revival inadvertently legitimised the use of indigenous performance genres as weapons of resistance. For, under the pretext of criticising King Mwanga II's brutalities, performers implicitly protested against Amin's atrocities.

Significantly, Kawadwa's appointment as the key administrator of the National Theatre meant that he carried the responsibility of building up an indigenous theatre patronage. Crucially, several conditions facilitated the rapid development of an already existing theatre-going culture at that time: specifically because after the institution of a Republican Constitution in 1969, the Baganda were affected by the changes and identified themselves with symbolic cultural welfare clubs as a means of maintaining cultural continuity. Outstanding among these clubs was Express Football Club, euphemistically referred to as *mukwano gwa bangi* or *ttiimu ya bantu* (the people's club/team), which had been founded by the Baganda. However, Abdul Nassuru, Amin's Provincial Governor of Kampala, intent on humiliating the Baganda, disbanded it in 1976, an action followed by the increased harassment of football supporters at matches. Coincidentally, cinema houses suffering from the backlash of Amin's 'Economic War' (they could no longer import films), were being transformed into playhouses. The lack of alternative entertainment, coupled with the insecurity mentioned above, forced the football-going community, as well as other members of the public, to resort to the theatre.

The unintentional consequences of Nassuru's actions were astonishing: once again, as one of the community at the receiving end of tyranny, the Baganda began to relate to the Uganda National Cultural Centre and the National Theatre as one of their iconic cultural symbols. In the meantime, Kawadwa's Kampala City Players had become the unofficial wing of Express Football Club because of its popular performances of Baganda based plays. The invasion of the theatre by these football club supporters brought a new dimension to theatre.[5] When their attachment to individual actors and responses to live performances became similar to that of crowds cheering their favourite team or player, it brought spontaneity and encouraged improvisation and exhibitionism in theatre, which were features of indigenous theatre that had been either overlooked or simply abandoned as unreflective of modern Uganda. At the same time, they formed an audience association; a pressure group similar to the Express Football Club Supporters group that aimed at influencing the staging of indigenously based popular shows in defiance of political authority.[6] Mbowa also notes the economic impact on theatre because the 'new practitioners' of playhouses and drama groups 'realised that they could supplement their living through theatre as there was a regular and uncritical audience for whom anything that produced laughter and gave grief to the government in power was good theatre' (1996: 91).

However, at the end of Amin's regime, those Ugandans who had gone into exile returned to create a new social class replacing Amin's Nubian class. The returning Ugandans, referred to as *ba-exilo* (exiles or returnees), forcibly threw the *stayees* (a term coined to describe people who stayed in Uganda, but with connotations of being traitors or collaborators) out of their properties at gunpoint. In order to avoid gun-wielding returnees, the public deserted drinking bars, preferring *bitanda* (private rooms or grocery shops) in localities where they were well-known. Likewise, theatre artists ejected from the playhouses took over the abandoned bars and nightclubs turning them into playhouses.

Kawadwa and the Theatre

Between 1969 and 1975, Kawadwa wrote and directed a number of plays based on Ugandan folklore, political and social experiences. These include *Serwajja Okwota* (1966);[7] *Sitakange* (1969), a translation and adaptation of Jean-Batiste Poquelin's *The Miser* (1967); and *Mitaafu* (1970), a translation and adaptation of Wole Soyinka's *The Trials of Brother Jero* (1969). In addition, in collaboration with the music composer, Wassanyi Sserukenya, he wrote three plays, *St Lwanga* (1969); *Makula ga Kulabako* (Kulabako's Beauty, 1970); and *Oluyimba lwa Wankoko* (Song of Wankoko, 1971). In these plays, Kawadwa underlines familial and cultural virtues and communal strengths as the best means of challenging anarchy. In the plays written before Amin's ascension to power, historical facts were invested with literary significance and up-dated for purposes of contemporary relevance. For instance, *Serwajja Okwota*, a proverbial title that reflects on the political scheming that got Obote into power, is 'the story of a lean, hungry dog that came to warm itself by somebody's fire, but drove the owner and usurped the space all to himself' (Mbowa, 1994: 123-135). *St. Lwanga*, *Makula ga Kulabako* and *Oluyimba lwa Wankoko* pointed toward musical plays, a new performance genre, which combined dialogue, songs, actions, and other aspects of oral performance that incorporated politically defiant comments and occupied an important critical space.

For Kawadwa, foregrounding an indigenous identity inspired his theatre practice. He used the royal institution as a metaphor to criticise the political status quo, because within the context in which he worked, his audiences could identify with the institution. Notably, the abolition of the Buganda Kingdom made it easy to draw on it for inspiration, without the playwright jeopardizing his personal safety. Further, the palace setting was easy to use as a platform for criticism: Baganda political intrigues had been widely duplicated in national politics; therefore, while the plays may have feudal themes, they draw implicit parallels with contemporary events. *Oluyimba lwa Wankoko*, *Makula ga Kulabako*, and *St Lwanga* highlight the political and cultural consciousness prevalent in Buganda beginning around 1966.

The comedic content of *Makula ga Kulabako* is graphically illustrated by the elderly fisherman, Semuvubi, a rich and verbose suitor who would be rejected by Princess Kulabako in preference for a poor but good-looking palace dancer. *Makula ga Kulabako* raises no direct political issues. However, *Oluyimba, Oluyimba lwa Wankoko*, informed by internal Baganda political intrigues, draws parallels with post-colonial political events. The play has had four major productions - 1971, 1977, 1989 and 2006. While there have not been any structural and major ideological changes for historical reasons, successive directors have adjusted its ideological thrust to address contemporary socio-political conditions.

Kawadwa articulates the cracks in the relationships between the individual and society, and the ruler and the ruled, through the trope of madness and possession by presenting characters that appear self-centred and oblivious to the needs of other people. Hence, in *St. Lwanga*, Mukajanga, Mwanga II's chief executioner, is the first creation of this type of character that came to be central in his plays. Other characters, for example, Semuvubi in *Makula ga Kulabako*, and Wankoko in *Oluyimba lwa Wankoko*, appear possessed or entranced, oblivious of the reality of their surroundings. Christopher Wrigley (1996) underlines attributes of retribution, *schadenfreude*, fickleness, treachery in the character of the Baganda that are also identifiable in the themes of these plays. For example, in his study of the Buganda dynasty, he hints at the political intrigues in the King's palace stating, '[T]he royal court was a place of peril as well as opportunity' (1996: 239). *Makula ga Kulabako*, *St Lwanga* and *Oluyimba lwa Wankoko* examine how class, politics, religion and indigenous conflicts affect the community.

St. Lwanga

Lord Fredrick Lugard, incensed by King Mwanga II's belligerent attitude, wrote in his diary, 'For my part I *detest* both having him here, or going to him. I have never made blood-brotherhood as he wished. We are on the best of terms but he is a murderer, and a public and open Sodomite - a mean despicable brute, and a notorious coward' (1959: 234). This statement sums up Lugard's impression of King Mwanga II when he arrived in Uganda in 1889 as the representative of the Imperial British East African Company. The entrenchment of rival religious organisations - Muslims, Protestants and Roman Catholics - in the palace, led to religious conflicts, which were underlined by intense power struggles between chiefs, the king, and inevitably the Baganda. This led to the Buganda religious wars from 1888 to 1893 within which, according to Kasozi (1994: 8), religion was to be used 'not only as a basis for identity but also a tool for political mobilisation'. Notably, they necessitated the formation of alliances between Muslims and Protestants (1888-89). The Roman Catholic converts were relegated to Buddu. The immediate after effects of the religious wars included the partition of Buganda and the division of political offices in accordance with religious beliefs. *St. Lwanga,* the historical play written to celebrate Pope Paul VI's visit to consecrate the Uganda martyrs' shrine at Namugongo in 1969, depicts King Mwanga II's reign, highlighting the forces responsible for sparking off the massacre that culminated in the burning of fifty boys on June 3, 1886. Apart from its purely religious relevance - focusing on the period of the execution of Christian converts in Buganda between 1885 and 1889 - the play analyses the background to the politicisation of religion in Uganda. The conflict is between Katikkiro (Prime Minister) Mukasa, *Abaami* (Chiefs) and *Abataka* (Clan Leaders) manoeuvring to keep their positions, on the one hand, and King Mwanga II with his young warriors on the other. Caught in between are the Christian missionaries and their converts. *St. Lwanga* places King Mwanga II in the context of the political intrigues of the time; therefore, emphasizing the religious factor in Ugandan politics. The massacres were the cause of King Mwanga II's deposition that resulted in the religious wars of 1886 to 1889.

At the time of the Christian executions, King Mwanga II's *abapere*, the 'tarnished' (John Iliffe, 2005) or vigilantes, so called because of their anti-social violent behaviour, eroded the influence of the old traditional chiefs. These young and arrogant gangs caused chaos in Buganda and 'spared no one except themselves' (M.S.M Kiwanuka, 1971: 198-201). The clan leaders, plundered and humiliated by *abapere* confronted the king with their grievances. Kawadwa depicts King Mwanga II as a victim of his own nature because of the political machinations of his father's old chiefs, religious rivalries, and colonial political conflicts. King Mwanga II's interest in women was in doubt since he did not father a child until he was twenty-nine. His homosexual practices - opposed by European colonialists, missionaries, Christian converts and Baganda elders alike - were a source of conflict. Balikuddembe, the chief page (servant), thought to be a turncoat by King Mwanga II, expresses society's concern about his amorous exploits:

> In our language, we describe some actions as shameful, immoral, filthy.... I am sure, my lord, you know the circumstances in which these words are applied.... Some of these foreigners may not have some of these concepts in their customs. Therefore, my lord, we should not emulate them wholesale...lest your behaviour embarrasses people.
>
> (*St. Lwanga*, p. 11)

By judging his morality, Balikuddembe, a mere slave, invokes King Mwanga II's anger and pays with his life.

King Mwanga II is driven by the desire to be master in his own house and protect the sovereignty of his country; he engages our attention in a soliloquy in which he debates alternative routes to end the political crises in the nation. Living in fear of losing his political power, and his ambition threatened by the increasing influence of the 'Bloody Whites' (*St. Lwanga*, p. 10) in his palace, he avenges himself by killing the pages. The ugly humour, contrived by the actions of the guards around the dying converts which underline the hideousness of the scene, echoes Uganda's experience under both Amin's and Obote II's regimes. Kawadwa could not have known what was to happen when he wrote the play in which scenes provoking the violent past of Buganda equated with the present. For instance, Kassimir (1991) notes the 'tragic irony' of martyrs in contemporary Ugandan history, specifically illustrated by Obote's military massacre of people at Namugongo in May 1984. Kawadwa engages us in a balanced assessment of the conflicts (religious and political) which led to the massacres. These tensions between Kawadwa's interpretation of the history of Buganda, and the colonialist recorded narratives, are ironically mirrored in contemporary religious and political discourses in which King Mwanga II and the martyrs are presented in contrasting positions. Some people consider King Mwanga II as worthy of compassion, while others draw similarities between him and Amin.

Makula ga Kulabako

In the new post-colonial world, after the Nakulabye Massacre and the 1966 Kabaka Crisis, a new consciousness emerged that altered the perception of identity and space, which troubled the people's relationship with the nation. The challenge for the new rulers was to develop cultural expressions that gave a feeling of nationhood. People, particularly the Baganda, could not give up their cultural expressions as the symbols of their identity; thus, the emergence of theatre performance as the leading voice of resistance corresponded with the people's re-awakened awareness of their ethnicity. Indeed, by 1966 the people had started to create a performance aesthetic response in reaction to a new tyranny. They had evolved forms of performance that would (re) locate them in public and private performance spaces, defying their presentation as outsiders. However, how did the artists deal with the crisis? How did they overcome the restrictions imposed on artistic expression? A close analysis of Kawadwa's work will allow us to discuss the different practices adopted by artists as they transformed indigenous theatrical expressions into dynamic contemporary forms. Three of the most important plays to have come out of this period - *Makula ga Kulabako*, *St. Lwanga* and *Oluyimba lwa Wankoko* - offer interesting evidence regarding the significance of the idea of resistance in performance.

Makula ga Kulabako, one of the earliest representations of theatre of resistance, is a play about life in the royal palace, which examines inter-class relationships. In a race to capture Kulabako's love, Nnyonyintono, the handsome, courteous, but ordinary court dancer, outdoes Semuvubi, an unsophisticated elderly tax collector. Semuvubi's behaviour distinctly points to the age gap between him and Kulabako, prompting her to reject him because he is not the man of her choice; she is indifferent to Semuvubi's wealth and to his confessions of love. Ugly, lascivious, loud, and what the Baganda would describe as *omukopi be kkopo kkopo* (country bumpkin), he is a contrast to Nnyonyintono. Kulabako's status and her expression of ordinary human desires, especially the dilemma she faces in relating to the ordinary but lovable peasant's son, Nnyonyintono, makes her character appealing. The decisiveness and determination she displays in the process is expressed in her song, '*Ono Omugenyi wa Ssuula* (My guest has opened a new Chapter)', which describes the changes her courtship introduces into society.[8] The setting of the play, which determines the plot structure, begins on Buvuma and Ssese Islands, moves to the fishing shores and ends at the mainland palace. The reed fences and Kulabako's reception room, ornamented with traditional bark cloth and reed decorations, evoke a courtly atmosphere. Alternate scene changes are flexible, illustrating the varied activities of the community: fishing, love-relationships and courtly life. Kulabako's appearance on the lakeshore makes it convenient for the women to present her to us as an admirable beauty. By presenting a royal princess on stage, Kawadwa adds excitement to his drama. Kulabako is an authentic character: vainglorious, snobbish, and behaving with the arrogance expected of princesses in Buganda. When Kulabako, with Nabachwa (her aunt), connives to smuggle Nnyonyintono into the palace, it is an exciting and colourful scene. Nnyonyintono, dressed as a woman, walks in among a group of women to deliver Kulabako's '*makula* (presents or a beautiful object)' in handcrafted baskets. The word play on '*makula*' reveals that Nnyonyintono is the actual present, hence, the title of the play.[9]

Through acts of reclamation of indigenous cultural symbols and theatrical expressions, as well as casting known performers, Kawadwa's practice can be seen in dialogue with the socio-political conflicts of the 1960s and 1970s. His dialogue focused on questions of (new) power relations, class and political privilege, native and stranger all rooted in Obote's political policies. The play examines these class tensions as complex discourses of differences in the palace (a microcosm of Buganda) where boundaries between the royals and the commoners were not firmly set and non-erudite individuals remained outsiders. Throughout his works, Kawadwa's characters are engaged with inter-class and intra-class relationships that existed long before colonisation. In fact, when she sings her soliloquy, '*Nnyonyintono*', Kulabako asserts that class boundaries are blurred by love.

For the first time in Ugandan theatre, folk music was used as part of the unified plot. The Baganda (Kiganda) performative folk culture forms are reflected in the extended use of dance, song and instrumental music, movement, and recitation that Kawadwa, with the help of Wassanyi Sserukenya, builds into this genre, which he described as 'musical plays'. Apart from making the play more enjoyable, Kawadwa uses music as a plot development devise. The chorus songs are used to create conflict between Ssemuvubi and the rest of the cast and to avail more facts for the audience. Additionally, it often highlights the character's contrast, especially between Nnyonyintono and Ssemuvubi; change in fortunes of the characters, and as a soliloquy by Nnyonyintono, Kulabako and Ssemuvubi, song is used to reveal their feelings. Other interesting scenes include the love scene in which Nnyonyintono and Kulabako verbalise their feelings through music. Ssemuvubi's dramatization of his feelings of dejection, when he learns Kulabako will not marry him, and Kulabako's marriage to Nnyonyintono at the end of the play, that includes the '*mbaga* (wedding)' dance, emphasizes the romantic plot, giving the play a successful conclusion. Once Kulabako falls in love with Nnyonyintono, the issue of their class differences disappears. The use of Luganda idioms, as well as folkloric reference to the Baganda language, rituals, *mbugo* and *kanzus* (bark cloth wrappers and white tunics), was complemented by scenery and stage designs based on a traditional Buganda royal palace. By celebrating the Baganda culture through a representation of popular theatrical expressions, costumes and the visual construction of the stage, Kawadwa references banned cultural values and practices, exemplifying the people's determination to resist oppressive institutions. Kawadwa crafts resistance in small, apparently insignificant but critical ways, and the audience knows how to continue the pressure of resistance on the oppressive state institutions.

Oluyimba lwa Wankoko (Song of Wankoko)

The satire, *Oluyimba lwa Wankoko,* is committed to revolutionary struggle. The success of the play depends as much upon the understanding of the political narratives of Uganda, as well as a shared understanding of the oral performance traditions, so that the dialogue between them transforms the play into a contemporary folktale.[10]

Whereas decrees and *Legal Notices* characterized Amin's military regime, Obote's first UPC government was identifiable with 'Documents' and 'Declarations', a trend similar to the movements in Tanzania and Zambia at this time. *The Common Man's Charter* (1969), *Document No. 1*, the first document of the series of five, was meant to address the 1966 events. Additionally, they were aimed at introducing self-reliance policies and uplifting the under-represented commoners, the policies exacerbated the relationship between

Ugandans from the northern regions, which supported the government, and the rest of Uganda. Kawadwa depicts a government at odds with traditional institutions. In Wankoko, the main protagonist, the play presents an ambitious commoner whose campaign for change, in all aspects of life, does not carry the community. As Christopher Wrigley has argued, in Buganda there was no strict class society; therefore, 'large numbers of individuals were constantly climbing or falling off the ladder of power and status' (1996: 239). When the play was staged at the Second African Festival of Arts and Culture (FESTAC) in Lagos in 1977, Amin's regime had reached its apogee and he was desperately clinging on to power. His government was under threat from freedom fighters whose abortive invasion via Tanzania had resulted in mass arrests, 'disappearances' and public executions (firing squad).

In this play, Kawadwa conveniently uses the colonized Buganda state, Buddu, Wankoko's (the Cock's) place of origin, which has both political and social significance in Buganda. Separated from the rest of Buganda by the river Katonga, it was 'the last major addition to the territory of the pre-colonial [Buganda] state' (Wrigley, 1994: 218). Wrigley notes that in post-colonial politics there was disagreement between Buddu and the rest of Buganda. This was because Buddu 'was the largest district to be assigned to the Catholic party as an early colonial settlement; and was then in some degree alienated from the continuing Protestant ascendancy' (Wrigley, 1994: 218-219). Apart from historical differences, Buddu supports the Democratic Party (DP) whose membership, until recently, has remained predominantly Roman Catholic; and in some quarters in Buganda it is regarded as anti-aristocratic. Consequently, while superficial, the confrontation is between 'BanaBuddu' (*Oluyimba lwa Wankoko*, p. 6) - residents of Buddu County - and the rest of the Baganda community; however, at the national level it represents the confrontation between feudal institutions and republicanism. Therefore, when Wankoko uses a regional Luganda dialect, LunaBuddu, Kawadwa is playing with linguistic variations to echo ethnic differences.

The plot centres on Barungi, a beautiful princess and resident of the palace, from Tooro Kingdom. Imagining '*olubiri* (the palace)' as the '*ekibuga* (town)' or a colonial administrative centre, as a contested space separated by social, military and political boundaries, Kawadwa represents the palace as a political island in the country. It is where the working classes, such as Wankoko and his companion, Nkwale (the Partridge), can define their identity. When Wankoko and Nkwale come to pay homage to the king, the palace workers joyfully welcome their arrival because their liveliness breaks up the monotonous chores of the palace workers. Nkwale symbolises hangers-on, similar to members of the General Service, Special Service (intelligence services in Obote and Amin governments), and the Special Forces, (a paramilitary police wing in Obote's governments). Wankoko, rejecting the submissiveness of the workers, remonstrates with the palace guards, an offence that leads to his arrest. Prince Suuna saves him with the hope that he will woo Barungi, the beautiful princes from Tooro, on his behalf. Suuna is shy and Wankoko becomes indispensable to him as a go-between. Wankoko takes advantage of this friendship to further his own career in several ways: first, by wooing Barungi for himself instead of Suuna; second, by using Suuna's trust to insinuate himself into the workers' confidence, thus gaining administrative ascendancy; and lastly, by ousting Suuna from his father's favour. The King disowns Suuna and expels him from the palace. Barungi, who from the beginning has been suspicious of Wankoko's ambitious designs, follows Suuna to the forest and returns to the King, determined to expose Wankoko's treachery. The King orders Wankoko's arrest, pardons Suuna and sanctions his wedding to Barungi. After his arrest, the guards tie Wankoko with ropes and evict him from the palace.

Wankoko dominates the play right from the beginning when, at his entrance he immediately provokes a quarrel with a member of the audience, accusing him of disgracing indigenous cultural and religious values. The audience, distracted by a sharp exchange of voices, turns to see a stout, fierce, unshaven man, wearing a tattered coat and carrying a small bundle of his belongings. He marches to stage centre and brings life to the chorus with a single command, '*Kale tutandike* (Let us start)' (*Oluyimba lwa Wankoko*, p. 1), and in the following act, he animates the chorus, even frivolously dancing with some of the women. At this point, the 'initiate' audience will know that in the past Wankoko's type brought relief and humour to the palace as clowns, with the privilege even to tease (with reserve) royalty without provoking their wrath. In this scene, Kawadwa details the sequence of movements in the stage directions to underline Wankoko's and Nkwale's provocative attitude. Dissatisfied with the applause at the end of his performance, Wankoko unashamedly demands more from both the cast and the audience.

> **Wankoko:** (*Inviting everybody, including the audience to clap*) I am grateful for this reception. Nevertheless, please, give me a more befitting welcome.
>
> (*Oluyimba lwa Wankoko*, p. 1)

Both men are intent on undermining the King's power and his reverence by the commoners. Through Wankoko's character, the play establishes a link between past and present; a connection between absolute monarchical rule and political dictatorships. Initially, he embarks on his mission by scorning a guard who attempts to restrict his freedom of speech:

> **Wankoko:** (*cynical*) I was merely noting the admirably beautiful tyranny pervading this palace.
>
> (*Oluyimba lwa Wankoko*, p. 8)

This defiance culminates in the song, '*Ffena Twenkana* (We are All Equal) restating his belief in equality and social justice. The song not only undermines collective allegiance to the King, but also belies his opposition to undemocratic institutions. In performance, there is a disjunction between the words of the song and his gestures, movements and voice inflections. He rejects the submissiveness of the workers, remonstrates with the palace guards, and they arrest him on felony charges relating to his disrespect of the King; afterwards, he is expelled from the palace. In this sense, Kawadwa draws parallels between Suuna's temporary banishment to the forest and the experiences of the exiled King Mutesa II, also a former President of Uganda.

The audience's ability to engage and identify with Kawadwa's play depends on the performers' portrayal of the characters, and use of gestures and music; in addition to this is Kawadwa's employment of the trope of madness to explore the gendered and ethnic politics of resistance. Wankoko, whose origins are dubious, fits his name. Whereas elsewhere he snubs the guards, dismissing their assumption that every name must belong to a clan, on this occasion, using the title song, 'Wankoko', he relates origins to his relentless search for trouble spots. Like the ferocious cock, Wankoko claims to use his over-grown claw to expose and eliminate 'political' trouble spots. He boastfully sings, '[*O*]*kusimbula ejjindu...buli omu aba ssanyu lye* (The moment I disengage my claw, everybody is joyful)' (*Oluyimba lwa Wankoko*, p. 1). The initiate audience may note the associations attached to the claw as a lethal weapon or a phallic symbol; but in addition, it clearly relates to Wankoko's rhetoric in which he underscores his power.[11] Since only full-grown cocks may possess a sharp claw, Wankoko's statement indirectly refers to his survival instincts. There are two possible explanations for Kawadwa's choice of this name. First, the name originates from the Luganda proverb, *Wankoko by'azaala bye bimununula*, which literally means the ransom of Wankoko's life is his/her children (chicks). Second, he may have been drawing on the humour contrived by the corrupted version of Sir Keith Hancock's name (the Chairman of the 1955 Buganda Constitution Committee) by the Baganda. As noted by D. A. Low in *Buganda in Modern History* (1971: 118), Luganda has no "H" sound; therefore, Hancock became 'Wankock' or 'Wankoko' meaning chicken, thus creating an amusing pun.

The play illustrates Kawadwa's exploration of folklore to confront authoritarian political regimes. In a 1991 interview, Macpherson observed that while basing the action of the play on snippets of Baganda fables and their dramatization, he alludes to two apparently deluded post-colonial rulers, Obote and Amin.[12] Wankoko's ambition to articulate himself in the world as both subject and citizen takes him on a journey (through a series of political struggles) that ends with banishment into exile, away from the country where only the privileged by birth may enjoy the fruits of independence. His confrontation with indigenous power structures, as well as his rupture with tradition, evokes specific cultural memories of resistance and uprisings against oppression and exploitation. As well as dealing with the relationship between the ruler and the peasant (common man), *Oluyimba lwa Wankoko* demonstrates that theatre can rehearse revolutionary changes. Wankoko's revolution is aborted and the workers forsake his re-imagined shared communal society, allowing the palace to go back to its routine. His understandings of the oppressive indigenous institutions are at the heart of his cosmetic reforms, even though his motives are self-centred. At the root of this conflict are the concepts of *ekitiibwa* (decorum) and *obuntubulamu* (humaneness), prerequisites for communal respectability in Buganda. Although he is initially courteous, Wankoko shocks the community by his blatant self-seeking and disrespectful behaviour, thus highlighting the contrast between the feudal traditional government of the kingdoms and the brashness of the Obote government. Wankoko is indifferent to court ethics and will be decorous only if he stands to profit from the situation, thus evoking critical remarks from the guards and workers alike. The guard's response to Wankoko's offensive behaviour (quite normal in Buganda, but implicitly offensive to other people) is a statement questioning his identity that seems more snobbish to an egalitarian society than to an aristocratic one: '*Y'ani oyo baaba? Ye ngamba mwana w'ani oyo*? (What is his family background? Whose son is he?)' (*Oluyimba lwa Wankoko*, p. 19). Similar to 'political lunatics' of his type, Wankoko uses Nkwale to propagate his revolution. Nkwale, small, fast, and seemingly slippery, is the *muleebeesi* (cheerleader), his co-bandit, praising him at every turn and silencing the opposition.

By targeting '*ennaku* (hardships), which implicitly refers to various forms of communal oppression and poverty, Kawadwa identifies with the shared destiny of the audience. The essence of Wankoko's argument is the need for collective action against oppression currently dominating the workers' lives. He expresses disgust at the workers' submission to tyranny that, as Nkwale alleges, is spreading throughout the palace like '*obuloolo* (fowl fleas)' (p. 19). Nkwale swears to confront and quash tyranny like '*ttingatinga enyiga mugoya* (a steamroller pulping the blind worm)' (p. 9).

Act I, Scene 4, referred to as 'the political scene' by the original cast, is a key scene because it provides the structure and ideational link between feudal and republican governments and peace and anarchy. In Kawadwa's most cogent expression of his opposition to political dictatorship, it alludes to Obote's attack on feudalism, tribalism and colonialism.[13] Wankoko parodies political rallies as he constructs a narrative that reveals his scheming skills and enables him to persuade the chorus to join his revolution. His speech draws on contemporary political catchphrases, clichés, euphemisms and slang to make the message immediate to the audience and insinuate the empty rhetoric of contemporary leaders. Each utterance is a subversive political statement or '*pokopoko*' (*Oluyimba lwa Wankoko*, p. 19) awakening the audience to the real meaning of their oppression. Nkwale, insultingly referring to the workers as 'sweepers, window cleaners, and the suffering lot' introduces Wankoko as their comrade, '*ekitangaala ky'enjuba evaayo* (the new dawn)' (p. 19). The Wankoko who appears to address the workers is a transformed character who is callous, determined, and uncompromising, but looking like a political prophet. For instance, when responding to the workers' ecstatic welcome he states, '*buli omu mugudde mu kifuba* (Let me give a hug to each of you)' (p. 20); a linguistic expression for a symbolic collective embrace to canvass their support. He shows a cunning understanding of crowd politics that enables him to exploit the occasion at once. His verbal skills and cynical humour carry the day as he sees factionalism as the cause of their agony and uses the lemon grass straw broom, the symbol of their misery, to persuade them that their salvation lies in collective action. His argument is that a child may easily snap a strand of grass, but strung together (to make a broom) it is strong; so a tyrannical ruler will fail to break a united workers' body. However, his motive is selfish, as we discover when he reads an already prepared document, which he purports to be '*Ekiwandiiko ekisooka*, (their first (Memorandum) document)' (p. 21). Wankoko asks the workers to endorse the memorandum and tells Suuna that it is a collective palace workers' document. It levies a tax of which he is to get the largest percentage as the workers' leader; he appoints himself in charge of all palace appointments irrespective of the status of the worker; he levies a tax on the first salary of all newly appointed workers to meet his clothing allowance. For all his rhetoric about the workers' humanity and right of choice, his solutions to the workers' misery are farcical. He promises to supply them with '*Byekwesewa* (a strong insecticide comparable to DDT, popularly used in the sixties to fumigate homes)' to treat head lice; to dig wells in their courtyards, and tarmac paths leading to their houses and the well (*Oluyimba lwa Wankoko*, p. 22). *Byekwesewa* was cheaper and stronger than DDT and the audience would be familiar with this insecticide. In this context, Wankoko's reference to an insecticide is double-edged: it is an insult to the workers (who unfortunately miss its implication) because Wankoko is imputing that they are vermin that should be exterminated with insecticide. Using physical force, persuasion and rhetoric, Wankoko terrorizes the workers into accepting his propositions.

Wankoko: Plenty of things (wealth or positive changes) are on the way. Ok. All those who are ready to work with me, please put up your hands. (*Most workers do not respond.*) Did you hear what I said? (*Wankoko barks at the workers.*) All those who say, yes, put up your hands.

Chorus: (*Only two or three workers raise their hands.*)

Wankoko: (*Furious, as he forcefully stretches the hands of the ones who have hitherto resisted giving him support. He commands them in Swahili and Luganda.*) Everyone, hands up. *Juu* (Up) Both hands up.

Chorus: (*They all raise hands.*)

Wankoko: Good. Well done. (*Cynical laughter*) Thank you for supporting me.

(*Oluyimba lwa Wankoko*, p. 24)

Music

The syncretic aesthetics rooted in the indigenous travelling popular performance traditions - the kinetic elements of music and dance - underpin the structure of the play. Call-and-response songs (see Devon Boan, 1998: 263 - 271) frame the structure of interaction between Wankoko and the chorus. Moreover, whereas in *Makula ga Kulabako* music is topical and used emotively to express ordinary human desires shared by the key characters, in *Oluyimba lwa Wankoko* it is crucial in the thematic development of the play. Aesthetically, music and dance help Kawadwa to achieve dramatic unity, which is an essential part of the whole. Songs performed by Wankoko himself or with the workers, and by other characters like Suuna, are part of their action. '*Ffena Twenkana*' dismisses social classifications in the community and '*Omuntu Muntu* (Man is Man)' contrasts man with beasts and calls for equal treatment. '*Ffe Basajja ba Kabaka* (We are the King's Men)' expresses allegiance to the king; '*Bamukwate* (Arrest him)' illustrates the fickle nature of the workers (crowds) because they disown him after their earlier support. '*Bakatujjeeko* (He has been deposed), marking Wankoko's first, and '*Wankoko Togasa* (Wankoko, you are useless)', are demonstrations of the unreliable nature of the crowd. Workers celebrate Wankoko's downfall, despite the support and praise accorded him on earlier occasions. Wankoko's arrest signifies society's verdict on Wankoko and politicians of his type. It is a litany of what Wankoko rejects as '*okuvunnama* (feudalism). Here, the chorus condemns his anti-social behaviour.

Chorus: His Majesty is 'husband' to us all.
That is why we kneel and prostrate when greeting him...
Why we never squat in his palace...
Whose son is he, he who is so disrespectful?
Where was he born?...
We have a great inheritance... a strict code of conduct that the elders taught us... The woman who sits indecently (*with her legs apart or crossed*), brings poverty to the homestead.
A woman must never whistle...
Those are our customs.
So, who is this fellow to controvert them?
Arrest him. Lock him up.

(*Oluyimba lwa Wankoko*, p. 10)

Wankoko exposes his true character when he leads the chorus in the song, '*Ffena Twenkana* (We are all Equal)', a demand for equal rights.

Wankoko: Listen, we may not be like the boss, but in this world, we are all equal. Why should a man...with brains...be oppressed? .... Why should a pretty woman be oppressed? .... If I were to die now, what would become of me? What would become of you if you were to die? What would you tell God? What profits would you take back to him? What have you profited from the talent of a brain he gave you… you have sacrificed it.... You have allowed yourself to be abused.... You are despised... You are exploited.... Who wants to go on living like this? (*pause*) This is my proposition: We are all equal.

Chorus: Yes. It is true. Let us all be equal.

(*Oluyimba lwa Wankoko*, p. 19)

A good example of Kawadwa's and Sserukenya's use of music is best articulated in Act I, Scene 4 when Wankoko, after addressing the workers, teaches them 'his' song, '*Omuntu Muntu*'. The song urges the restitution of human dignity and leadership with a human touch. Wankoko argues that unlike other animals, reptiles and birds, they share a common heritage because their mothers like his, suffered birth pangs; moreover, they speak, get angry, and experience hunger. In addition, since the physical features, behaviour, and status of insects, beasts and birds differs from that of human beings, the latter merit better treatment from politicians. Therefore, he urges the workers to wake up to their plight, wake up to reality, and he identifies the cause of their oppression; otherwise, they will all perish out of their own folly. The chorus of workers gradually transforms into caricatures of beasts, birds, insects, and worms as it sings the refrain, '*Ekiwuka* (The insect)' (*Oluyimba lwa Wankoko*, p. 25). It is at once a collection of masked figures, as well as a bunch of rebellious workers, responding to Wankoko's impassioned statements.

Wankoko: Listen, no one was born to suffer; to be exploited by hisfellow man. Are you human beings? Are you birds?
Chorus: Noo.
Wankoko: Are you Beasts? Are you Insects?
Chorus: Noo. We are human.
Wankoko: True. You are human beings. You are men and women. (*Breaks into a jig. The workers join him and they all dance to celebrate their liberation from tyranny.*) Therefore, let us have change. Feudalism is old-fashioned. We must eradicate backwardness, corruption and bribery, nepotism, and beggary. Support Wankoko and you will be rewarded with wealth.

(*Oluyimba Iwa Wankoko*, p. 25)

John Conteh-Morgan (1994) comments that in traditional African drama, '[M]eaning is not prosaically represented in words alone but…finds "objective materialization" in movement, gesture, and sound' (p. 12). In drawing parallels between Wankoko and contemporary military leaders' behaviour and gestures, Kawadwa is attempting to reconstruct the audience's memory. Yvette Hutchison (2005) underscores this when she states, "Memory and history are important because they are the means by which we contextualise ourselves, both as individuals and nations, in relation to the past, and thereby define the future…. how these 'memories' are constructed and reconstructed defines whom we are, or become..." (pp. 354-362).

Throughout this performance, as elsewhere in the play, Wankoko, seemingly possessed, acts like a cock - pecking, clawing, and intimidating both the chorus and the audience as he draws freely from current physical gestures of contemporary politicians. However, these may differ from production to production. For example, during the production that followed the 1989 Liberation War, Wankoko's militaristic tone and posture was comparable to present day performances of political leaders.

To take the extreme view shared by some Ugandans, particularly during the period of civil strife, the song, '*Ffena Twenkana*' reflected on the North-South divide, whereby the Bantu ethnic groups from Southern Uganda treated the Acholi, Langi and Lugbara, and other people from the northern region, as the 'other'. Notwithstanding this, the Northern group, specifically the Langi and Acholi had their divisions. In Luganda, a Bantu language, *abantu* (people/human beings) is plural, while *muntu* (a person/human being) is singular. The opposite of *muntu* is *kisolo* (singular) / *bisolo* (plural), meaning beast, which are generic as well as derogative terms used to refer to people from both Northern and Eastern Uganda. While it may be speculative, the subtext of these words may have sparked off the conflict between Kawadwa and the state. Kawadwa's relationship to Ugandan ethnic values (political, moral and aesthetic) raises questions about the adoption of 'non-traditional' political models and cultures by politicians, as well as sections of the community. While he does not escape the critical problems that arise from writing plays focused on Buganda, Kawadwa makes an effort to distance himself by his attempts to explore syncretic performance forms, comment on political leadership, evaluate the role of religion in the community, and redefine Ugandan popular performance. Believing in equal rights for all Ugandans, Kawadwa created a theatre that critically responded to the problems caused by the European encounter, beginning in the 1870s. He constructed a theatre tradition rooted in indigenous performance forms, while borrowing aspects of European theatre elements.

Given its political context, characterised by feuds, treachery, tyranny and attacks on feudalism, the title *Oluyimba lwa Wankoko* (Song of Wankoko) may sound flippant. What does song and dance have to do with political oppression? The title is meant to invoke not only the political narratives of the tyrannical regimes, their deliberate use of theatricality to terrorise the people and to demonstrate the relationship between various performances and resistance. The play demonstrates how autocratic systems transform people into objects for political repression. Thus, it is not surprising that Kawadwa's resistance theatre ultimately led to his death at the hands of the government agents.

Chapter 4

FARCE AND BIBLICAL ALLUSIONS AS A RESPONSE TO OPPRESSION IN WYCLIFF KIYINGI'S THEATRE

The importance of Wycliff Kiyingi for the theatre was that he was the first person to realise the importance of, and to start, formal theatre in Uganda. His work examines the interrelationship between theatre, society, religion and politics in the post-colonial period since the 1960s. In his plays, staged from 1959 to 2000, Kiyingi engages in examining and developing theatre while making it a relevant critical tool in contemporary contexts. The plays juxtapose off- and on-stage performances, drawing the audience's attention to the socio-political situation in the country. That way, he uses his writing and theatre work to influence change in different ways, including through resistance. The significance of his work is the contribution to the theory of theatre in Uganda, particularly his insistence that all formal theatre productions should be based on written scripts. Secondly, he asserts that it is purposeless to insert songs into a play if they have no thematic relevance. It would, he claims, produce a harmful effect on the message the audience would receive' (Kiyingi, 2009). The following interview was recorded in Uganda on 5 December 2009 with Kiyingi and his manager, Kagimu Mukasa. The questions focused on the highlights of his sixty years as a writer and producer.

SK: What language would you prefer to use during our interview?

WK: I prefer *mu* [in] Luganda to English.

SK: Where did you meet Kagimu Mukasa?

WK: I met him at King's College Buddo where we performed plays. Later, in 1954, we met and decided to form the first Ugandan drama group, which we named, African Dramatic Association. At that time, there were two other amateur groups: KATS and the Goan Institute group owned by European expatriates and the Indian community, respectively.

SK: Where does the ability to master words come from? For example, in one episode of your radio play, *Wokulira*, you use the phrase, '*antunuulira nga ente entomezi*' [eyeing me like bull which is about to charge] to describe an angry and vengeful character.

WK: I write about everyday life so I have to use ordinary language. For example, when I want to satirise a character or a situation I either create or use existing comic expressions. I always use satirical expressions

SK: What influenced your development as a professional playwright?

WK: The most significant influence was that at the formation of the African Dramatic Association, where the constitution included a clause that identified me as the writer and director of drama; and in addition, another clause stated that the association would not stage improvised plays, but all our productions would be based on written scripts.

SK: Why don't you write exploring the indigenous theatrical expressions (dance and music) as Byron Kawadwa and Robert Serumaga do?

WK: To begin with, I am not musical. I attended Namugongo Primary School that had a Roman Catholic foundation. Unlike the Protestant missionaries, the Roman Catholic missionaries did not support musical activities; therefore, by the time I went to Buddo, (a Protestant missionary school) I had lost interest in music. In my view, it is purposeless to insert songs into a play if they have no thematic relevance; it would produce a harmful effect on the message the audience will receive.

SK: In your plays, there is a tendency to 'navigate' between social and political worlds. What accounts for this?

WK: Why do governments think they have a right to enforce policies that are meaningless to the ordinary man? It is for that reason that I create characters who do not understand politics; these are mere human beings existing in society. They lead a purposeless life and have no idea why they are in this world. I always like to present a true picture of people's life (to the audience) from the Ugandan perspective. For example, in Wokulira, the *omupakasi* (labourer) is not concerned about national politics - he concentrates on his existence. He knows that he cannot influence the larger issues in society.

SK: In your plays there is a tendency to 'navigate' between the world of religion and politics. For instance, someone watching *Olugendo lwe Gologoosa* without locating it within the political context may think it is a religious play. What accounts for this?

WK: Both, in colonial times when the whites were still ruling this country, and throughout Obote's first government, one always tried to avoid trouble by desisting from commenting on political issues. *Naye, olina engeri ebyobufuzi gyobikozesa naye ate nga bo tebakitegedde.* (However, you have to find ways of embedding critical statements in your script without alerting the government.) In the early post-independent period, all the party stalwarts - Democratic Party, Kabaka Yekka and Uganda People's Congress - wanted to patronise our group. Hence, a play such as *Ekiwonvu kye Ssenya* (The Ssenya Valley), which was critical of Obote's government and the manner in which party politics in general was affecting ordinary people, was supported by all political representatives who turned up to watch the production at the National Theatre.

SK: Why didn't you stage it again?

WK: My radio plays were very successful; therefore, I started to devote my efforts on radio drama.

SK: Why didn't you give it to another drama group?

WK: At that time there were few local drama groups performing scripted plays. Most artists improvised their theatre productions because they did not want to learn acting lines.

SK: How do you get ideas for your plays?

KM: Let me help you with that question. I have worked with Kiyingi for a long time. Sometimes you travel around the city centre and at the end of the journey he will ask you whether you noticed the behaviour of X or Y. Of course, you would not have paid any attention to their behaviour. However, because he is very observant, he will highlight aspects of their behaviour or actions.

SK: What kind of support have you had from your group?

WK: Because at the beginning they put pressure on me to focus on writing, I have ended up being the first professional playwright in Uganda.

KM: Our ambition was to allow him to concentrate on writing; therefore, we relieved him of other duties including financial management and administrative responsibilities.

SK: Why don't you always direct your plays?

WK: I end up quarrelling with the cast.

SK: Why did you cast Dan Sabwe in the role of Kimaama, the village labourer?

WK: Kimaama is an ordinary man who did various jobs in the village. I needed someone who could interpret the role of this character. Sabwe was a great actor and very talented; unfortunately, later in life, he turned into a social drinker.

Kagimu: (*to Kiyingi*) Could you please give us more details about Kimaama's character?

WK: He is a common man who has no idea who he is and has no status in the village. *Talina kyali. Ku nsi nga abeerako bubeezi.* (He merely exists.) He is *omupakasi* (labourer) who runs errands for the residents. *Ajjuza bujjuza nsi*. (He fills empty space of the world).

KM: In spite of his behaviour and status, the whole village knows who he is. *Buli ekigwa ku kyaalo Kimaama aba akimanyi. Era byayogera n'oli by'anayogera ... naye olaba ekyalo kyona bw'okiwuumbyeeko naye nga oyise mu Kimaama* (Kimaama knows everything that happens in the village because he talks to every resident. If you can talk to Kimaama then you will know and understand the whole village.)

WK: He is an ordinary person.

SK: Which one of your plays is your favourite?

WK: All the plays are very good. However, while *Wokulira* is very good, *Lozio Bba Sessiriya* is the better play especially because of the way it portrays characters that use their privileged wealthy positions to abuse everyone in society.

KM: *Wokulira* made him popular; people always looked forward to the weekly Sunday afternoon episodes

WK: It engages with a range of issues; for, as the saying from which it derives its title states, by the time you reach adulthood you would have witnessed a lot of dramatic (and excruciating) happenings.

SK: Why did you write *Olugendo lwe Gologoosa*?

WK: It was an Easter play. While I wanted to represent the biblical events on stage, my intention was to make it relevant to contemporary reality. They prevented us from staging it at the National Theatre; therefore, [we] put it up in an alternative playhouse, The Centre.

It is obvious from the above conversation that, beginning in the colonial period, Kiyingi and the artists who worked with him viewed theatre as a space that could be used to explore social and political issues relevant to the Ugandan audience. Elsewhere in this interview Kiyingi noted that his play, *Pio Mberence Kamulali* (1954), satirising post-colonial chiefs, was the first 'formal' indigenous play to be staged in a community centre.

Throughout the colonial period, therefore, there were a series of confrontations among the European colonial officials, Indians and indigenous Ugandans. Additionally, Buganda as well as the other parts of Uganda, 'disliked' the 'penetration into its midst of Asian entrepreneurs both as owners of factories processing African peasant-grown primary products', particularly coffee and cotton, 'and as the dominating influence in rural retail trade' (Low, 1971: 156). Hence, in 1959, Augustine Kamya, the leader of the Uganda National Movement organised a trade boycott that aimed 'primarily against the grip which Asian entrepreneurs in particular had established over the economic life of the rural areas' (Low, 1971: 201). The campaign did not only include boycotting their business, but also involved violent attacks and arson directed at the Asians and people dealing with them (A. D Low, 1971: 156-158). Kasozi, the Ugandan historian, explains that while the boycott was 'limited to Buganda and was crushed by the colonial state' the 'anti-Asian sentiments did not disappear' (Kasozi, 1994: 46). As discussed in Chapter 1, competing performances (displays) of power staged in the colonial period were evident after independence, particularly during the Buganda 1964 and 1966 crises, Amin's *coup d'état* and his expulsion of Asians in 1972, and the suppression of popular uprisings during Obote II's reign. What is significant about this crisis and others in the postcolonial period is the theatricality of political events at which pronouncements of political agendas are made and the performance spaces, which include open spaces such as football stadiums, the City Square, Kololo Airstrip, or *bomas*. Thus, set against this background is Kiyingi's drama, which is grounded in particular historical (social and political) events and people, specifically, the political and religious leaders, moments of social change and political crises. For instance, details of the foregoing historical event are the focus of one of Kiyingi's earlier play, *Wokulira* (1961-2000) and *Ekiwonvu kye Ssenya* (1965). Undoubtedly, the off-stage performances, both political and military, inevitably inform variable on-stage performance responses and influence the theatrical styles, developed by Kiyingi, Kawadwa, Serumaga and other playwrights, that generate resistance. The plays discussed here cover a thirty-nine year span, from 1962 - 2000, and all of them demonstrate Kiyingi's strategy of using a shared communal experience, and collective memory to achieve his theatrical aim.

These plays illustrate the systems of exploitation and oppression and the experience of social disintegration leading to the development of a theatre of resistance. In the hostile political environment, particularly in Amin's period, as social fragmentation climaxed into anarchy, political witch-hunting, disappearances and murder, Kiyingi adopted theatrical styles that enabled him to hide his message from government agents. His plays of the late 1960s and 1970s offer insights into his and other playwrights' styles, adopted as the grimy acts by government agents spread across the country. In this sense, Kiyingi attempts to subvert the government's control of information, always asking the audience to reveal their perception of events. Indeed, in the Obote II period, people were more likely to ask their friends or colleagues whether they had listened to the *Wokulira* (1962 - 2000) radio serial than to the government's announcement. In relation to the political circumstances that shaped them and which they shaped, the audience's engagement with the play demonstrates the relationship between drama and politics; the performances upstaged the oppressors by opposing the oppressive regime's off-stage performances intended to terrorise ordinary people.

Kiyingi's theatre comes from the audience's awareness of the actors as people sharing the audiences' lived experiences. Their (known) position in society enables them to offer a critically viable position. To this end, he acknowledges folk performance forms, while attempting to signify the intersection of multi-layered national identities, colonial, and contemporary urban and rural realities. Echoing Taylor's views on the development of Latin American theatre, developing a dramatic style that sets the plays 'against the historical fact of disintegrating moral, judicial, and personal frameworks' is important for: 'Traditional dramatic forms, with their own historical contexts and ideological assumptions, no longer serve to depict the horrifying new reality' (Taylor, 1991: 123). To achieve this, Kiyingi manipulates the folkloric trickster form and similar to Kadongo Kamu musical artists, 'construct[s] hilarious and riveting dramas that allude to social fragmentation and excessive consumption' (Mugambi, 1997: 214). Hence, although indigenous myths and folklore may form other contemporary artists' theatrical imagination, Kiyingi employs the trickster figure and farce in a new way, while at the same time presenting subversive scenes and moments which allow the audience to ask questions about their condition. In the context of his post-Amin play and musical performances, in particular, aspects of performance that had been taken for granted are reworked and injected with new issues such as immorality, promiscuity and violence to prove that even the most contemporary drama can contain theatrical elements that offer critical statements. In this sense, *Omwana w'Omuntu* (1969) and *Olugendo lwe Gologoosa* become archetypes of abstract allegory where the Biblical content alludes to disappearances linking it to Amin's killing fields. Other plays that evidence these theatrical practices and demonstrate Kiyingi's revolutionary theatre are *Muduuma kwe Kwaffe*, *Wokulira*, *Omwana w'Omuntu* and *Lozio bba Ssesiriya.* My intention in using such a combination of plays is to demonstrate how postcolonial theatre, specifically Kiyingi's drama, interprets and examines postcolonial tyranny and social discontent through its self-conscious manipulation of indigenous theatrical elements and the trickster motifs.

Kiyingi's 'urban-created' (Mugambi, 1997: 207) radio and television dramatic narratives are interesting in the way they attempt to redefine the function of traditional narratives and the storyteller, which he has placed in a new political context. At the heart of Kiyingi's work is the concern to present Muduuma, his fictional village, a microcosm of Uganda, as a hostile place where cultural, moral and political values lose their essence. Mugambi's (1997) discussion in her essay, 'From Story to Song: Gender, Nationhood, and the Migratory Text', provides a way of discussing the work of performing artists, such as Kiyingi and Kawadwa, whose dramas, although different, use 'migratory texts' allowing them to critique society. The 'migratory elements' he uses, to borrow a concept used and delineated by Mugambi (1997: 211), include traditional narrative elements, for instance, 'the narrator's explicit declaration of the function of the story, incorporation of several genres into the narrative, formulaic openings and endings' and 'traditional motifs' including the trickster (Mugambi, 1997: 206). The 'manipulation of these migratory elements' enables him to 'appropriate' the indigenous storyteller's function as well as the 'unquestioned authorial and legislative power' embedded in oral narratives which he uses to 'perpetuate or reconstruct' individual and national identities in his dramas (Mugambi, 1997: 207). His use of such texts is critical to his work and resonates with Mugambi's comments on contemporary (Luganda) radio songs, a form that she describes as 'urban-created narratives' that 'are composed of aesthetically flexible, migratory elements derived from traditional pre-urban oral narratives' (Mugambi, 1997: 207). Katumbula, the main protagonist in Kiyingi's *Wokulira*, self-consciously expands the 'spatial boundaries' of Muduuma beyond its outskirts questioning the behaviour of the villagers. Indeed, Mugambi also reflects on the performances of Matiya Luyima the Kadongo Kamu artist who, similar to Katumbula, composes and imposes 'his laws, not only for his immediate audience, but also for all citizens of Uganda as a nation' (Mugambi, 1997: 208). Mugambi argues that these 'strategies of re-creating power indicate that contemporary' performers 'function not as passive transmitters of genres, but as astute or crafty narrators' since 'they transfer the functions of ethnic group's narrative to the radio' performance's 'vast national audience' (Mugambi, 1997: 208). She offers a model for critical analysis, which, in the context of this discussion, is applicable to radio, television, and staged performances.

Katumbula's character in *Wokulira*, or, Kyeswa's in both, *Buli Enkya, Buli Ekiro* (Day In, Day Out, begun in 1962), *Nebuba Enkya Nebuba Eggulo* (1970 - 1973) and *Obwavu Musolo* (1973) (played by the same actor, Dan Zirimenya), as 'a provocateur', 'self-aware and comic' (Campbell, 2010: 252), is based on both the trickster and the travelling musician's role. In her essay on contemporary radio song texts previously mentioned, Mugambi reads the trickster motif in ways relevant to Kiyingi's use of it. She asserts that Kadongo Kamu artists' interpretation of Wakayima 'embrace[s] the multi-layered connotations of *bukalabakalaba*' in Luganda. Wakayima, according to Mugambi, 'confuses, and sometimes misleads others into behaviour that gets them into trouble' because of his 'limitless expression of ingenuity.' His ability to 'successfully evade punishment or retribution even when caught in the most hopeless of situations', or, 'to instantaneously invent novel solutions when facing conditions where defeat appears inevitable', is not apparent in the English version of the trickster (Mugambi, 1997:214). Thus, to '[impose] the English term "trickster" on figures in traditional orature, specifically Wakayima, the Hare, clearly impedes access to the possibilities inherent in the more appropriate Luganda term *bukalabakalaba*' (Mugambi, 1997: 214). In Kiyingi's plays, the motif is 'transformed' into a 'crucial rhetorical devise' (Mugambi, 1997: 214-216) for interrogating oppressive systems. The key traits that Katumbula or Kyeswa display that resonate with Wakayima are his success in using his 'brains, not physical might, to triumph over adversaries'; hence, his reputation as *kalimagezi*, a witty character or cunning fellow. (Mugambi, 1997: 216) The trickster, therefore, becomes a potent tool with which Kiyingi opens a dialogue with the audience, discussing their shared history and reality. Throughout most of his professional practice, Kiyingi has worked with a collection of actors including Dan Zirimenya, Saabwe and Kezia Nasejje, who established a rapport with the audience. Zirimenya provided an interesting focus for the examination of Kiyingi's exploitation of the trickster motif.

Across his dramas, Kiyingi constantly keeps Dan Zirimenya's identity as *kalimagezi* fluid, casting him in similar roles as Katumbula Omusomesa (Katumbula the Catechist/Preacher), Katumbula RC (Katumbula the Resistance Committee Chairman),[1] Lozio, Lebeni or Kyeswa (commonly known as Bwana Kyeswa), always attributing him new meanings and new tricks; hence, these multiple identities marked him out as *kagezigezi* or *ka-kalimagezi*. Zirimenya's characteristic laughter, (*enseka ya Katumbula*) and quips: '*Oba Muduuma akutte kkubo ki?* (I just wonder where Muduuma [this country] is heading!)', '*Muduuma tagwaako byewuunyisa* (Muduuma is full of surprises), and '*Engeri Muduuma gy'afaanana ebyalo ebirala* (Muduuma, just like every other village in Uganda)' work on the audience, linking radio drama to storytelling, to urban and village communities, and drawing attention to the shared reality. This way, the trickster identity that he seems to represent resonates with that of the trickster elsewhere in African and Native American communities, 'mobile, always different *and* differing itself into' plays/roles, 'and unable, therefore, to become fixed and contained' (see Campbell, 2010: 253) by his oppressors. The audiences' identification with Zirimenya, and the other members of the cast, whom they knowingly refer to as *abazanyi baffe* (our actors), demonstrate the popularity of these plays.

The concept of *katemba*, discussed in Chapter 1, is useful here for understanding the relationship between Kiyingi's drama and the *abadongo* (travelling musicians) genre. For Kiyingi, *katemba* exists as a space of resistance to tyranny and negative forms of modernity. Today the term *katemba* is used pejoratively to mean a charlatan. Nevertheless, *katemba* can be seen as a critical tool that artists use to interrogate people's concerns to demonstrate their connectedness (and difference) to all forms of performance and to their world. Kiyingi's drama presents a reframed *katemba* that shows an awareness of the people's concerns, linking their reality to history, cultural values and lived experiences. This theatre, therefore, is *katemba* (critical theatre), and plays such as *Wokulira* and *Bwebukya ne Buziba,* are significant elements crucial in the study of the kind of resistance performance that appertained in radio and television dramas. Similar to Serumaga and Elvania Zirimu, Kiyingi, whose dramas testify to his position as a master of contemporary reality, is not interested in including indigenous theatre expressions or oral performance. He uses allegory and farce within a Western performance framework to represent critical oral performance. Dialectic interplay between oral performance, lived experience and postcolonial culture is critical in post-independent dramas but it is most notably demonstrated in Kiyingi's theatre. In his practice, *katemba* presents the notion of transformation of the individual actor, as described by Davies, from 'the daily circle of life, work and struggle to an emotional level [state], to 'a level of history', and finally, as *munnakatemba* (a performer), to the context of deconstruction and interpretation (Davies, 1996: 200).

This way, it 'allows the individual [performer] to occupy a different location in relation to the community' (Davies, 1996: 200).

In functioning from within *katemba* and *abadongo*, the established performance genres, the artists consciously travel 'outside … the boundaries of restriction and oppression' (Davies, 1996: 201). It is arguable that in a society, which has undergone several dislocations, beginning with colonisation to post-Amin liberation, this transformation allows the 'creation of an alternative physical, political/performance space, outside of the terms of the dominant society' (Davies, 1996: 203). Thus, in Kiyingi's practice, *katemba* may refer to his 'articulation' of the needs of Ugandans in a more responsive performance space both within and outside of the conditions of the oppressive state in which they live. Nevertheless, it would be a mistake to view *banakatemba* (performers) as marginal, as critics and a cross-section of society sometimes do, for, as Kiyingi's work demonstrates, they do not exist on the margins of society but are located and work in the midst of society.

Lozio bba Ssesiria (*Lozio Ssesiria's Husband*) (1974)

The subtext of the play, *Lozio Bba Ssesiriya*, is the story of a marginalised people in Muduuma, a village within a ten mile radius of Kampala city. Similar to the title of his other play, *Ssempala bba Mukyala Ssempala* (1968), this epigrammatic title exploits the word play on the words '*bba*' and '*mukyala*' which mean husband and wife, respectively; Lozio's actions and demeanour present him as Sessiriya's wife. As I have written elsewhere, culturally among the Baganda, *kuwasa* and *kufumbirwa* refer to the masculine and feminine roles, respectively (Kasule, 1993). Therefore, if a woman controls a man, especially if she is wealthier, society would comment, *b'amuwasa/y'afumbirwa* (he got married), cynical expressions implying that the person lost his masculinity. Similarly, in this sub-culture, age, death and funerals are exploited to further individual gain. The play is a satire of emasculated men (such as Lozio and Girigooli) living in a world that has been turned upside down; where concepts of home, marriage, husband, wife, and woman have taken on new meanings. Notably, between 1971 and 1986, home had lost meaning; indeed, in many cases home was no longer safe while in others it did not exist anymore. The residents include Lozio,

Sessiriya's partner, whose parasitical existence represents a cross-section of Ugandans scrounging for a living; Sessiriya, a divorcee whose status as a *nakiyombekedde*[2] is loathed by decent society; Sessiriya's daughter, Jane, recently graduated from the university; Dr Luninze, is the local medical doctor; Yolamu, Lozio's uncle and Kimaama, the *omupakasi* or labourer. Apart from Dr Luninze, a medical doctor but impoverished because in this material world education has no meaning, most of the ordinary residents are people who have no voice in the wider national community.

Kiyingi's artistic endeavours aim to give people a voice through theatre, and to this end, he asks controversial questions about politics and power, and the continuance and relevance of cultural values in the changing socio-economic environment. This suggests that as he transforms the space into a place of public discussion of human experiences through the questions the performance provokes, the problems of post-independent governments are exposed. The focus on the politically volatile atmosphere of Obote 1 and Amin's political reigns, where the General Service Unit and the State Research Bureau kidnapped and imprisoned people, and unemployment, poverty and alcoholism were rife, enables an interrogation of the roots of a dysfunctional nation. Illicit sexual relationships with wealthy *banakiyombekedde* and *banamwandu* (this concept refers to unmarried women and others widowed by the regime) symbolised the degeneration of society where wealth not individual worth was recognised (Kasule, 1993). However, it should be stated that wealth has always been important in marriage to a lesser extent. It is in this sense that Kiyingi identifies with the South African writers of the apartheid period or Kenyan and Tanzanian writers (see Kavannagh, 1985; Ngugi, 1998; Coplan, 2008). Their point of intersection can be found within the presentation of independent enterprising women who operate *shebeens*, emasculated men, and a society in the grip of an oppressive political system. In considering this play from the theatre of resistance perspective, one may take Ngugi's assertion (1998: 39) that, since colonial times, East African nations have been uneasy about performances. For, '[w]hile the state performs power, the power of the artist is solely in the performance, either of their own or of the other, but they have the audience as their common target.' A significant feature of *Lozio bba Sessiriya* addresses these aspects of the performance space as a site of resistance performance. Kiyingi, in resonance with Ngugi's view on the relationship between artists and their society, wants his audience to deal with its reality and to understand that the fundamental contest between the state and the people is the source of the degenerating socioeconomic condition.

Action takes place in Sessiriya's home-cum-bar where she sells *enguuli* for a living. Her mud and wattle house with *malebe* (paraffin and oil tins) sheeting is furnished with discarded wooden and tin containers that serve as seats for her customers. Kiyingi deliberately uses the euphemisms such as '*kali*' and '*akagiraasi*' to create rapport with the audience aware of the words coined to describe illegally brewed gin. Lozio, summing up Sessiriya's character to Yolamu, calls her a woman with a wicked heart who, for example, manipulates her real age to fit her desires. In circumstances rife with jealousy, rivalry and corruption, Lozio's hopes for a rich inheritance are dashed when Sessiriya, loathsome of the freedom he is about to acquire, steals his father's Will and accuses Girigooli, Lozio's friend, of the robbery. However, Lozio and Yolamu later discover the will hidden in her wooden box (safe). On this occasion, Yolamu states: '*Oli kkondo tulina okukuyisa nga kkondo* -You are an armed robber' - (*Lozio bba Sessiriya*, p.50). Sessiriya's actions, which lead to the conviction, imprisonment and death of an innocent man (Girigooli), are comparable to those of armed robbers and political oppressors. This way, the play demonstrates repression through the presentation of Muduuma residents as victims of 'cruelty and entrapment' (Severino Joao Albuquerque, 1991: 141); for example, Lozio is the object of Sessiriya's entrapment. Sessiriya, by stealing the will left by Lozio's father, robs him of the inheritance; by extension, her action denies Lozio the opportunity to escape her repression. Similar to Griselda Gambaro's Youth, in *Las Paredes* (*The Walls*) (1964), whose watch is stolen, in this context, 'the theft affords' Sessiriya, 'the [tormentor] an additional opportunity to blame' Girigooli, the 'victim of the victimization process'[3] (Albuquerque, 1991: 138).

Wokulira Ng'olabye Bingi (Life is an experience) (1961-2000)

Kiyingi's radio drama, which some critics have dismissed as simplistic and peripheral, reveals his role as the modern day storyteller who, since the introduction of radio in Uganda in the late 1950s, has engaged with wider audiences than any other artist in Uganda has.

Crucially, as an oral audience, people receive Kiyingi's radio and television plays not just aurally, but critically with an indigenous knowledge and perception of the significance and meaning and purpose of the Luganda language and storytelling. The plays evoke the traditional storytelling genre - not only were they broadcast/televised but, as mentioned earlier, for over forty years they were performed by the same cast who formed a relationship with the 'listening [and watching] invisible national audience' (Mugambi, 1997: 211). Therefore, Kiyingi manipulates both radio and television (drama studio) spaces to present resistance and interethnic discourses; this way, his plays transform into a medium that links urban and rural issues, the past to the present, but above all acts to 'establish his credibility, enabling him to validate new stories' (Mugambi, 1997: 211).

Kiyingi's abstract allegory is the long running radio series, *Wokulira*, which can be considered to be a record of Uganda's history; in the 1960s and 1970s it warned the listeners of Uganda's gradual descent into dictatorship. The play, broadcast between 1961 and 2000, is about the community in Muduuma, affected by national changes, and is simultaneously a critical examination of local and national, political and social policies, moral values, political tensions, corruption and institutional violence. While drawing on newspaper reports, phrases from radio announcements, church or government pronouncements that are rendered with humour and sarcasm, particularly between 1974 and 1977, and again between 1981 and 1986, our attention is drawn to representations in which recognisable local linguistic expressions have ominous implications. In developing particular themes from his previous work, the dramas repeat versions of history and 'personal' narratives that the characters claim to be the reality, but which frequently turn out to be subversive comments on the reality; in a way, this reflects the experience of life in post-war Uganda, which is as varied as people who live in Muduuma. All the moral, political and social abuses that can be found in Uganda are represented in Muduuma; the extraordinary life of Muduuma as underlined by Malita, one of the residents, '*Muduuma okiyita kyalo kya kusema* (Muduuma village is indescribable)' (*Wokulira*, Episode 109), embraces all the above aspects. One statement helps to connect the themes in this play and other issues discussed previously: 'Theatre *ye paliyamenti yaffe*. (Theatre is our parliament)'. Benoni Kibuuka, the

President of the Uganda Theatre Association, made this remark when I asked him about his view on the role of theatre in contemporary Uganda in 2010. At the heart of this statement, on the one hand, is the acknowledgement of the rapport between theatre and the audience, while on the other, it underlines the tension between theatre and the state. Kiyingi, as noted above, blending humour with sharp satire, and his deep understanding of the people, uses the historical and social elements to present dysfunctional families, and eccentric characters - '*abatamanyi kye bali* (people who have no sense of identity)'[4] - to examine society and challenge the audience's view about the political status quo.

Apart from Katumbula, other characters include, Daudi, his brother, Malita, a divorcee, market trader and bar owner who co-habits with Daudi. Others are Dominiko, the Finance Secretary to the Village Resistance Committee, Kasumali, the shop owner and trader, and Mbalyowere, Malita's daughter. Similar to Sessiriya in *Lozio Bba Sessiriya*, Malita is a common village character, self-supporting, providing social services to the villagers. Another character, Dominiko, a divorcee, whom Katumbula describes as, '*tamanyi kyaali* -he does not know his place in society' (*Wokulira,* Episode 111). In radio serials broadcast in the 1980s and 1990s, the residents of Muduuma are subjected to economic domination by the new merchant class (who replaced Indian traders) represented by Kasumali, and on the other hand, by an intimidating political system, introduced by the National Resistance Movement, viewed by residents as a means of grooming a new breed of political stooges. The play captures Uganda through the lives of these characters that, apart from Mbalyowere, previously lived under the colonial government and since independence, have witnessed the circle of violence. They are witness to a post-war nation whose political systems are not developing as coherently as they should since the social environmental factors that gave rise to the recent conflicts are still in place.

In the play, Katumbula occupies two roles: before 1986, he was cast in the influential role of *omusomesa* (a catechist) whereas in the Museveni era, he is the Resistance Council Chairman and 'ex-*musomesa*'. Both positions afford him a powerful vantage point to criticise the government and society. He appropriates these positions, transforming the spaces into locations for socio-political discourse that centres on Muduuma village and broadly, the whole nation. In one scene, Kiyingi takes advantage of what Mugambi (1997: 212) has termed the 'virtual audience' to comment on how materialism is crippling religious institutions. The scene below demonstrates his point.

Katumbula: *Naye laba lino evvubuka lye twaziika jjuuzi…*
Mbalyowrere: *Liriwa eryo?*
Dominiko: (*Dives in.*) *Kkondo omututumufu mu gwanga…*
Katumbula: *Abasomesa kata bagwe nemuntaana.* (*Mbalyowere aseka.*)
Mbalyowere: (*Amused.*) *Batya?* (*Katumbula aseka.*)
Dominiko: (*Dives in.*) *Anti nga balwanira ebifo okubeera ku mwanjo -*
Katumbula: (*Dives in.*) *Ku ntaana….* (*Beat.*) *naye owa Alwizi twayigga muyigge …*
[Katumbula: Do you remember the young man whose funeral took place the other day?
Mbalyowrere: Which one?
Dominiko: (*Dives in.*) The most notorious robber in the nation …
Katumbula: The funeral was attended by so many priests that they almost fell into the grave. (*Mbalyowere laughs.*)
Mbalyowere: (*Amused.*) How? (*Katumbula laughs.*)
Dominiko: (*Dives in.*) They were jostling for positions around the grave -]

(*Wokulira*, Episode 112)

In another scene, he castigates Dr Mukasa's practice of extorting money from his patients by comparing it to that of professionals and contemporary political leaders. In conclusion he remarks cynically: '*ENNYONYI ENKULU NGA EKYAYIGIRIZA ENTO okupama mu kisu; siraba ssente z'abandi we zinawonera ne nguzi.* (AS LONG AS THE OLD BIRD CONTINUES TO TEACH THE YOUNG ONES how to defecate in the nest, the theft and embezzlement of public funds will not stop)' (*Wokulira*, Episode 111). His comments allude to other extortionists, '*abasajja abatumbuufu* (the bloated untouchables)' who include '*Ba-Zaidi, Ba-Kasumali ne Musoke owa Kalina* (the Zaidis, the Kasumali's and Musoke who owns a two storied house - Zaidi is a wholesale trader while Kasumali is a shopkeeper)' (*Wokulira*, Episode 111). Once again, in fulfilling his intentions of portraying contemporary reality, Kiyingi exploits commonplace idioms, phrases, and other forms of register, identifiable with urban dwellers, and in addition, creates words and phrases to describe and ridicule Ugandans with obscene wealth and power. For, instance, '*abatumbuufu* (the bloated untouchables)', which relates to the *mafutamingi* in Amin's military regime.

In post-liberation context after 1986, Kiyingi mocks the new government whose people (soldiers and politicians) abuse the ten point National Resistance Army Code of Conduct[5] - which he compares with Moses' Ten Commandments - specifically abusing human rights and engaging in corrupt practices. Thus, similar to the Jews, who 'turned Moses into an attendant of toddlers, all the time holding them by the hand as they get entangled with his legs', the NRM cadres had become 'the bloated untouchables', behaving like 'toddlers' and blocking Museveni's attempts at transforming Ugandan society (*Wokulira*, Episode 112). These are comments about a society in the 'Money Age', characterised by moral decadence and a repressive political system. Moreover, as Katumbula asserts, in this society the ordinary person is part of the 'Silent Majority' (*Wokulira*, Episode 112). Kasumali, one of the bloated untouchables, is not human but '*muntu-nsolo* (meaning a commando or person with a bestial behaviour)'. He is an unscrupulous trader whose extortionist practices remind the villagers of the business practices of the expelled Asian traders as well as the illiterate *magutamingis* of the 1970s whom Kiyingi depicted in his earlier play, *Muduuma Kwe Kwaffe*. Not surprisingly, to Katumbula, he is 'an elephant standing astride a field of stunted grass' (*Wokulira*, Episode, 112).

Kiyingi, unlike cheap artists who wanted to stage performances for financial gain, helped to fulfil the need for a complex, provocative theatre that could engage with the new political issues. Although his plays, blending contemporary events and themes, can often appear to favour the ordinary person and focus on themes of empowerment, human dignity, human rights, community and individual identity, Kiyingi does not overlook the role of the people destroying their lives. Thus when Katumbula reproaches Mulisi, one of his guests, whom he calls, '*embwa eyawangukamu amannyo ey'olubungu* (a toothless barking dog), for non-participation in the (New National) Constitution Committee seminars, he aims to sound a warning that whatever the ruling party's wishes, collective responsibility not the so-called constitution will restore peace and integrity to the nation (Episode 113).

Allegory: *Omwana w'Omuntu and Olugendo lwe Gologoosa*

Once again, it is important to focus on the socio-political conditions and moments that influence the creative process and production of the performances of this period. This idea is discussed in relation to the view that *katemba*, a further extended form of critical theatre, must evolve from the encounter of socio-political reality so that non-violent performance established by artists such as Ssekinoomu, one of the Buganda Royal flutists, complements an armed rebellion. In *Omwana w'Omuntu* (1969) and *Olugendo lwe Gologoosa*, the discourse of resistance comes from new presentational practices, and a new politics of ethnicity located in *katemba*.

When the violence related to political instability, the breakdown of cultural values and fragmentation of social structures led to increased incidences of disappearances, detentions in army barracks, and ungazetted detention houses such as Naguru Go-down and the Nakasero State Research Bureau headquarters. The story of Jesus' Passion provides Kiyingi with a framework to examine society's passive resistance. When Kiyingi wrote *Omwana w'Omuntu* in 1969 using the hostile security atmosphere as its background, the government banned the stage performances at the National Theatre. Nevertheless, to criticise the political and military dictators, Obote, Amin and Paulo Muwanga among others, who presented themselves as saviours of the people, Kiyingi reworked the script and named the new play, *Olugendo lwe Gologoosa*. Unlike his other dramas, the setting of these plays is not Muduuma but instead open spaces that could be *mbuga* or village-meeting compounds. In both plays, he compares the political leaders' behaviour, represented by Pilate and the Jewish leaders, with that of the Roman occupiers of Israel. Within both plays, evidence of collaboration between the Jewish leaders and the Roman oppressors signifies the collaboration between ethnic leaders and the post-independent oppressive governments. Thus, while subtly signaling to the people the true saviours of the nation, the 'competing sets of performances', on and off stage, 'share a nationalistic faith in the act of sacrifice' for the sake of Uganda. (Purga, 2008: 73) These plays, while offering a perspective on theatre's critical examination and exposition of militarised government systems, and alternatives of communal resistance, use specific historical moments of the 1960s, 1970s and 1980s as the backgrounds of the action. Amin and the governments that immediately followed his expulsion, the Uganda National Liberation Front's Military Commission and the UPC government, used the emerging political and military resistance to justify the eradication of suspected bandits and saboteurs. Similar to Argentina's socio-political crisis of the 1960s, Ugandan 'Society [underwent] a normative transformation as the abnormal' suddenly became 'the norm and the unnatural [replaced] the natural' (Taylor, 1991: 99).

Omwana w'Omuntu is staged with a neutral backdrop (although Kiyingi states that the producer may alter the setting) while the backdrop for *Olugendo lwe Gologoosa* combines a red cross painted against a dark background. The latter set design 'heightens the atmosphere of terror'; the 'visual framing', specifically the painted backdrop depicting a red cross painted against a forested landscape 'leads us beyond the boundaries' of the performing space to the 'dangerous, invisible spaces into which people disappear' (Taylor, 1991: 134). To blend into a dark setting the chorus is dressed in red cassocks and presents a visual image that blurs the boundaries between 'the individual and the political, past and present' (Taylor, 1991: 170-171). Similar to the 'visual framing' of Ruganda's *The Floods* or Gambaro's *Information for Foreigners* (1972), the juxtaposition of the performance space and the hidden illegal detention houses, forests, lakes and rivers in Buganda and elsewhere prompts us to expand our inquiry to cover the 'broader' national picture.

As the central character in the play, the Narrator uses words from the Bible to satirise politicians or make direct political statements immediately relevant to the audience. For example, his opening statement makes indirect references to the intensification of organised resistance against the government, particularly between 1980 and 1982, and the beginning of the notorious *panda gari* (board the truck) operations. Starting in April 1981, the armed forces (police, paramilitary, military police and the army) started conducting massive operations, known as *panda gari*, on the pretext of cleansing the country of *bandits* and guerrillas. Soldiers would gleefully announce to the abducted, *Aa ha, Scania nakufika. Muntu yote panda gari* [Aa ha, Scania [the truck] is here]. Everybody board the vehicle. On other occasions, the military also drove around in a bus, popularly known as, *mpaawo atalikaaba* (everyone shall weep), which they used to transport people kidnapped from roadsides[6]. Kasozi also confirms this when he writes, 'Soldiers would station their vehicles at places where people collected, such as markets, sports matches or religious places. They would select young people from the crows and have them board trucks or other military vehicles by force, shouting "*Panda Gari*"' (1994: 147). Whereas in *Olugendo lwe Gologoosa* Kiyingi uses a Narrator who reads poignant and critical verses from the Gospels, a significant feature of *Omwana w'Omuntu* is the inclusion of the Chorus as the Narrator, which allows Kiyingi to comment on the communal terror. The Chorus, which includes ordinary people who have been victims of violence, reveals to the audience that they have enough self-determination to resist tyranny. One of the most powerful statements of resistance is made in the scene after '*apparently a gathering has just been broken up by Roman soldiers*' (*Omwana w'Omuntu*, 1982: 26).

> (*Buli omu asiisitira emboko y'Omuroma w'emukutte - omutwe, okugulu etc.*)
> *Kakati tukubirwa ki*
> *Tukoze ki*
> *Twaza ki*
> (*Members of the crowd beaten and lashed by the Romans feel their body - on the head, legs and arms, etc*)
> What crimes have we committed?
> Why are we being tortured?
> What have we done wrong?
>
> (p. 26)

Moments later, a soldier arrests Yoswa, one of the leaders. The Chorus represents the people's resistance to Obote's suppression of traditional kingdoms and the militarisation of politics between 1964 and 1971. In the above scene the political and the aesthetic cannot be separated from one another, anymore than the authorial instruction to stage the scenes of protest against the background of thematic songs can be separated from the public rejection of oppression and imposition of foreign/strange rulers or army of occupation. This combination is what differentiated one of Kiyingi's most critical theatre performances from the drama of any of his contemporaries.

Omwana w'Omuntu is framed by a Chorus, which, through song, challenges the audience to respond to tyranny. Similar to oral storytelling performances, 'action and narrative unfolds through songs'; songs can be taken up by the audience 'who by so doing [become] part of the unfolding of the action' (Ngugi, 1998: 110). The Chorus sings politically charged songs that comment on the narrative; the 'non-initiates' may not understand it but the target audience understand the meaning of the message. For example, at the beginning the Chorus sings a song that directly talks about institutional violence:

> (*Omuserikale omu Roma ajja nga akutte Bendera. Mpange ku muti - crosses the stage - CHORUS yesasa nayitawo. CHORUS egudde ku ttaka etandika okuyimba mu ngeri ewakanya n'okuvumirira.*)
> *Genda ogambe Pilato*
> *Ategeeze Kaisari*
> *Bendera ye mu Yerusalemi*
> *Mu kibuga kya Katonda waffe*
> *Tugiganyi;*
> *Wabula okufa okugwawo*
> (*The Roman soldier comes in carrying a flag attached to a flagpole - crosses the stage. As he crosses the stage, the CHORUS moves to one side. Out of fear, they lie prostrate themselves and sing songs criticising the oppressors.*)
> Go back and tell Pilate
> To inform Caesar
> We reject his flag
> This city belongs to our King
> We do not want here
> We would rather die than have the Roman flag flying in the city.
>
> (*Omwana w'Omuntu*, p. 16)

The singing stops when the soldiers engage in a running battle with the Chorus while the Jewish priests, who come to the stage accompanying Pilato (Pilate), watch from a distance. Through song, the Chorus discusses issues of social justice, makes direct comments on the (offstage) reality that 'unfolds' before the audience, and asserts their claim for peace. At the end of the play, although attempting to identify with the Chorus, the play alludes to local community representatives who acquiesce with the oppressor to gain favour and wealth: '*Nedda, nedda, abantu tebannagamba/ Wabula mwe mugamba/Kubanga obugagga bwamwe/Obuyinza bwamwe/ ebitiibwa byamwe/Bibafudde emisege emiruvu.* No, no, people haven't said it/ those are your own words/Your wealth/Your power/Your privileged positions/Have turned you into gluttonous beasts' (*Omwana w'Omuntu*, p. 30). The Chorus and the audience still regard the Jewish leaders as collaborators who are directly responsible for the oppression of their own people. It is defiant and it knows how to maintain a critical gaze, one that is resistant to tyrannical institutions.

It is impossible to read or watch Kiyingi's *Omwana w'Omuntu* and ignore the issues undergirding the violence and oppression that marks the conflict within the 1970s, 1980s up to the present Uganda. As Mbowa suggests, the play was written as 'an outcry against the oppression of the Baganda by Obote's soldiers [but Kiyingi] molded it into the Easter story of the tortured Christ and his followers' (Mbowa, 1984: 126). Yet, the play is self-consciously farcical and therefore more entertaining than it would otherwise be. As in *Olugendo lwe Gologoosa*, the unbearable is rendered endurable by means of a performance practice of presenting what the audience can or cannot feel or understand at given times: political protests, disappearances, politically motivated imprisonments, murder of innocent citizens. Kiyingi's dramatic evocation, of a disappearing Buganda and political freedom, which alludes to the Roman occupation of Israel, attempts a creative 're-enactment and reclamation' of the audience's shared social reality/history.

In theatre, abstract allegory, as Puga states, 'deploys ambiguous, fragmented, multiple levels of meaning often concealed one inside of another' (Puga, 2008: 15). Therefore, the use of Biblical or 'historical allegories exemplify a theatrical strategy that often surfaces under conditions of political oppression, when the urgent need to express dissent coincides with the urgent need to disguise the expression of dissent' (Purga, 2008: 73). *Omwana w'Omuntu* alludes to those Ugandans who tried to ignore the poisonous environment of false accusations and imprisonments, news about kidnappings, tortures, murders and disappearances in Obote 1 and Amin's regimes. Indeed, Kiyingi's use of the Roman Empire echoes the Brazilian playwrights' use of The Inquisition during military dictatorships. For, the Roman Empire's methods of interrogation are a metaphor for the relationship between the murderous Uganda military and their victims. There are many parallels between the dramatic action in *Omwana w'Omuntu* and *Olugendo lwe Gologoosa*, which creates similarities between two historical periods, the Jews under the Roman imperial rule and the twentieth tyrannical political systems in Uganda. The audience is encouraged to draw allegorical equivalences that are broader than the national allegory. Accordingly, 'within this allegorical frame' (Puga,

2008: 78) the soldiers and Jewish political leaders are any twentieth century soldiers and indigenous political leaders accused of betraying the people, on the other hand, the Chorus represents the subversive grassroots organisations, accused of betraying the nation and labelled *bandits* by the second Obote government. The parallels between the Roman colonial state, the British colonial state and the postcolonial oppressive government are striking and these inspire Kiyingi to write *Omwana w'Omuntu*. In the play, the Roman colonial oppressive state is worried about the gatherings in the open space, that is why they disperse the crowds (chorus); it is not just about people singing in the courtyard, the state is sensitive to the 'collective expression' (Ngugi, 1998: 65) of dissent and to the soldiers, and Pilato, this may represent a crime. The blending of the Sermon on the Mount and elements of the Passion from the Gospels, and folk theatrical elements is relevant to the audience which needs historical, religious and contemporary shared experiences as reference points to support the silent majority to confront reality.

Staging violence, as Susan Sontag suggests (1989: 139), may invoke different reactions from the audience, which, on one hand, acts to reinforce stereotypes, or empathy, forcing them to react; in *Omwana w'Omuntu*, for example, the violent clash between the Chorus and Serikale (Soldier) allows the audience to understand the background to their suffering. The spectacle consists of the soldiers' infliction of physical punishment on the Chorus, in Act 1 Scene 1, and later in the play, on Yoswa and Jesus. The effects of the brutality are experienced by three sets of audiences: the onstage audience, the Chorus, the people watching the play or paying audience, and what Taylor (1991: 132) has referred to as the '"silent majority"' outside the theatre, who are silenced by the ongoing practice of torture by the militaristic rulers. Kiyingi does not stage atrocity but he alludes to the theatricality of torture when he stylises violence and turns it into a spectacle. To a certain extent, I would agree with Taylor's argument that since torturers 'are not self-employed' but 'work for a state', the use of 'torture, as an instrument of the state, is tied into power structures far exceeding the most bizarre fantasy' (Taylor, 1991: 133). In this way, both plays, *Omwana w'Omuntu* and *Olugendo lwe Gologoosa*, demonstrate Kiyingi's articulation of the native and stranger binary, between ordinary persons (victims) and the rulers/military (victimisers) as well as victims and collaborators, the 'two obvious participants in torture' (Taylor, 1991: 112) some of whom are from pre-colonial rival indigenous states. *Omwana w'Omuntu* echoes Taylor's assertion that the 'theatricality of the victimizers' which 'sets the drama in motion …is *real*' since 'victimization could not continue without it. Victimizers, however theatrical, do not represent something else, such as the "human condition", they are not make-believe "bad guys" that delight audiences. They kill people.' (Taylor, 1991: 100) In this sense, '[t]he victimizers see themselves as victims defending themselves from annihilation' or 'from dangerous *others*' (Taylor, 1991: 100). The effect of using soldiers in *Olugendo lwe Gologoosa* and *Omwana w'Omuntu*, whose actions allude to those of the Ugandan marauding armed forces, demonstrates their split personality. In order to underline the beastly behaviour of the Roman (Ugandan) soldiers, Kiyingi presents two images, humans and beasts, side by side onstage; this recalls similar binary sense in Kawadwa's *Oluyimba lwa Wankoko* in which Wankoko, in his protest song, delineates the difference between people (*abantu*) and beasts (*ebisolo*) or soldiers/political leaders. *Omuntu*, human being, in the title, is ambiguous, it could be an adaptation of Jesus' statement in the Bible, 'the son of man'; from a parochial perspective, it connotes the Baganda as opposed to strangers or non-Baganda from Northern and North Western regions, as Obbo (1971) explains, but a national view would include the ordinary person. At another level, *omuntu* as the opposite of *ensolo* (animals) in Luganda, references the treatment that is being meted out to the people as if they are animals. The Chorus identifies with the audience, 'compassionate onlookers' (Taylor, 1991: 134), victims of the soldiers or beasts, the main protagonists in the play.

Omwana w'Omuntu signalled a new kind of theatre for resistance, which '[depicts] a new kind of violence, a terrorism that is itself highly theatrical' (Taylor, 1991: 136). It presents the stage as the new space for 'intense political confrontation' (Taylor, 1991: 136) as symbolised by the confrontation between the Chorus and the soldiers; conversely, outside theatre, between playwrights and government censors in the Ministry of Information. Although playwrights submitted their scripts to the Censor board, as Omutaka Dick Kasolo (playwright and director) admitted to me in an interview with him in 1990, the directors staged scripts with subversive messages since the government agents rarely attended theatre performances. Once again, the play resonates with Ruganda's dramatisation of Amin's atrocities in *The Floods* in which 'acts of cruelty take place offstage' (Taylor, 1991: 136). However, echoing the practice of the torturers both in Amin and in Obote 2, at the right moment in a move that is intended to deter the Chorus (and the audience) from engaging in subversive activities, in Act 2 Scene 1 the soldiers bring Yoswa onstage, bruised and bleeding. From their boastful statements to the priests, we learn about torture, murder and other dehumanising acts:

Kabona: (*Musanyufu*) *Ssebo wange onkubidde omusajja nange nensiima.* (*Amukwata mu ngalo.*)
Kayafa: (*Musanyufu - alwanira engalo*) *Iii basajja mwe mumanyi okukuba.*
Serikale: Iii, *omulimu gwe tukola buli lunaku, lwaki tetwandigumanye* . (*Enseko.*)
Kabona: *Hee-ee, omulimu mwaguyiga.* (*Amangu ennyo Pilato akomawo.*)
Serikale: *Awedde okukolako Mukama wange.*
Pilato: *Kaakati…?*
Serikale: *Akubidwa bulungi nnyone bano ne basiima.*
Kabona: (*Jovial.*) My dear, I greatly appreciate the manner in which you lashed and tortured that man.
(*He offers a handshake.*)
Kayafa: (*Jovial. Quickly grabs his hands.*) Iii, you guys are good with the lash and methods of torture.
Serikale: *Iii*, why shouldn't we? That is our daily routine. (Laughs)
Kabona: *Hee-eee.* You were well-trained. (*Pilato comes back.*)
Serikale: My lord, we have finished with him.
Pilato: So?
Serikale: We have administered the torture so well that even these people have appreciated our methods.

(*Omwana w'Omuntu*, p. 29)

When, in his description of the state of Yoswa's battered body, the soldier alludes to a shell-less egg, we realise that this apparently innocuous remark relates to the communal terror in the country. The audience is aware that among the 'disappeared' and murdered artists had been Kawadwa and Galabuzi Mukasa, a Principal Cultural Officer, and in addition, Pio Zirimu who had allegedly been poisoned by Amin's agents. New words that described these actions included *yabuze*, *bamubuzizawo*, *bamuwambye, bamuyodde*, *bamututte* (he disappeared, they disappeared him, they kidnapped him, he was picked up or he was taken). When Kabona and Kayafa praise Serikale's skills of torture we know that they are as complicit in the abuse of the citizens as is Pilato and other Roman leaders; this dispels the differences between government, military leaders' (strangers) and local chiefs' love for power. That the local chiefs may accuse the 'strangers' of abusing the ordinary people's human rights while, on the other hand, they are willing to sacrifice anyone threatening their position, resonates with the comments about *schadenfreude* as a characteristic trait of the Baganda (Lloyd Fallers, 1964). In many ways, Kiyingi's capacity to juxtapose religious ideas with reality reveals the complex task of preaching 'love' to people living under tyranny. For instance, in the following dialogue, the play alludes to the Sermon on the Mount.

Kayafa: *Musa yatugamba nti twagale atatwagala?*
Kabona: *Yatugamba ku mukyawa.*
Kayafa's Group: *Erinnyo ku linnyo.*
Olusambaggere ku lusambaggere
Kifuba ku kifuba.
Luyi ku luyi.
[**Kayafa**: Did Moses command us to love our enemy?
Kabona: He commanded us to hate him.
Kayafa's Group: A tooth for a tooth.
A kick for a kick
A push and a shove for a push and a shove
A slap for a slap.]

(*Omwana w'Omuntu*, p. 14)

Elsewhere, offstage reality intrudes into onstage action as Jesus and the audience are presented with witness statements about the suffering experienced by the people. We are reminded that the play is not about the historical experience of the Jews, or oppression of one ethnic group, nor about one militaristic regime, but is as much an indictment of the audience as silent observers who have unconsciously helped support the abuses. 'Torture', Taylor states, 'works on several levels simultaneously. It annihilates the victim; it destroys the victim's family' and 'it undermines the immediate community, which, however threatened, is unable to put an end to torture' (Taylor, 1991: 142), as *Omwana w'Omuntu* and Ruganda's *The Floods*, show. Arguably, Kiyingi's motive is to force the audience to confront their self-destructive tendencies.

The grisly scenes on stage make people rethink or create a new language to describe its performance (and postures), therefore, introducing a new (grotesque) vocabulary into their 'normative' language as a way of handling fear. For instance, *y'akasudde, akalagajaliridde, ebiryo byavunda*[7] (he dropped it [the skull]; he was negligent with his skull; the pumpkin is rotten) were sometimes used to report death. *Olugendo lwe Gologoosa* is a presentation of how a community which has endured hard times either on the run,[8] or as *ba ekizayiro* (internal exiles), have watched the nation gradually transform into a place of skulls. Similarities are drawn between the historical political intrigues in Jewish society during the time of the Roman occupation, and twentieth century Uganda. Kiyingi's aim is to incriminate the audience as being responsible for the betrayal of trustworthy leaders[9]; an action best summed up in the vital and significant parallel of the Chief Priests and Pharisees midnight plot to arrest Jesus with the National Consultative Council's[10] all night meeting that passed the vote of no confidence in ex-President Yusufu Lule. The audience may recognise the reference to the dubious methods by which people 'disappear' at the hands of the security forces. While Kayafa's selfish actions are politically motivated, Yuda's are materialistic. Kiyingi so presents the *magendo*, dubious dealings in human commodities by *abayaaye*, *abalebeesi* or *bakibanda,*[11] with its climax in the exchange of Jesus for thirty pieces of silver that the audience can compare the Pharisees and Yuda's obsession with wealth and power with that of contemporary leaders.

Kiyingi's *Omwana w'Omuntu* and Olugendo *lwe Gologoosa* capture some of the issues of suppression and resistance associated with these years of crisis and the way the conflicts affected the ordinary person.[12] The positions from which his main characters project their dilemmas or points of view are informed by their consciousness of how their future had been destroyed (by their own leaders not colonialists) and that they were partly to blame for their fate. While some of the earlier plays, for example, *Gwossusa Emmwanyi* and *Bwebukya ne Buziba*, mainly focus on social issues demonstrating the development of a class society, *Wokulira* is a systematic record of the degeneration of the socio-political institutions, and *Omwana w'Omuntu* and *Olugendo lwe Gologoosa* are theatre of resistance that focuses on the individual experience of terror. The scenic design of *Olugendo lwe Gologoosa*, for instance, resonates with the experiences of the government's massacre at Namugongo, the location of the Baganda Martyrs Shrine that, previously in 1877, had been the scene of Mwanga II's massacre of Christian converts. As noted earlier, on May 1984, government forces, irked by the Roman Catholic Church's criticism of its anti-people policies, invaded Namugongo and the surrounding villages, shooting, raping and looting property. In addition, they killed a protestant priest and desecrated a mosque when they 'slaughtered, barbecued and ate a pig in the prayer house' (Kasozi, 1995: 182). These incidents are not comparable with King Mwanga II's purge of Christians in the early years of European occupation.Nevertheless, Kasozi observes that 'Once again, after almost one hundred years, the fires of Namugongo were shaping the destiny of the country' (Kasozi, 1995: 183).

Kiyingi's theatrical work, with its focus on social, economic and political issues, is perhaps more identifiable as a theatre of social/political protest. His aim is not to distance himself from the issues but to develop and underline the importance of the construction (and examination) of a theatre that resonates with the people's concerns. It is theatre that 'signals protest covertly in proverbial and figurative language', which, as evidenced by his *Olugendo lwe Gologoosa* (1982), uses 'titles that [serve] the purpose of allegorical finger-pointing to national, social and religious situations' that interests Kiyingi and forms the basis of this study of a theatre of resistance. (Mbowa, 1984: 126) In the interview at the beginning of this chapter Kiyingi states, '*Njagala nnyo okulaga picture ey'omuntu owa bulijjo nga bwafaanana, social life nga bweefanana* - I want to present the ordinary person's picture [reality], his social life experiences -' (Kiyingi in conversation with Kasule, 2009). Of course, the aim is to find a critical position to create a discourse that will not only question old forms of performance but also destabilise the power structures and subvert the oppressive systems. By representing the perspective of the people and not that of the political and religious leaders, Kiyingi alerts the audience to view performance as a source of new possibilities of transformation and resistance, blending reality and fiction.

Chapter 5

FOLKLORE AND TRADITION IN THE DRAMA OF CLIFF LUBWA p'CHONG

Cliff Lubwa p'Chong whose works include: *Generosity Kills*, *The Last Safari* (1972), *The Minister's Wife* (1982), and *The Madman* (1989), in addition to a collection of poetry, *Words of My Groaning* (1975), described his writing as being 'very very, political' (Lubwa p'Chong, 1991). He was a realistic and direct dramatist who belonged to the 'song school'. The song, being emotive and the most popular indigenous performance genre became the major motif of the writings of p'Bitek and many other Ugandan writers. This form adapts and transforms indigenous idiomatic expression into English, making the end-product appeal to literate and semi-literate audiences alike. It develops the stylistic features of traditional orature as a means of re-awakening communal and collective consciousness and responsibility in society. Lubwa p'Chong's sensitivity to socio-political issues and humaneness, as alternatives to political absolutism, is evident in the play texts discussed in this chapter.

What is interesting about Lubwa p'Chong's earlier plays, *Generosity Kills* and *The Last Safari,* is that he uses various indigenous forms of expression and shared myths, legends and folktales; the performances present witness accounts of the lived reality under Amin. Once again, echoing the earlier plays, *The Minister's Wife* and *The Madman* specifically draw our attention to the conditions of political violence that became the reality of Obote II's regime. In the years following independence, specifically after Amin's expulsion of people of Asian origin in 1972, theatre had to interact with fragmented and transformed cultural, social and political institutions. These conditions varied from government to government: in Obote I's so-called revolution, the political institutions inherited from the colonialists were dismantled and, as discussed earlier, there was an ideological shift to socialist structures or what Obote called, the Move to the Left.[1] Amin's regime that started with intentions of 'revers[ing] the Socialist moves of the last years of the Obote regime' was characterised by chaos and violence.[2] (Obbo, 1983: 313) The four post-Amin governments were divided along ethnic and party lines, so much so that the 1980 elections (organised by Paulo Muwanga's Military Commission to restore democracy), which were allegedly rigged, were the beginning of autocratic rule, plunder, and violent ethnic strife. The crisis extended to the post-Obote II governments where, as noted earlier, the conflict between various armed groups intensified because of their greed for power and wealth. Amin, Muwanga and Obote between them transformed politics into a performance art. Lubwa p'Chong's plays capture the 1980s drama associated with *coup d'état*s, counter-coups, political campaigns, riots, and the violent suppressions of resistance. While *The Minister's Wife*, using the 1980 elections as its background, provides an insight into the processes used by the government to rig elections, *The Madman* examines the abuse of power by modern chiefs. These plays offer a greater sense of the systematic practice of terror or what Bukenya calls 'the six types of terror' that include '"taking [away]', that is, violent abduction; detention; execution; killing", i.e. massacre and murder; rape and assorted tortures' (2000: 19). Collectively, these plays 'make visible' the atrocities 'committed by military dictatorships' and tyrannical governments of the 1980s; '[T]hey also make visible the lasting trauma suffered by families of the disappeared and the country as a whole' (Taylor 2002, p. 152). *The Minister's Wife* presents a good example of Lubwa p'Chong's evaluation of what went wrong in Uganda; for instance, ethnicity, greed, hatred, immorality, and jealousy, while urging the audience to understand its responsibility in the post-independence violence. *The Madman* presents Ugandan leaders' acquisitive urge and fascination with violence; it provides an opportunity for exploring the notion of resistance in performance, since it demonstrates how playwrights in the 1980s attempted to incite people to rebel against rampant acts of violence, rape and murder. The onstage world, deliberately constructed to echo the militarised institutions' offstage performances, is terrifying, especially when the Madman describes how Chief's bodyguards exterminated his family: 'They tore the baby from her [my wife's] arms, put it in our mortar and pounded it to pulp! They threw the mortar and its contents into the burning hut! My wife tore at them with her nails and teeth, screaming …. They twisted her neck until it broke! Then they raped her corpse one by one!' (*The Madman*, pp. 62-3).

Generosity Kills

Generosity Kills, a dramatisation of a legend, belongs to Lubwa p'Chong's earlier works and contextualises the disorder in Uganda's history. It was written for performance during the Makerere Arts Festival Week of 1971. In the plot, Latina discovers a new recipe for beer; in her excitement, she brews it and generously serves the whole community. The Chief of the village consumes a substantial amount, passes out, and is mistaken for dead. On waking from his stupor, he demands to see Latina to congratulate her, only to be informed that the villagers in the mistaken belief that she had poisoned the Chief have killed her. This act fulfills the Acholi proverb 'Generosity kills the generous ones'. Latina's brewing skills, her inventiveness and generosity led to her death. Lubwa p'Chong adapts the form and structure of the folktale, which illustrates how excessive well-meaning behaviour can be detrimental to an individual.

The Prelude to the First Movement begins with excitement as a group of people drink beer at Latina's house. It is a traditional evening setting complete with storytelling, dance, and music. The characters in this scene are only referred to as 1ST Man, 2ND Man, and 3RD Man, who are villagers or representatives of a community whose voices may easily be mimicked by the narrator. On behalf of an Elder, who arrives too late to share the brew, the Boy warns the Girl to 'leave a remnant/In the bottom of the pot' (*Generosity Kills*, p. 2). After goading the Elder to explain how 'generosity', which has 'no hands/For holding knives, sticks or Spears/To kill', could have killed Latina, the Elder becomes the Narrator-cum-Diviner and the scene is transformed into a re-enactment of Latina's legend. He uses a diviner's cloak and gourd rattles to invoke the spirits of Latina and her adversaries. Weird sounds signify the response of the spirits to the invoking sounds of the rattles. In performance, the Elder and his audience would join the secondary audience in the circle off the stage to witness the re-enactment of the legend. The Elder, as Diviner, appeases Latina's spirit which is approaching earth from the underworld, beckoning her to 'Come in peace ... Slowly, slowly...' (*Generosity Kills*, p.3). Latina, and her daughter, Lawino, appear centre stage and are later joined by Oluma, the husband. After Lawino has accomplished her 'creation', Oluma drunkenly dances and laughs while Lawino yodels to climax.

Dramatic irony is achieved when Twon-Coo and the neighbours initially dismiss the brew as 'soppy bread' or the sickly vomit of a dog', only to discover its potency. The point to note is the communal spirit of the society, which collectively responds to the alarm (ululating) - this time resulting from excitement - and willing to share the achievements and failings of their neighbours. Latina observes communal ethics when she takes her brews to the Chief and for,

> ...our people say
> If you kill an animal, however small it may be
> One leg belongs to the Chief.
> Chief ... here is your share.
>
> (*Generosity Kills*, p. 14)

The Chief gulps the drink and talks wildly, delivering his heroic recitations to the background of exciting music. Lubwa p'Chong's ridicule of the Chief (and by inference, contemporary political leaders) is highlighted in the following extracts.

> (*He [the Chief] again drinks it non-stop. He begins to sway. Gets up, dropping the calabash, and begins to talk wildly.*)
> I went to hunt,
> A buffalo came,
> It came as if singing:
> 'Children, children, children.
> See, see, see,
> My liver, my liver, my liver ...'
>
> And later,
>
> (*He looks at one of the court jesters who is not even standing near any of the Chief's wives*)
> **Chief:** You, you, what are you doing?
> **Court Jester:** Nothing, Chief.
> **Chief:** Nothing, Nothing, Chief.
> Do you think I am blind?
> Do you think
> I did not see
> What you were doing?
> (*staggering towards him drunkenly*)
> How dare you, a commoner,
> touch the Chief's wife?
>
> (*Generosity Kills*, pp. 15 -17)

Laughter is provoked from the audience by his attempts to chase the Court Jester round the stage. As the Chief strikes the Court Jester the latter ducks and falls on the floor. More laughter is 'milked' from the audience by his abortive attempts to stand, before he finally lies prostrate, dead drunk. Like a 'commoner', he is embarrassed on waking from his stupor by the throbbing drums and cold water poured over him. The awe, embarrassment, shock and communal guilt are expressed by the silent moment, as the Chief looks round searching for Latina. The projected image of the Chief in this state is meant not only to criticise chiefs who behave in a manner not in keeping with their positions of responsibility in the community, but also to caution people against the evils of taking strong drink.

The poetic effect of the play is realised through images, symbols, similes, proverbs and metaphors that relate to the cultural environment and are very much part of the audience's life. For example, describing the potency of the beer, the 3RD MAN says, 'See how it [the beer] vomits clean froth' and Latina describes Lawino's emerging breasts as 'pawpaws' (*Generosity Kills*, p. 5). The lyricism of the language is highlighted in Oluma's description of the brew as,

> …not *gasia* (*tastes*)
> This is sour-sour. (*tastes*)
> Bitter-bitter. (*tastes*)
> Sweet-sweet. (*shakes his head*)
> Strong-strong …
>
> (*Generosity Kills*, p. 10)

Similes, metaphors, praise-names and other images are used by the characters to describe each other, such as Oluma's description of Latina as, 'the mother-in-law of birds' whose mouth has been beaten with 'the testicles/Of a he-goat' (p. 5).

Glorious mention of one's roots by the naming of clan and praising of parents is an instinctive response in the people's daily life. It is done to summon one's courage in moments of danger, to show pride, warn off potential antagonists and display determination:

> **Oluma**: Woman shut up!
> Let me drink this drink in peace,
> (*Drinks and belches*)

I am the son of my mother!
I am the son of the woman
Whose teeth are white
Like dry season moon!
I am your wife beat you with pestle...

(*Generosity Kills*, p. 9)

It is the praises and the subsequent cajoling adjectival phrases, which make the scene in which Oluma's neighbours share his brew, light-hearted, humourous and memorable.

(*Oluma holding the calabash in one hand shakes hands with him [Twon-Coo]. They call each other praise names.*)

Oluma: *Yaa* Twon-Coo!
Twon-Coo: *Yaa* Oluma *yaa*!
Oluma: *Yaa* a dog urinated in your wound!
Twon-Coo: *Yaa* Your Wife Beat You With Pestle!
Oluma: How are you man?
Twon-Coo: Healthy as sunrise.
Oluma: Put your buttocks down man.
Twon-Coo: (*sitting*) Thank you, friend.
What are you drinking?
Oluma: We are drinking millet bread
which our child dumped in water.
Twon-Coo: So you drink *Gasia*, rubbish?

(*Generosity Kills*, p. 10)

In juxtaposing ritual, divination, invocation, and legend, Lubwa p'Chong transforms the traditional story-telling genre into a theatrical mode. The result is a mutually shared experience of the legend by both audiences - the primary audience assisting the narrator to animate the story and the secondary audience watching the dramatization.

The Last Safari

This play is a dramatisation of a folktale indigenous to Acholi and Buganda, centred on Keetimo (or Mpoobe in Buganda), a hunter of great repute, who defies ominous signs of fate. When Keetimo goes hunting, he ends up in the Kingdom of Death in the underworld. Death releases him on condition that he should never reveal his experiences. When he breaks the promise, Death strikes him.

Lubwa p'Chong focuses our attention on the spear, the strongest symbol of the homestead in many Ugandan communities. It is the pride of the homestead, source of food, and 'guard/over all!' Neglected and rusty, the spear is discovered by the Young Man who raises the alarm, calling the actors to the stage. The Old Man interprets the sacrilege as the cast bursts into a mournful dirge indicting the community for having neglected and allowing the Young Man's father's shrine and spear to rust. The Old Man proclaims that social chaos, disorder, rape and robbery will prevail and the community will have to pay the price. The dirge highlights shared social guilt. It is a dirge for a community plunged into chaos by reckless individuals who should have been guardians of the people's consciousness, physically symbolised by the ancestral shrine. The whole community has participated in the erosion of the human essence, the cultural mores that made it whole. The state of the neglected spear is parallel to the state of a community that has become powerless, defenceless, and helpless.

The First Movement is full of ominous signs such as the sounds of cockcrow, hoots of the owl, and Keetimo's sneeze as he cleans his hunting spear. His wife, Binen, dreams of Keetimo sitting under a 'big *kituba* tree/While young men are digging a grave' (*The Last Safari*, p. 26). Contrary to her interpretation of the dream - that Keetimo should not go hunting - Keetimo predicts a successful hunt. Further, Binen, Keetimo's mother, draws his son's attention to the multiplicity of ominous signs hovering over the homestead:

Binen: Mh, my son, do you call that
Success.
Don't you know
Meat is red
Like grave soil?
To make the matter worse,
An owl was hooting
Just before you sent for me.
When owls hoot at dawn,
It means death, sure death.
Therefore, this owl
Was announcing someone's death;
And that person
Must be close, close,
For the owl was sitting on your roof.

(*The Last Safari*, p. 27)

It is signals such as these that Lubwa p'Chong exploits to create a fresh indigenous theatrical shorthand.[3]

The play is a multidimensional reconstruction of Acholi attitudes, thought-systems and social ceremonies relating to death and human destiny. Tragedy is a communal concern to be shared by friend and foe. Through imagery, Lubwa p'Chong reminds the audience that they should not laugh at victims of death like Cock:

Clan Leader: For a moment keep silence,
….
When death occurs,
Even worst enemies
Come and mourn together
I know sometimes
When death occurs
As it has,
Some people pretend
To be mourning
But deep in their hearts
They celebrate.
The cock crows:
Diki Wang ca rommo neo pala!
A Man: Tomorrow the knife
will sink past
The ram's throat!
Clan Leader: And the ram answers:
In kono ibid ok kwere ki abnila pa kwana?
A Man: What about you, cock,
How will you escape
Being sacrificed at the ancestral
Shrine?
Clan Leader: (*addressing everybody*) The death
That killed your brother
Will be the death
That will kill you

(*The Last Safari*, p. 41)

Binen, through the extended eulogy (and metaphor) and the thematic content of the dirges, expresses the iniquitous nature of death (fate).

Binen: Then my son must be dead.
My clansmen, Come and see me,

This cruel world has knelt on me
And crushed me completely.
[....]

BINEN and Lapobo begin wailing. Companion tries to comfort them. Mourners enter from different direction, wailing. They start a funeral song and they perform the funeral dance.

Binen: Stop and listen here!
[....]
For to-day, the sharp axe
Of death, the unkind one
Has felled Keetimo, my beloved son
[....]
Maybe cruel death
Has struck and thrown into water
Keetimo, the chief of *bulu* young men,
And now he is being eaten
By fish and crocodiles!
[...]
Like boiling oil,
Like red pepper
Put on wounds
My grief drowns me
In tears

(*The Last Safari*, p. 39)

She personalises death, drawing a picture of a cruel, beastly, and bloodthirsty person who fells people like trees. As p'Bitek (1974) explains, among the Acholi, Fate is described with hunting images of 'kneeling and crushing'. These derive from the manner in which a wounded buffalo, for lack of strength, falls and crushes its victim with its massive weight. As she refers specifically to the body being eaten by 'fish and crocodiles', her words echoed the offstage communal performances of the time since the play's premier coincided with Amin's genocidal attack on the Acholi (Lubwa p'Chong's home region) in 1975. Notably, between July 1971 and September 1972, there were four attempts to overthrow Amin. On all these occasions, July 1971, February 1972, June 1972 and September 1972 he suspected that the Acholi and Langi were instrumental in plotting his downfall. Thus, he took opportunity to eliminate them. For instance, in March 1971 between two hundred and five hundred Acholis and Langis were massacred while similar numbers were later collected from various barracks, taken to isolated farms or forests and massacred. On another occasion at Makindye Military Barracks, in March 1971, Acholis were herded together, dynamited. In February 1977 Archbishop Janan Luwum, Erunayo Oryema and Charles Oboth Ofumbi, all Acholis, were tortured and killed by Amin. Thus, killing innocent Ugandans and leaving their bodies to rot in isolated places or feeding them to crocodiles in Lake Vitoria was a crime that became increasingly common in Amin's Uganda. In calling our attention to the possible cannibalisation of Keetimo's body by crocodiles, Lubwa p'Chong also underlines the ways by which security agencies disposed off their victims' bodies.

The climactic conclusion to the tragedy is a synchronized mime of omnipresent Death and his assistants dancing to the rhythm of an Acholi dirge, stalking, shouting and wooing Keetimo to his death. The Acholi metaphysics visualize Keetimo being locked in battle with Death, while his people helplessly watch him receding beyond the horizon. As Joe de Graft has suggested (1972: 64), the audience may:

> [J]ust sit there stone still in their seats though alive in every fibre of their being to every little movement or sound or impression that is being projected to them by the actors ... intensely silent, but intellectually and emotionally active [in] participation.

The ritual presented in its entirety in the play is the blessing of the hunters' spears by Binen. Keetimo and his friends hold their spears and stand forming an arc, while the elders are standing behind them. A liturgical prayer, intended to placate the ancestors, inspire the hunters, and woo animals to their traps, is chanted in a litany. As Binen sprinkles ritual water on the spears, she leads the chant and the elders respond with the last line of her incantation. The hunters do not respond until the last lines of the prayer. Binen prays to the ancestors to bless the spears so that they may 'Drip red with animal blood' (p. 31). She asks the evil spirits which live in rivers, big trees, dark mountains, shady forests, caves and holes to give way to the hunters. This part of the prayer illuminates the metaphysical and cosmic nature of Acholi belief and the possibility of communing with evil as well as good ancestral spirits.

Sacrifice and ritual are important facets in the development of the plot. Keetimo's return from the bush is a representation of a funeral crowd 'unfearingly' speaking their minds for the good of the victims of Death and the community. The elders emphasize to Keetimo the importance of instant sacrifice for falsely shed tears - to be instantly washed away with a bull's blood - or else he would end up in the 'stomach of the earth' (*The Last Safari*, p. 45). Using mimicry, the Elders recall Lekamoi's words:

> I still do not have a bull,
> I still do not have a bull...
> Now where is the young man?
> Is he not in the stomach of the earth?
>
> (*The Last Safari*, p. 45)

Lubwa p'Chong uses language with intensity, as in the speech when Binen mourns her son's death with the poetry of a funeral ceremony's declamation. Elsewhere, the Clan Leader and the men argue about staging a cleansing ceremony for Keetimo because, 'If you want to kill a snake safely,/Kill it in the egg,/Don't wait till it breathes' (*The Last Safari*, p. 46). In addition, an Elder warns him that evil, like 'Dog's dung, must be removed/From the floor/While it is still steaming (p. 46). Elsewhere, Binen draws attention to her plight by dramatizing her sorrow as she imagines her son, 'rotting/Somewhere in the grass/Like a dog!' (p. 39) In anguish, she decries the hyenas, bald-headed vultures and worms laughing at her son's body, breaking bones, eating out the intestines, burrowing into his beautiful eyes, ears and mouth (p. 40). She further carries the audience into the abyss by alternating images of Keetimo's body being ravaged by land as well as aquatic creatures. The images used by Binen intensify the tragedy because they are within the immediate social experience of the people, as again they are allegorically referring to their experiences under the Amin regime.[4]

The Madman

This play, written after an interlude in which Lubwa p'Chong changed his style, marks his maturity as a playwright. The central argument in *The Madman* is that ultra-egotism and myth making have contributed to the state of dictatorship and the gun culture endemic in Uganda's politics. The play laments *Matunda Ya Uhuru* (Fruits of Independence), which have not been delivered, thus causing a paralysis in a society where human and temporal clocks have stopped.

For instance, Adolf Enns (1985: 53) in his article, 'The Clocks Have Stopped in Uganda', notes how, in a society where the elite at Makerere (the national university) drive their 'Mercedes on the sidewalk right up to the door of their office building', the clocks symbolise the state of the nation. Significantly, the clocks performed and perform the paralysis in the polity and in socio-economic and cultural spheres.

> The clock at the prestigious Mulago Hospital's eye-nose-throat clinic reads 4:56. On the tower of Makerere University's administration building the clock reads 12:20. Above the main entrance to the high court in downtown Kampala, it reads 11:14. Inside the main post office, it reads 12:27. All over Kampala clocks have stopped---at different times.

In *The Madman*, the legend of Walukagga has been so dramatized that at each stage the parallels with the contemporary political crisis can be recognised. In style and form, the play illustrates the theatrical trend in Uganda by which artists use folklore, pre-colonial themes and traditional structures to interpret and criticise contemporary conditions. As in the earlier plays, the Narrator plays a central role in the plot. He outlines the conflicts in the plot, underlining the fear experienced by the villagers, 'for each morning the sun rose with news of some new orders...and nobody's life was safe' (*The Madman*, p. 5). The Narrator highlights the misdeeds of the Chief, noting his manipulation of the people through plunder, torture and murder. Chief's warrior vigilantes follow his instructions without 'caring about right or wrong ….They operated anywhere at any time, and in full public view...ran wars of intimidation and terror...looted and destroyed property, killing and maiming, raping young and old women....widows...sowing yaws [AIDS]!' (*The Madman*, p. 6) The people reached their nadir when the royal warriors, in executing their 'painful duty' of collecting human tears and hair, broke bottles and used the pieces to shave heads. In the end, 'popular anger' (*The Madman*, p. 6) forced Chief to relinquish power to a committee of elders. The Narrator uses the end-form of folktales in Buganda when he describes how the people celebrated Chief's downfall:

> I came away to tell you the story. (*Plays a tune briefly [on his bowl-lyre]*) And up to this day in Uganda, there is a proverb which says: A man will take his problem to a madman when sane men fail (*Wokubira omulalu mu kyama nga omulamu gwolaba*).

(*The Madman*, p. 10).

One of the characters in *The Madman* is the blacksmith, Walukagga, who in Kiganda folk traditions is a heroic figure.[5] On the one hand, Chief represents despotic rulers while Walukagga, on the other hand, represents the will of the people and the unspoilt elements of harmonious communal existence and humaneness. Lubwa p'Chong exploits the conflict between a megalomaniac, self-centred Chief and the peasant Walukagga. Chief mistrusts crowds and only visits on short notice. When he eventually appears on stage, he rolls his 'frightened...eyes terribly' (*The Madman*, p. 7) to frighten the villagers. This physical or bodily action parodies the manner in which both Obote and Amin faced their audiences at the ebb of their rule. Using phrases and words relished by dictators, he orchestrates forced applause from the villagers. The people are his 'masters' and he is their 'humble servant', the '*shamba* boy', labouring in their gardens for their own good. For this reason, they are fat and must '[c]lap for your happiness' (*The Madman*, p. 7). His images and metaphors are beastly and obscene showing a person whose brain has been crippled by power, wealth and spilt blood of the innocent. For example, he illustrates his contribution to the welfare of the villagers by comparing their physical state at the beginning of his reign to 'chickens drenched by some heavy rains...cows suffering from dysentery' (*The Madman*, p. 23). However, now they are 'sleek like lion's cubs! ...like well-fed puppies...bubbling with life like well brewed *kwete* beer!' (*The Madman*, p. 24)

Chief's intellectual dwarfism and insensitivity are further exhibited in the riddle he gives the Women to solve. He is oblivious to the sufferings of his people, failing to interpret the Women's answer to his riddle in which they echo the suffering unleashed on the community because of his greed. They tell him that after eating a lot of 'saliva-bringing food' (p. 30), his hunger goes to a poor person in his kingdom, and so does his illness after he is cured of an illness. The Women's solution to the riddle means that Chief's rule has merely putrefied society. Then Chief makes a decree that no one else in his chiefdom is to be referred to by the title 'CHIEF' any more, and all holders of the title will henceforth be called 'Clan-overseers, Village Heads, [and] Communal Organisers' (*The Madman*, p. 25). Dramatic irony is effected when we realise that the Chief Hunters will effectively become Head Hunters. The pun is not lost on the audience as the villagers, at 'spear-point [gun-point]', chant refrains parallel to contemporary party songs, 'One Chiefdom, One Chief' (*The Madman*, p. 25).

The ritual of peasants offering gifts to visiting 'dignitaries' is structurally used to precipitate the conflict between Chief and his people. Village Head 1 offers a hammer to Chief; Village Head 2 offers a chain; Village Head 3 a *panga* (machete) and Village Head 4 offers a spear. Chief is the chief murderer, the master blacksmith, forging dead bodies out of his human subjects. The audience is aware of the apparent misuse of these symbols of torture and cruel death, so that the euphemism for Amin is *kijjambiya* (machete) and his regime is *omulembe gwa kijjambiya* (the machete's reign). The intended parallelism of Chief's regime with Amin and the post-Amin state security organs [Head Hunters] is quite clear. Chief, incensed by the display of praise for Walukagga, dares, 'our clever blacksmith [Walukagga] ...to forge me a man who can eat and starve, can cry and laugh, can love and hate, can kill and be killed' (*The Madman*, p. 39). Because jealousy, rivalry, ambition and greed have become a way of life in the community, abductions and extermination of work-mates, neighbours and relatives are commonplace. In the conflict between Walukagga and Chief, the latter is supported by the evil blacksmiths. Walukagga's adversaries preoccupy themselves with mud-slinging, spreading *ladit* (nepotism and corruption), backbiting, bickering, gossiping and rumour mongering.

Lubwa p'Chong's dramatic vision is evidenced by his choice of folklore material from East, West, South, North and Central Uganda to represent the 'various types of madness of our time and place' (Lubwa p'Chong interviewed by Alex Tetten-Lartey, 1985). In the interview given after the premiere production of *The Minister's Wife* he remarked, 'particularly after the fall of Amin...about 90 per cent of Ugandans' heads are not correct' (Lubwa p'Chong, 1985). In using madness as a motif, he is contemplating the plight of Ugandans who continue to suffer at the hands of a few mad politicians. He traverses post-colonial Uganda history identifying positive and negative forms of madness in society. His target is the negative and destructive madness of politicians, which has moved the leadership in Uganda from reconciliation to intimidation, to the systematic elimination of citizens in the Amin regime, and the near-genocidal massacres under

Obote. The addition of the madman in the play is a thematically important feature. He represents the peoples past, present and probable future. He is a living example of those people who have paid a price for resisting Chief's orders. He enters, 'wearing some human bones around his ankle like ankle bells, and carrying a human skull in one hand laughing at [with] the skull' (*The Madman*, p. 52). He cross-examines the human skull, his only companion, and the symbol of death and terror existing in society.

> To whom did you belong? What was your sex? Place of birth? Age? Work? Tribe? Religion? Marital status? How did you meet your end?
>
> (*The Madman*, p. 52)

The question about the skull's identity echoes the statement made by Muwanga, a former Ugandan Vice President, to the effect that he should not be charged with the atrocities [in the 'Luwero Triangle'] because the skulls in Luwero are unidentifiable.[6]

> **Madman:** (*lifts up the human skull*) This is Chief's royal drum! (*beats it briefly: Talking to the skull.*) Yes, everything and everybody in this chiefdom is not a reality. My friend, you are the only Reality of this chiefdom…
>
> (*The Madman*, p. 61)

The reference to the skull - which he assumes to have belonged to his wife who 'disappeared' from his home - is the reality of the chiefdom and its substitution as its symbolic drum marks the denouement. 'Disappeared' (*yabula* or *yabuze)*, as discussed earlier, was a euphemism coined to describe the method used by the state to exterminate its opponents. As Bukenya explains in his essay, 'An Idiom of Blood' (2000), terror in the state, usually described by other euphemisms including 'taking [away]' or 'violent abduction' (p. 19), related to arrests and abductions [that] led to almost certain execution' (p. 21). In Madman's wife's case however, the state agents killed and gang-raped her body; afterwards he states, they 'took away [her] dead body and dumped it I don't know where' (Lubwa p'Chong, 1990: 63).

The character of Madman has multi-layered metaphorical significance in this play. Like Serumaga's Majangwa (in *Majangwa)*,

Madman is the conscience of society, indicting the audience for mistreating the sick in their midst. They,

> [T]hrow cruel jokes at me! You set your dogs on me! One of you one night scratched me all over the body with his barbed arrow for sleeping on his verandah! Your children throw stones at me but you don't reproach them! A bad animal comes from a bad bush. You and your children are the same: mad! You are like Chief! Mad! You enjoy inflicting pains on people. Like Chief!
>
> (*The Madman*, p. 61)

Within this play, Lubwa p'Chong underlines the mad sense of humour prevalent in the community, which makes people

> *Nyah, nyah, nyah, nyah*! [laugh] at the misfortunes of others, at everything.... Even when Chief says or does something that pulls our hair, and makes anger choke us, we burst out, *nyah, nyah, nyah*! *Nyah, nyah, nyah, nyah...nyah*!
> (*The Madman*, p. 68)

This demonstrates how contemporary society expunges its frustration, and moral and physical corruption, on the mentally sick, turning them into carriers of evil. There is dramatic reversal when Madman comments that the madness in society has reached such abominable depths that ancestral prayers relating to society's cosmology have changed.

> North is now south, and south is now north. The sun rises in the west and sets in the east.
>
> (*The Madman*, p. 60)

Contrary to the Acholi world-view by which people pray for evil to descend with the setting sun, the prayer asks:

> All the evils
> That are coming,
> Let the setting sun
> Take them down
> In the East!
> And so they are taken down
> In the east!
>
> (*The Madman*, 60)

Madman's image of the 'man' who can effectively tackle Chief is Lubwa's metaphor for a strong ruler, capable of purging the country of all the evils symbolized in Chief. He offers Walukagga a solution to his dilemma through a riddle to be given to Chief. Sarcastic about Walukagga's troubles, he states that Chief's virility may be on the wane; otherwise, he would not require a 'man' forged from steel. He requests Walukagga to:

> [F]orge us a man who will tackle Chief head on. A real man who will wrestle with Chief and throw him down. (*Grabs Walukagga and throws him down.*) Like that! To teach Chief some sense. Stupidity has built a permanent house over Chief[7].... [A] man not with two balls only but five balls, who will grab Chief's big balls and pull them hard for us. Chief has fondled our balls for too long!
>
> (*The Madman*, p. 56)

If Chief wants Walukagga to forge a man, Madman explains, he must provide him with five big sacks of charcoal burnt from human hair and five big pots of human tears. Chief orders his warriors to collect the items from all 'four corners of the chiefdom...today before the sun sets' but they only manage to collect a pouch-full of hair and a bowl of tears. Dissatisfied, Chief orders everybody to 're-shave hair, and re-shed tears' (*The Madman*, p. 86). Should the villagers refuse, the warriors must:

> [S]laughter all the people therein! Raze their huts and granaries to the ground! And drive all their livestock to the royal herd! ... Kill everyone then hang yourselves on the nearest tree! I must see only corpses tomorrow!
>
> (*The Madman*, p. 86)

This is the turning point in the plot, for 'popular anger' turns the villagers against Chief and they demand his resignation. In spite of promises for reform, Chief and his Chief Murderer, Ssenkoole, are tied up and the Elders take over the reins of the state. Lubwa is optimistic that society will one day revolt against the dictators.

The use of indigenous images and phrases makes it easy for Lubwa p'Chong to make believable his themes and effectively communicate with the audience. Two Women in the play (called Woman I and Woman 2) give us the impression that the issue of a multitude of edicts, decrees, legal notices and pronouncements is to the Chief's delight.[8] Ethnicity is used by the Chief to manipulate his subjects as illustrated by his latest order by which everyone must stick to their places of indigenous origin. Woman 2 graphically describes the divisive and isolationist strategies of Chief as a game of 'dividing, sub-dividing and sub-sub-dividing' society. The Women are sarcastic about the nature of obedience prevalent in society:

> **Woman l:** Our children are now like little machines...
> **Woman 2:** When Chief presses Button A...
> **Woman 1:** They move...
> **Woman 2:** When Chief presses Button B...
> **Woman l:** They stop...
> **Woman 2:** Like well-oiled little machines!
> **Woman l:** Obedience!
> **Woman 2:** Obedience!
> **Woman l:** Obedience has become madness in this chiefdom.
> **Woman 2:** We have become obedient like bulls trained for ploughing.
> **Woman l:** We are submissive!
> **Woman 2:** So subordinated that even Chief's favourite expressions have become fashionable throughout the chiefdom.
> **Woman l:** Everyone wants to be his Master's voice!
> **Woman 2:** Everybody dies to talk like Chief!
> **Woman l:** To smile like Chief!
> **Woman 2:** To walk like Chief!
> **Woman l:** To stand like Chief!
> **Woman 2:** To dress like Chief!
>
> (*The Madman*, p. 12)

The climax of the play-in-play is achieved when both women turn to the audience and in unison consult it on whether they should turn their Chief into a 'Chiefdom deity [President for Life]' (*The Madman*, p. 13). The scene illustrates the power with which Lubwa p'Chong uses folklore motifs and expressions to enhance his drama. The stick he carries, for every person straying from 'the herd...is beaten back' (*The Madman*, p. 12), which symbolizes absolutism and the demagogic position of Chief in society. Implied in this image is the contemporary African leaders' ridiculous use of fetish-like paraphernalia such as sticks, flywhisks, and handkerchiefs. Talking through riddle and metaphor, the women satirize the maddening aspects of power, comparing it to the fang of a poisonous snake.

Woman 2: [T]he longer the person stays in power the longer his fang grows.
Woman 1: Until it grows out of his mouth like the teeth of a warthog.
Woman 2: Yes, power possesses man, with evil spirits!
Woman 1: And when a man is possessed with some evil spirits of power, he can wake up one day and tell people under him, 'I anta this mountain levelled down!'
Woman 2: Yes, when power has possessed a man in power, the unthinkable becomes thinkable!
Woman 1: The impossible becomes possible!
Woman 2: And the useless becomes useful!
Woman 1: I tell you, power turns us into mad people. (*They both burst out laughing.*)

(*The Madman*, p. 22)

The theatrical devices in the play include music, song and dance. Most outstanding is his use of the Luganda (sacred) folk song '*Walugono*' which is performed by the villagers during the preparations for Chiefs visit: 'In mothers' wombs/Walugono twists babies' hands/He enlarges heads of babies/When they are born/They are deformed' (*The Madman*, pp. 16-17). *Walugono* is a pugnacious god whose relationship with the community is as demanding and retributive as Chief's is. Throughout the performance the actors involve the audience to imply that they share the guilt for the country's decadence and must, therefore, help to remove the ogres in their midst.

Lubwa p'Chong, just like the playwrights discussed in previous chapters, effectively articulates the problems of society. However, because he writes in English his plays have a limited audience and one can only hope that they will begin to be translated into Acholi, Luganda and other indigenous languages. Oboteism and Aminism, the madness that spurs the themes analysed in *The Madman* and *The Minister's Wife*, are the same forces affecting the transformation of popular theatre. Transformed folk expressions, when combined with communal contemporary experiences, have given this theatre its identity. The urgency to communicate their message to a wider community has forced the theatre practitioners to extend Kiyingi's evolution, of a Ugandan theatre lingua franca (overriding the problem faced by Lubwa p'Chong), to a form combining several languages in use in society.

Chapter 6

THE DRAMA OF ELI KYEYUNE, JOHN RUGANDA, NUWA SENTONGO AND ELVANIA NAMUKWAYA ZIRIMU

The presence of 'critical performing artists' (Ngugi, 2007: 4) in the East African countries of Kenya, Uganda and Tanzania, has been significant to the transformation of the indigenous oral forms into a contemporary genre that disrupts a theatre inherited from the colonial regimes; it is also a genre that is capable of exposing, challenging and subverting abusive post-colonial governments. The idea of transporting forms and models from oral and other cultural traditions to the stage, as a way of suggesting new discourses or ways of performances, was crucial to theatre. For ultimately it is here, at the intersection of indigenous and Western forms, when critical performing artists view new dramas and their own work as interconnected with but restricted by orature, dance, music, and storytelling that one can find the work of criticism and theory continuous and contiguous with indigenous ways of performance. Thus, the representation of the popular indigenous theatrical expressions in theatre juxtaposed with the delineation of serious political issues and social concerns since Idi Amin's regime is the focus of this chapter.

The work of four playwrights, Elvania Zirimu (1939 - 1980), Sentongo (1942 -), Eli Kyeyune (1936 - 2000) and Ruganda (1941 - 2007) presents characteristics of a typical theatre of resistance. In many ways, in their attempts to achieve a sense of reality of the Ugandan situation on stage, these playwrights were more concerned with performance rather than publishing. Additionally, similar to playwrights discussed in previous chapters, they blended music, dance, dialogue and song in order to create a dialogue with their audiences. Attempting to convey on stage the post-colonial world in which conflict, disappearances, murder myth and legend are indistinguishable from everyday reality, these works present another theatre that nonetheless relates to what we call *katemba.* By appropriating theatrical forms, and incorporating them into the structures of Western theatre performance modes, these writers achieve a subversive manoeuvre that challenges the audience to reevaluate their lived experience. Such intervention in the transformation of performance can further explain the subversive ways in which, apart from Serumaga, other playwrights, such as Ruganda and Elvania Zirimu, draw on aspects of folklore to offer provocative dramas that challenge society to confront autocratic leaders.

As Austin Quigley has explained, modern theatre 'invites audiences not just to receive entertainment and instruction but to participate in an inquiry that questions both what we know and how we know it' (Quigley, 1985: p 53). In this way, Sentongo and Ruganda are not as interested in the content of indigenous folktales and rituals, but in the way in which they inform and shape debates of current events. So, if we are searching for a close connection between theatre and politics some of the best examples would be in the works of Ruganda, Sentongo, Elvania Zirimu and Eli Kyeyune. An interesting aspect of Ruganda and Sentongo's plays is their exploration of how motifs, rituals and other aspects of orature from specific ethnic groups can be used to address nationalistic concerns. For instance, the night dancers' ritual and *akakookolo* (the trickster) are used to illustrate how such motifs can effectively work on stage. Thus, at first glance, the plays are imaginative recreations of indigenous rituals, legends, myths and dance and music festivals shared by various communities. However, as previous discussions have shown, these plays were written to perform acts of resistance in unpredictable ways. For instance, in Eli Kyeyune's *Bemba Musota* (1984), archetypal in its use of myths, history, music and dance, one can identify political elements in the subtext. He utilizes the alternative version of the creation myth of the Baganda to create a part allegorical, part satirical play challenging tyranny. It is a play reflecting on intra-ethnic conflict and institutionalised violence, pre-colonial history and myth.

Eli Kyeyune's *Bemba Musota*

Like Ruganda, Eli Kyeyune wanted to deal with themes such as autocracy, brutality and greed, setting his play in King Bemba Musota's Buganda and Kintu's hideout on Buvuma Island in Lake

Victoria. Buvuma Island, which forms part of the Ssese Islands on Lake Victoria, is regarded as the major sanctuary of the Baganda gods. Combining elements of the legend of Walukagga the blacksmith, also used by Lubwa p'Chong in *The Madman*, and the history of Buganda, Eli Kyeyune based the play on the notorious King Bemba Musota, a psychopath who, like *enswera* (the black mamba), murdered his own people. In *Bemba Musota*, his disregard for human life and callous disrespect for the dead is illustrated when he kicks his soldier's dead body. Collectively, his actions alert us to the internecine conflicts in Uganda as well as central themes of autocracy, anarchy and mass atrocities in the play. Notably, in the play, Eli Kyeyune glorifies Kintu, the first king of the Baganda, as a life-giving individual whose personality radiates peace and freedom. On the other hand, Bemba Musota (Bemba the Viper) is depicted as the despotic ruler of Buganda during the second half of the fourteenth century. Kintu starts as a simple protagonist but as the play unfolds around their conflict, we are reminded of his significance as the founder King of Buganda. He is now displaced and must fight to return to his ancestral home. The connections between *Bemba Musota* and *The Madman* are particularly resonant. Both plays are responses to Elvania Zirimu's transcription of the Luganda folktale about Walukagga and the Madman. Both plays draw on indigenous rituals and theatrical expressions, especially those that inform developments in post-colonial performance. Thus, as well as engaging with the discussion of Ugandan's history and contemporary political experiences both plays engage with the discussion of anarchy, authoritariarism and self-determination.

In the opening scene of *Bemba Musota*, Bemba receives news of Kintu's impending invasion, and hence, begins his mission of bloodshed. His mission is to defeat Kintu, avenge himself on the opposition and seal his power. In this context, Bemba represents the contemporary arrogant, vicious rulers with a fearsome reputation for committing mass murders. He commands Walukagga, the blacksmith, to mould soldiers of steel to help him defeat Kintu and other enemies within the kingdom. However, Katumba, Walukagga's deputy, criticizes him for debasing himself, trading his skills for personal safety. Daring him to make a test run of the assembled frames to see how best they take commands, Katumba mockingly asks, '*Simanyi n'ebigambo nga boogera bya byuma*? (Will their utterances be of steel?) (p. 6). He warns Walukagga not to report to Bemba's palace; otherwise, similar to other victims his body will be mutilated (pp. 11-13). As they argue about the possibilities of fulfilling the task, the confrontation between Walukagga and Bemba, which frames the play, represents both, the similarities between Amin, Obote and Bemba and the struggle by the people to depose the murderous dictator. In the end, the gods who advise him to request ten sacks of human hair and ten pots of human tears from Bemba as the basic ingredients in turning the steel soldiers into living beings rescue Walukagga. For, as a result of Walukagga's request, Bemba reaches the nadir of his excesses when he issues an edict to the chiefs to collect hair and tears required by Walukagga to transform his fabricated steel soldiers into living beings. The audience recognizes Walukagga's desperate need for survival and consequently finds it exciting to see the underdog, sharing as he does, similarities with the guerrillas fighting a contemporary dictator.

Nalwoga, a vestal virgin and one of Walukagga's assistants, leads the civil rebellion against Bemba. Acting as a mole in his palace, she recruits fighters for Kintu and leads communicants in prayer to the gods of war. In one scene, she alludes to Bemba's manhood to illustrate the measure of his excesses and society's disdain for his rule.

> **Nalwoga:** *Tubulewo. Kati tumuleke yeyambise ku bawala abaweese. Ndowooza balimuzaalirayo ne ku baana ab'byuma abatafa yadde okulwala.*
> [Let us disappear. Let us leave him to copulate with his fabricated girls. I hope that they will bear him children made of steel who will neither fall sick nor die].
>
> (*Bemba Musota*, p. 18)

On the pretext of fulfilling Bemba's command to collect hair and pots of tears, Nalwoga combines with Walukagga's assistants, Luswata and Lugejja, to unleash vengeance on Bemba's concubines. The language used is appropriate to the obscene actions of Bemba's tyrannical state machinery. For example, Nalwoga says to the women, '*Njagala zziga lyo. Kati. Kati. Lya buliwo. Tewali kuwoza.* (I need a "drop" of your tears. Now. Now. Now. Presently. No excuses.)' (p. 82). In this context, Nalwoga's actions allude to extortionist acts of Bemba's vigilantes.

Bemba, frustrated and confused by the opposition, swears to employ the services of god Sserubwatuka Mukasa to desecrate their tombs - smash and burn their jawbones. Apparently insane, he grabs a spear to kill god Kibuuka, an act that invokes the god to challenge Bemba to a duel. This and other inglorious acts alienate the gods, ghosts, and spirits. From this point in the plot, Bemba in a confused state drives himself to insanity, creating more comedy for the audience, which may laugh at his self-inflicted fate. At the end of the play, Bemba's men neither follow him into exile nor carry the royal drums off the stage, thus making it clear that he can no longer hold the instruments of power.

At the same time as it constructs the history of oppression, resistance and transgression in Ugandan society, Eli Kyeyune's drama might be said to underline the significance of theatrical forms in post-colonial performances. Instrumental court music, sacred song and dance are blended with drum signals for structural and thematic purposes. Traditional court music and clan-signals symbolise Bemba's position as king of Buganda. In contrast, a carnival atmosphere is created in Kintu's 'hide-out' through the syncretic performance of ritual dance movements, cult praises, sacred music, possession and prayer, as well as thunderous war drum music. The dance movements are vigorous, war-like and are accompanied with provocative gesticulation. Amaggunju, a ritualistic dance specifically danced for the king by members of the Butiko (Mushroom) clan is blended into the war dance to signify Kintu's position. The sacred and secular aspects are personified in Nalwoga's solo performance moving in and out of possession. The images in the war song associated with slaughtering chicken and poultry, for example, the refrain '*Maanya*' (p. 56), imply plucking, dismembering/disembowelling/slaughtering the enemy. On the other hand, the chorus response '*kaabya*' (p. 55), literary translated, torment them until they cry or torture them, resonates with actions widely practiced by Amin and Obote's soldiers. The brave warriors are 'a*bamaanya* (slaughterers)', those who slaughter people or '*abakaabya* (tormentors)' those who make people cry through torture (pp. 55-6). This apparent contradiction between bravery and brutality is a reflection on the status of Amin. This is a vivid example of the use of communal experience by contemporary Uganda playwrights. In this context, the experience is contrived through the juxtaposition of folklore with contemporary experiences of performers and their audience. Thus, Eli Kyeyune follows the contemporary trend, seen in many postcolonial Ugandan plays, of conflicts between mythical characters and authoritarian rulers but in the plot, he opens up the debate about the past role of women in political liberation. There is a dialogue between the past and the present and within this dialogue, the play examines complex issues of self-determination.

John Ruganda

John Ruganda, similar to Sentongo, Serumaga and Elvania Zirimu, was a Senior Creative writing Fellow at Makerere University as well as being the Representative of Oxford University Press in Eastern Africa until 1973 when he went into political exile in Kenya. His published plays include *Covenant with Death* and *Black Mamba* (1973), *The Burdens* (1972), *The Floods* (1980), and *Music Without Tears* (1982). *Black Mamba* criticises academic and sexual corruption in society caused by a disintegrating community infrastructure. Odhiambo, the main protagonist sums up the conditions in the country as extremely sordid. The discourse in the play raises other issues such as institutionalized disrespect for individual privacy, displacement of priorities and corruption. Ruganda's work is shocking and provocative, aimed to arouse the audience. In his drama, as in other contemporary dramatists such as Serumaga and Sentongo, he blends history, storytelling and personal memory to articulate the new experience arising from post-colonial terror and massive bloodshed. Like *abadongo* before him, Ruganda constructs a new performance space in order to articulate resistance to a new form of oppression. He turns to folklore and language (in its broadest sense) as the key tools with which to find the space and recreate people's post-colonial experiences. Again, Taylor's work on indigenous Latin American performance traditions of performance of protest and resistance has remarkable points of intersection. In her writing on performance protest in Argentinean theatre, she reflects on the ideas of 'performance strategies' or the 'DNA of performance' (2003: 169), which, in addition to Ngugi's strategy 'of using performance against institutions of power' (Gikandi, 2000:162), are critical to the discussion of Ruganda's works. Evidenced in these plays, which, similar to the Argentinean *Abuelas* and *Madres* employs 'performance strategies' (Taylor, 2003: 169) that parallel the *abadongo,* are 'various iterations of performance protest involving' the transformation of songs and folktales into hybrid theatrical expressions of protest. In this context, as Gikandi has said of Ngugi, using 'plays as forms in which art can resist the hegemonic performances and rituals of state power' (Gikandi, 2000: 162), Ruganda enables the audience to reflect critically upon their socio-political reality. From his first play, *The Burdens*, to his later plays, in particular, *The Floods*, Ruganda's performance functions as a representation for intra-cultural performance, hybridity and politics.

The Burdens

In *The Burdens* (1972), first produced in 1972, Ruganda consciously protests against anarchy. At the centre of the plot is Wamala, a discredited Cabinet Minister who, following his involvement in a plot to overthrow the government has sunk to abject poverty. His wife, Tinka, a daughter of a chief who now illegally brews *enguuli* (a locally made spirit) for survival, blames Wamala for their fate and constantly prejudices the children, Kaija and Nyakake, against him. Tinka and Wamala accuse each other of being the 'burden' that drove the family to destruction; the 'millstone round his neck' that brought him down. However, she retorts that his father was never '[a]s high up as men like Isaza, or Isimba', for, '[a] lamb is not a lion' (*The Burdens*, p. 6). In this way, Ruganda presents her as a as a malicious, jealous and possessive woman.

The social conditions are so abysmal tat even *kondos* (armed robbers), and night dancers, have become desperate. For example, Tinka relates to Kaija how *kondos* stole a suitcase from a taxi only to find the body of a dead infant. The bereaved mother could afford neither a coffin nor appropriate transport for her dead child. To underline the gap between the poor and the few wealthy individuals, Ruganda contrasts Wamala's living conditions with those of Kanagonago, a Cabinet Minister. Wamala draws our attention to the stench of sewage that 'meets the nose' and the site of 'neighbours' children defecating all over the place' (p. 54). While Wamala uses empty tins as seats, Kanagonago's settee is covered in *moquette*. Since Wamala spends days ruminating about the past and drinking *enguuli* (locally brewed gin), Tinka sarcastically remarks to her son that his father thinks prostitutes and alcohol will solve his problems. Wamala's efforts to make adapt to his new status and provide for his family are symbolised by his 'slogans with taste' (p. 28) which he hopes to sell to commercial company marketing executives. His aim is to buy a bed for Kaija and pay Nyakake's medical treatment, but Tinka believes that this business venture will never succeed for he has lost his political influence. As Wamala's slogans indicate, in a morally and politically corrupt society, humour and comedy can only be contrived by the use of vulgar language, which in turn is an indication of a sick-minded society.

Wamala: (*Interesting.*) Easy, old girl.... Mine are slogans with taste Nothing like the 'PUT A TIGER IN YOUR TANK' stuff. My Slogans must emphasise self-pride. Must exploit international prejudices against the African. Must redeem us from the rags of our humiliation.

Tinka: (*Sits.*) Give me one.
Wamala: (*Off the cuff.*) 'WARAGI WINS THIGHS'.
Tinka: What?
Wamala: 'DRINK VAT FOR VIRILITY'.
Tinka: Good God.
Wamala: 'REX AND SEX
FOR A MAN OF TASTE'

(*The Burdens*, p. 28)

At the end of the above scene in which Wamala demonstrates his new money making scheme, he cynically states that dirty minds and sex are the new religions in contemporary society.

Significant to Ruganda's and Serumaga's practice is their transference of the performative nature of orature to the stage where, as previously stated, members of the audience become active participants in the performance. By invoking and appropriating folk forms, these writers' strategy is to open a dialogue between the audience and the performance, inviting them to analyse their own meaning, and the process. In this way, their writing shows that rituals, legends and other performances can be reimagined and reinvented to engage with the discourse of resistance. Noticeably, in Ruganda's case, this becomes more evident as oral performance and Western theatre converge without apparently substituting the aesthetics of orature. Employing these strategies, he intends to find his own path in theatre, one that expands the margins of orature and transgresses oppressive structures of tyrannical institutions. Ruganda frames his play with a familiar trickster folktale, *Olugero lw'Akakookolo*, (The Leper's Tale), and with specific self-conscious references to tradition and contemporary real life experiences.[1] To many Ugandans, *Olugero lw'Akakokoolo* reveals the power of performance, the possibility to empower an apparently weak individual to a position of power and privilege. In the Baganda narrative, the suitors eat to the point of sickness while Akakookolo (the leper) watches from a distance.

Ruganda employs the trickster discourse of *Akakookolo* in order to unmask the pretentious actions of contemporary leaders and open a discussion on gender and equality, and the notion of the stranger (See Obbo). The main character's name, *Akakookolo,* is generic and may mean a leper or a mask. The allusive link between the two is the fact that lepers used to lose their noses and, because there would be no physical nose carved on a mask (in Buganda), the two are said to resemble each other. Significantly, since there are no rituals attached to masks in Uganda, whenever the mask is used, it creates comedy. Moreover, whereas in the original versions of this story, suitors were chiefs from Buganda, contemporary re-workings of the story offer a representation of the various other indigenous groupings in the country.[2] Contrasting behavioural and other performative characteristics, plus language and enunciation, make the plot immediately relevant to the audience. *Akakookolo*'s character is established by the manner of speech, behaviour, appearance and costume - he is palsied and disfigured, therefore, behaves strangely. Although conceived as a base character, disfigured and rustic in behaviour, he is usually projected as an exceptionally gifted musician. The story of Nyenje and the leper provides critical commentary on the political situation. The audience recognises both the original plot of the legend, idioms and symbols used to update it. Re-telling the story to Kaija, Tinka allegorically compares her plight to Nyenje's, the chief's daughter who was married to a leper (Wamala). As well as highlighting Ruganda's sympathy with the position of women in society, the play savagely attacks greed and materialism. Wamala, the main protagonist, sums up the conditions in the country:

> Everyone orders you to walk with your tail limp between your thighs. They don't want you to raise your head. They want you to know that your life is in their hands. [....] They can break it like a dry stick, if they choose to. And they always do, because it gives them the feel of power. They want you to know they are now on top, sitting on your head. And you beneath their buttocks, suffocating.
>
> (*The Burdens*, p. 35)

Critical in *The Burdens* is the idea of Tinka and the audience attempting to recognise how folktales are recreated to reflect on her contemporary experiences. In Act 1 Scene 2 starts when Kaija is listening to Tinka's story about the leper and Nyenje, Ngoma's daughter. The story is not told chronologically, a strategy that enables Tinka to focus on the end and to relate the meaning to her plight. Nevertheless, Kaija leans one important lesson: 'The meat of enemies can be under, sometimes/Can be tender when the heart's full of sorrow' (*The Burdens*, p. 15). Additionally, he learns that it is important to remember how history affects his life and influences contemporary conflicts. The play becomes a dialogue that explores conflict, intercultural and personal issues.

> **Tinka:** There was a hill from which ran a maze of paths. Do you remember the old name of the hill?
> **Kaija:** I've forgotten.
> **Tinka:** Never mind. In the middle was a big palace.
> **Kaija:** Now that is a new addition. The palace.
> **Tinka:** There must have been a palace because it was blown down. First a strong wind that whirled through the leaves and frightened the chicks. Then came the storm that wrecked the foundation of the palace and battered down the reed fence. The thatch scattered far and wide.
> **Kaija:** Last time you narrated this story, there was no palace and no storm either.
> **Tinka:** Memory fails you, son. There must have been a palace or else the song would never have been composed.
> **Kaija:** The song? What song?
> **Tinka:** 'Guns to Play the Drums', it's called. (*Recites*)
>
> (*The Burdens*, p. 14)

The play pre-dated Amin's regime and had 'clear echoes of the first period of Obote's rule' and his marriage to a Muganda, Miria Kalule, in 1963, following his political alliance with the Baganda Kabaka Yekka Party (Abdu Kasozi, 1994: 68). The audience recognises both the original plot of the legend, idioms and the symbols used to update it; moreover, in an attempt to purge her emotions, Tinka links the relationship between the leper and Nyenje with her life as the wasted daughter of a chief.[3]

The Floods

In *The Floods* (1980), first performed in 1979, Ruganda employs a form that reflects on the Hare (trickster), using idioms, cultural beliefs and values to enable Kyeyune, the main protagonist, to subvert the dictator's motives to make him disappear. Ruganda's aim is to draw on orature; writing in that tradition necessitates a creative response reminiscent of *abadongo* poetic exchange that allows the audience to see beyond the live performance. In this play, Ruganda expands the themes from his earlier play, *The Burdens*, to relate to wider issues of impunity surrounding corruption, disappearances and murders that have caused fear across the country. Significantly, after writing a play that draws on familial and individual conflicts regarding comments on post-colonial political crises, in *The Floods*, Ruganda concentrates on the clash between ordinary people and the state, represented by security agents, the Headman of the island and Bwogo the head of the State Research Bureau (SRB). Using the concept *katemba* to describe Ruganda's theatre might appear frivolous. How could a performance presenting torture and death on stage be entertainment? Does *katemba* trivialize people's pain?[4] As I have argued, *katemba* can be critical and daring, questioning the social and political, specifically in order to show its rootedness in society, and its role as the people's conscience. In this way, Ruganda's drama can be seen as a theatre of resistance within which performance is not artificial, not staged or negating reality, but it offers the actors and the audience a means of dealing with their pain and converting it into action and resistance. Ruganda's exilic condition (he wrote *The Floods* while living in exile in Kenya) allowed him to appropriate orature, blend and manipulate his audience's embodied (folkloric) and post-colonial memory, with his own knowledge to interrogate their contemporary traumatic experiences.

In *The Floods*, some people have been kidnapped or disappeared from their homes or places of work, while others, such as the residents on the island, have been duped into leaving the island with threats of heavy floods. First, the islanders are promised a safe exit from the island; they gather offstage and we can hear '*shouts, cries and all manner of noise from stampeding men, women and children*' as they flee the island (*The Floods*, p. 1). In the play's main plot, Kyeyune, an old experienced fisherman, unlike the other islanders, is engaged in avoiding becoming a victim of the murderous State Research Bureau (SRB) squads. We are told that he was once the best fisherman on the island (p. 8). Nankya, another resident, is a pseudo-intellectual and girlfriend of Bwogo, the Head of the State Research Bureau. In addition, *The Floods*' multiple voices include: the goddesses Nalubale and Nyamgondho, the dead and disappeared, Mukanga, the Brigadier found 'with three long nails in the skull [and] his genitals sticking in his mouth' (*The Floods*, p. 10), and ordinary people reverberating through Kyeyune's and Nankya's stories about the life in Uganda. Rather than dramatising Kyeyune's legendary skills, Ruganda's play examines both, his last fishing trip and the deceptive radio announcement concerning the floods to reveal the atrocities that constitute the history of the tyranny in postcolonial Uganda. For instance, in the first scene, one Fisherman relates his father's fate: 'Three dark figures came to the homestead one evening and took him away' (p. 6). Through Kyeyune and Nankya's personal memories, Ruganda revisits and examines the politics of fear and disappearances. Hence, the lake where the gruesome evidence hides provokes his examination of Amin's reign as a dark spot of Uganda's post-colonial history demonstrating that in the communal silence there is much to be told.

Kyeyune's stories connect performers and the audience who share the experiences and, therefore, are searching for forms of resistance. For example, in order to underline the sense of fear pervading the community, he comments: 'we are no better than a drunkard's cockerel - unsure of ourselves any one moment. Each dawn is as surprising as it is painful' (*The Floods*, p. 12). When, following the radio announcement, the Headman orders him to board the boat he replies, 'What did the radio say about Mukanga? That he was run over by a tractor. And didn't all of us see them dragging him from his hut - or have you forgotten' (pp. 8 - 9). This is the complex post-colonial history of Uganda's political landscape:

> No one bothers. Too engrossed in grabbing and hoarding. The [country] is falling to pieces, corpses upon corpses along the streets, in the jungle and in the lake. [N]o one takes heed of he squeals of terror in homesteads being deserted.
>
> (*The Floods*, p. 50)

Thus, Ruganda, similar to Eli Kyeyune, challenges the audience to view the play in ways that relate it to their sense of contemporary history, which includes the use of the lake as a burial, ground as well as a source of food.

Through Kyeyune's personal narratives, the audience views Ruganda's shifting images of the lake, from dead bodies, blood stained waters, bullets and bombs to a more placid space where Kyeyune and other fishermen catch their fish. In one scene, Bwogo, the Ogre's hatchet man, referring to the moment when soldiers shot at the boat, cynically states:

> 'He who eats well is always insatiable'. This lake can't complain, though. It has been the tomb of many men. [....] Lorryfuls of wailing civilians, driven to their deaths, over the cliff, at the point of bayonets. The crocodiles have never been more thankful.
>
> (*The Floods*, p. 19)

Hence, the boat, Kyeyune's hut and Nankya's bungalow tell the story about the island and the lake, as terrifying. We are invited to engage in a dialogue with Kyeyune, to acknowledge that he is not mad. In a bizarre scene, Kyeyune describes the moment when he caught the Brigadier's head in his fishnet.

> Then all of a sudden the net on my right became heavy. It weighed down the right side of my boat. I knew it was a bit catch. [....] A military man. Dead. Three long nails in his head, his genitals sticking our in his mouth. A big stone round his neck. His belly ripped open and the intestines oozing out. I looked at the body... and froze with fright. [....] But if there are men

> who can rip our bellies open, drill nails in our skulls and stuff our mouths with our won genitals, why have I lived long enough to see my head grey?
>
> (*The Floods*, pp. 9-10)

Kyeyune's words reinforce Ruganda's political purpose and underline the warnings against the oppressors continuously reflected in his work. For example, he tells Bwogo, 'when the beckon calls, he will gallop into the net. Big or small no one can resist the call of the beckon. It is a matter of time' (p. 12). Here, Ruganda's 'big or small' includes the Ogre or Boss, his henchmen such as Bwogo and the Headman of the island who, collectively, are the 'instruments of pain and misery' (p. 61).

Kyeyune's dialogue, similar to Majangwa's, interweaves folkloric linguistic and cultural expressions, plus theatrical and historical elements, to articulate his views and narrate people's lived experiences. He can move swiftly between statements incriminating the regime for misleading the peasants, to the story about the dismembered Brigadier's body that was caught in his fishnet, to Nalubale's (goddess of Lake Victoria) wrath for the indiscriminate dumping of dead bodies in Lake Victoria. As Bwogo cynically comments, 'The lake can't complain' because '[i]t has been the tomb of many men …. Lorryfulls of wailing civilians, driven to their death over the cliff, at the point of bayonets. The crocodiles have never been more thankful' (*The Floods*, p. 19).

Similar to *The Burdens* and other plays discussed in this book, *The Floods* places women at the heart of the action. It has a significant young woman, Nankya, whose former boyfriend, Lutalo, was murder by her Bwogo, her current lover. In an unconscious statement of resistance and insubordination, after the islanders' violent murder, she torments Bwogo:

> The dead are no longer dead, Bwogo. They are up in arms to right their wrongs. They have risen from their deep slumber at the bottom of the lake and are carrying shrouds of vengeance towards you.
>
> (*The Floods*, p. 46)

In a way, Kyeyune and Nankya, are trying to work together to bring an end to the bloodshed on the island. Rather like Nankya,

Kyeyune tells a frightened Bwogo, 'When death has spotted a quarry, master, it never exudes its odours' (p. 47).

Regardless of whether we approve of Nankya's relationship with Bwogo, there is a particular historical reference point; the 1966 Buganda Crisis marks Obote's militarisation of politics in Buganda, that defines this theatre of resistance. She defies Bwogo's attempts to label her mother a whore by relating her personal narrative. In a play-in-play she relates how she was raped by government soldiers.

> [My] mother is only sixteen. They look at her and burst out with laughter. Mother freezes with fright. Taut like a bow-string. One of them rips her bra open. Horrible laughter. He commands her to lower down her skirt. [...] Horrifying bursts of laughter. Soon the four men are on top of mother, one after the other, before she passes out.
>
> (*The Floods*, p. 98)

Hence, we find that we have come full circle; she is the physical link between the past and present. Indeed, the statement, 'Horrible laughter', strikes one as it reminds us of Kyeyune's description of the callousness of the military and State Research Bureau (SRB) officials.

Nankya and Kyeyune's dramatized realities echo the experiences of the audience, further highlighting the idea of the inseparable connections between communal and individual suffering. The historical circumstances that gave rise to the Argentinean 'theatre of crisis' that locates the performance space against the backdrop of lived experiences resonates with Uganda's intersections of horror with surreal performances while signifying the shifts happening in notions of performance, ethnicity and nation. Kyeyune, who mistrusts the radio and refuses to board the boat, reports the site of 'Floods of [blood] in the lake, oozing and spurting out of the boat and the waves ferrying it across to the island' (*The Floods*, p. 37). Later he describes how the 'ambassadors of darkness' had ambushed the boat: 'Then suddenly, spouts of gun-fire and fierce arrows of brilliance penetra[ted] the body of the lonely boat'. He saw, '[t]hunder claps bounding off the body of the boat and sending reverberations of death across the islands and beyond' and '[m]en, women and children [were] toppling over from the boat into the lake' (*The Floods*, pp. 37-38).

At the end of *The Floods*, the 'beckon', who has been tracked by the audience throughout the play, calls on Bwogo who is taken away by the soldiers. Kyeyune, who escapes the murder machine is associated with the lake through his fishing knowledge and rituals, is used as an iconic figure just as Walukagga in Lubwa p'Chong's *The Madman*. Hence, *The Floods* refers self-consciously to other dramas, histories and narratives of abuse, torture and resistance.

Nuwa Sentongo's *The Invisible Bond*

Nuwa Sentongo, who teaches creative writing at Makerere and Nkumba Universities has researched indigenous folklore, and participated in theatre and other creative writing activities. One of the founder members of Ngoma Players, he has written several plays that include, *The City Game* (1972) and *The Invisible Bond* (1972). *The Invisible Bond* is fascinating, especially the way it explores the theme of political cannibalism using the nocturnal mythical metaphors. He uses a subtle artistic style in his play to probe the nature of performance and our response to it, both in theatre and in real life.[5]

Sentongo edits, updates and dramatizes the thematic concerns of two Luganda folktales, *Kibaate* and *Olukokobe*, that warn people against anti-social behaviour and disrespect of cultural and ritual norms. *Kibaate* is about a man who, having revealed the secrets of the forest spirits, is cursed to spend his life traversing the forest searching for the central pole for his house. 'Olukokobe' tells the story of a youth whose anti-social behaviour and nocturnal life led him to his fate. The complex 'bond' between the corpse, and its protagonist, Kibaate, the nightdancer who digs it up from its grave, shocks the audience, forcing it to face the reality on the outside. To begin with, the Luganda word *olukokobe* (albatross) immediately suggests the mythological character of the albatross, half-man and half animal, bloodthirsty, stubborn, wicked and vengeful. The word has other meanings, for instance, it is used to suggest someone who has long nails, is evil, stubborn and hard to persuade. In the story it pretends to be an old woman who persuades the drunken youth to give it a piggyback ride; however, by attaching itself to his body, using its long nails, it forces him to obey its orders. Sentongo draws on the nocturnal cult of *abasezi*, sorcerers or night dancers, a most feared group in Buganda. *Abasezi*, similar to other groups of sorcerers, invoke/employ *ekitambo* or 'mystical powers' who possess other people or 'dig up graves to remove human flesh' (John S. Mbiti, 1990: 195). Mbiti, who has researched and studied African religions, comments on various aspects of sorcerers in different African societies:

> For African [people] sorcery stands for anti-social employment of mystical power, and sorcerers are the most feared and hated members of their communities. It is feared that they employ all sorts of ways to harm other people or their belongings. For example, they [...] spit and direct spittle with secret incantations to go and harm someone; they dig up graves to remove human flesh or bones which they use in their practices; they invoke spirits to attach or possess someone.

The play's representation of the *abasezi* cult is based around some of the characteristics identified by Mbiti. In this respect, Sentongo's work, sharing much of what Mbiti describes above, examines both society's inept response to anarchy and the regime's murderous acts. Sentongo uses the cult's motif, *ekitambo* - a magic spell that *abasezi* are believed to use to effect the state of possession and to put a curse on their victims and corpses - to comment on the killers' state of mind and their cannibalistic behaviour. Nevertheless, although the 'Olukokobe' folktale ends with a scene where the community unites to rid the boy of his tormentor (they entice the *lukokobe* to share their barbecue), Sentongo's play neither offers relief for Kibaate nor for Ddamulira's desecrated corpse.

When the play opens, the mourners are gathered for Ddamulira's burial. The Third Night Dancer dupes the mourners and performs a cult ritual on the corpse using a needle and thread. This spell later enables them to extract the corpse from the grave. Kibaate meets the corpse abandoned on the wayside and in the process it forms an invisible bond with him and dominates him. Structurally Sentongo interweaves the scenes with episodes in which the Night dancers' wives eavesdrop on their husbands. These episodes build up the tension emphasizing the mythic nature of the cult.

The resistance within this most provocative play is underlined by the Corpse's desire to torment and stifle Kibaate's voice and the evil domineering characteristics, most noticeably the simple act of piggybacking which is a comment on acts of torture practised by Amin's henchmen.

Corpse: Will you take me back to the bench?
Kibaate: No I won't. I'm not your slave.
Corpse: O.K. We shall see. (*The corpse becomes animated. It attacks Kibaate, piercing him with its finger-nails. They both fall onto the ground. Kibaate can't disentangle himself. He cries loudly. The corpse stands up over him gaining a commanding position.*) You have to do what I tell you.

(*The Invisible Bond*, pp. 35-36)

Through persuasion and force the corpse gradually dominates Kibaate amplifying the overtones of the euphemism, *lukokobe* and terminating his right of choice to act. The corpse turns Kibaate into its subject who must obey commands.

Corpse: Will you take me to the bench?
Kibaate: No, I won't. I'm not your slave.
Corpse: Ok. We shall see.
(*The corpse becomes animated. It attacks Kibaate, piercing him with its finger-nails. They both fall onto the ground. Kibaate can't disentangle himself. He cries loudly. The corpse stands up over him gaining a commanding position.*)
You have to do what I tell you.

(*The Invisible Bond*, pp. 35-36)

To the audience, the Corpse's insistent commands to Kibaate to lift it and set it on the bench are comical. Initially, despite the Corpse's attacks on Kibaate, the audience does not recognise it as torture since the victim is a nightdancer and the victimiser a corpse who holds no instrument of torture. However, to the Corpse, the punishment meted out to Kibaate is necessary since the nightdancers, in this context, represent political leaders and the armed forces, who torture the dead and the living.

> They never allow the dead any rest or freedom. They come bouncing on us, terrorizing our existence. [....] There is no more freedom left to the dead.
>
> (*The Invisible Bond*, p. 23)

The bond between Kibaate and the corpse is a powerful theatrical creation traversing the breadth of the audience's emotions from shock, to comic amusement, from empathy to anger.

Traditional mourning is realistically presented on the stage through shrill voiced wailing while, according to Sentongo, the night-dancers should exhibit the most intensive use of stylized dance performed by semi-possessed people, sorcerers and witches. The scene in which the night-dancers haggle over the body parodies the sharing ritual of game hunters in Buganda where the specific role played by a hunter in trapping an animal determines their share of the carcass. The grotesqueness of the scene is demonstrated by the night-dancers' weird behaviour around the Corpse. The political sub-text is realised when the Corpse challenges Kibaate's (political leaders and the army) commitment to human rights:

> They never allow the dead any rest or freedom. They come bouncing on us, terrorizing our existence... There is no more freedom left to the dead.
>
> (*The Invisible Bond*, p. 23)

The production of animated corpses on state complete in barkcloth costumes is a dramatic realization of the belief in the night-dancers' powers of sorcery, trance and hypnotism. In one scene when the nightdancers insist on sharing the corpse equally between the families, Sentongo underlines the ruthless behaviour of Amin's security forces. Sentongo insinuates that only men interested in feasting on human flesh can behave like hyenas. Thus, the nightdancers' performance, as demonstrated by the following dialogue, mirrors the cannibalistic behaviour, which is purported to occur throughout the nation.

First Voice: I'll eat the arm.
Second Voice: The ear is mine.
Third Voice: I like his full-blown lip and the think chin.
Fourth Voice: I'll eat the eyeballs.
Fifth Voice: I like these fat buttocks.
Sixth Voice: I want the toes.
Seventh Voice: Who will eat the thighs?
Leader of the Night-Dancers: Stop! Stop I say! Are you a bunch of hyenas and vultures? Are you human beings or beasts? Don't you have any sense of decency and patience? Now listen to me. We have to do this job in a descent manner.

(*The Invisible Bond*, p. 16)

The personal confessions of the nightdancers about how they helped to cause Ddamulira and other people's deaths is a savage indictment of the military regime whose soldiers rely on brutal power and the gun to enrich themselves.

The society that Sentongo depicts in *The Invisible Bond* is the same society that Serumaga explores in his dramatic works. Similar to other artists discussed in this chapter, Serumaga and Sentongo are interested in a theatre, which, as Quigley explains, 'invites audiences not just to receive entertainment and instruction but to participate in an inquiry that questions both what we know and how we know it'. This is 'an inquiry', he states, 'that also helps us to recognise the complex dependence of our knowledge on our ways of knowing both in the world of the theatre and in the worlds beyond it' (Quigley, 1985: p 53).

Elvania Zirimu

Elvania Zirimu, who remains perhaps the most prominent Ugandan female artist working both in English and indigenous language mediums, made the stage a site of resistance, not only against the tyrannical post-colonial governments but sexual discrimination as well. Her views on the relationship of theatre with society, her concept of *obuntubulamu* (humanness), and controversial debates on gender issues, are set out in her published critical essays, plays and poetry. Elvania Zirimu's views on Ugandan cultures, politics and performance had no ambiguity. In her essay, 'Your Experience is Your Own Truth' (1976, p. 1) she declares:

> [I] do not see it as possible to create art without a meaningful cohesive community in which the individual is free to express the self and develop what is within him or her, a community in which the individual feels important, accepted, wanted and valued.

By referring to 'a meaningful cohesive community' as a prerequisite for artistic creation, she raises the question of postcolonial political disruptions, and ethnic strife. Moreover, a society, which is not at peace with itself, cannot effectively relate to the outside world.

In the period between 1973 and 1980, Elvania Zirimu defined her position through the performance of relevant dramas and poetry. In this way, her work and politics were linked to the post-colonial spirit of freedom, which was committed to changing the sociopolitical conditions of and resisting tyranny. This is evidenced by her directing of *Omulambuzi wa Gavumenti*, a Luganda translation of Nikholai Gogol's *The Government Inspector* (1975), in 1975; an adaptation of Bertolt Brecht's *Mother Courage* (1975) in 1978, and T. S. Eliot's *Murder in the Cathedral* (1935) in 1977, following the murder of Archbishop Luwum. In a way, the selection of plays and the timing of the productions, reveals her fortitude to use the stage as a soundboard for society's views on socio-political issues. At the time when the military was in power, the plays represented active public performance protestations against Obote and Amin that was uncommon during the 1970s and 1980s. The staging was interesting because the pressure it created was the beginning of vocalised resistance to oppression albeit witnessed by modest numbers. That this resistance was organised by a female artist is pertinent; apart from the recognition of the need to acknowledge women's rights it underlined the fact that people knew they had the rights of free speech and were prepared to stand up for their rights. Secondly, the protest brought into focus the ability of theatre as a medium of resistance.

As Osita Okagbue writes, 'The uniqueness of African and African-Caribbean theatre(s) derives from the fact that both incorporate a lot of folk theatre and performance elements' (2009: 191). Indeed, within these theatre practices, '[w]hat determines the impact and meaning of a performance is the association' that the events in the play 'call forth in the minds of the spectators' (2009: 192). Key to this audience reception is what he describes as the 'notion of totality' that derives from the collective 'elements of the folk performance traditions, which easily lend themselves to manipulation by dramatists'. Okagbue concludes that '[t]hese elements are … all blended harmoniously to achieve a high degree of involvement of and/or participation by actors and spectators. (2009: 192-193). Such a totality of theatre is conveyed in post-colonial theatre and, in particular, Elvania Zirimu's conceptualisation of resistance theatre that, when appropriate in *katemba* (and *abadongo* genre), has the characters talk back to the oppressors. Elvania Zirimu's *When the Hunchback Made Rain*, in different ways, adopts 'performance strategies', to borrow Taylor's phrase used earlier, that not only allow subversion, but also the transformation of performance spaces. (2003: 169)

When the Hunchback Made Rain (1975), originally an experimental and collaborative effort between the playwright and the original cast is a reflection on Amin's campaign of double production, among other issues such as religion and institutional corruption. As discussed in earlier chapters, rather than rebuild the economy and restore stability that had crumbled under Obote I, Amin's action was to expel Indians and Europeans thus accelerating the economic decline. The effect was a decline in agricultural and industrial produce. Hence, between 1972 and 1973, he removed traditional chiefs and district administrators, replaced them with soldiers and politically sympathetic leaders, with directives to enforce the agricultural programme that he called 'Double Production' (See, Petter Langseth, and Rick Stapenhurst, 1997). In Kigezi, Western Uganda, farmers planted the hybrid maize seeds distributed by the new chiefs; however, following traditional farming practices, they kept some grains to plant during the next season because they had not been told that you could not replant them. Not surprisingly, they did not germinate and the farmers were angry. In the spirit of double production, the government forced farmers to plant cotton seeds instead of food. However, to spite the chiefs, they boiled the cottonseeds during the night and planted them the following day. Afterwards they argued that the soil was infertile and they were never forced to plant cottonseeds again.

The conflict of tradition and modernity is metaphorically expanded in the play to embrace criticism of aspects of old sacred and secular institutions including sacrifice, bribery, nepotism and corruption. As traditional folktale, religion, and ritual are transformed into theatrical images their relevance in contemporary society is analysed showing Elvania Zirimu's awareness of, and sensitivity to the changing role of tradition in society. Her opinions specifically highlighted in this play made her become regarded as anti-establishment and a daredevil. The plot is reminiscent of folk story themes in which the *mulubaale* (diviner) plays a central role in analysing and providing solutions to the problems of the community. The setting is a village devastated by drought. Drought, physically afflicting man, animals and nature, may literally be taken to be a metaphor for the socio-political drought pervading the community. Nsereko and Kabogozza, representing the peasants and determined to get rain at all costs, complain about Kirabira the Hunchback, also known as the 'terrible one' (p. 11). Nsereko and Kabogozza, representing the peasants, are determined to get rain at all costs. However, the Hunchback, mediator and aide apportioned power by God in the form of a 'rain sheet' (p. 27) that empowers him to give rain to peasants becomes vainglorious and his obnoxious. Once infuriated, Kaboggoza kills him, hence, inviting divine wrath and vengeance. In this way, the 'rain sheet' is similar to the gun as a cynical symbol of political and economic power alluding to Amin's reference to the gun as the father and mother of soldiers. While in its possession, Kirabira terrorizes supplicants and threatens: 'I brain anyone who dares to offend me. I'll brain your bungling brats' (27). While sacrifice is an indispensable ingredient in traditional prayer, in her discourse, sacrifice and offerings become synonymous with bribe and institutionalized corruption. Kabogozza informs us that although every peasant in his village is afflicted, and children's whose legs are 'no bigger than drum sticks' (p. 9) are trudging up the highway to ask for rain, Kirabira still demands bribes from the supplicants. Indeed, in their struggle to free themselves from the fetters of the drought people have offered God their best millet and chicken. Although sacrifice is an indispensable ingredient in traditional prayer, Zirimu questions the concept of sacrifice and offerings in the contemporary context. In her view, sacrifice and offerings become synonymous with bribe and institutionalized corruption. Thus, when Nabikolo informs God that she could not turn away supplicants God cautions her, '(*thundering*) That's bribery! (*contemptuously*) Offer-offerings! So that's how they go around you, eh? With bribes!' (p. 16). God, distanced from the humans by his register and manner of speech, is further given credence by the rituals performed on him by Nabikolo. Interestingly, in order to criticise sacred and secular gods for adopting a cynical attitude towards the community's needs, Elvania Zirimu presents on stage a God character in flesh and blood. A daring theatrical device exposes the secrets that lie behind the bark cloth screen in sanctuaries.

God: Do you think it is an easy thing to be God? Do you think it is a laughing matter to listen to thousands of humans begging for millions of trifles which do not carry the slightest meaning to me, one way or the other? Males who want females, females who want males, wretches wanting children, misers and cut-throats who want more of that thing they call money? What does it all matter to me? What does your lot think I am?

Nabikolo: Why don't you tell them?

God: Hhm, tell them! As if I didn't know your kind! All they know is that I am God? I can't change the earth any more than I can make a fig tree bear mangoes!

(*When the Hunchback Made Rain*, p.14)

The argument in the above discussion further exposes the weaknesses of the conservative view of religion. In the play, God is human to the point that in his eyes the Hunchback must give prioritise people according to the value of their sacrifice.

While Kirabira, the Hunchback, may be taken to represent the sanctuary keepers who terrorise supplicants, at the metaphorical level he is a symbol of soldiers, security guards and personal secretaries who have become demigods in society. Like them, he possesses all the vices such as corruption, nepotism and opportunism. He is a scavenger, 'bloated with fat' (p. 9) which ordinary people have given for sacrifice. God's act of delegating power to Kirabira indicts society for entrusting their destiny to people known to have scanty wits. While in its possession, Kirabira terrorizes supplicants and threatens: 'I brain anyone who dares to offend me. I'll brain your bungling brats' (p. 27). The Luganda equivalent of the word is *kubetenta*, associated with beating a snake's head to pulp or smithereens. Kirabira's attitude to the peasants is transformed by power, as he demands that God must now give him a guard to 'keep all vermin at the Gate' (p. 32). His reference to supplicants as 'peasants' (p. 32) is cynical, connoting *bakopi*, base, in Luganda. In a monumental declaration exhibiting feelings of a socially insecure person, he harangues them for being oblivious of his power: 'I have the power to give you what you want, or power to refuse, (grabs *his arm*) Hey, you, Do you think I can't give you rain?' (p. 26) He is a vivid example of upstart military rulers of the 1970s and 1980s, and *mafutamingis*.

The use of Swahili in the following extract underlines Kirabira's role as a caricature of the new bourgeoisie as he pompously insists on speaking English to the peasant.

Kirabira: (*seizing him by the arm*) What are you doing here you vermin, you?

Nsereko:	(*frantically jabbering in Kiswahili and English*) Ah, *mimi....mimi nakuja hapa....*
Kirabira:	How did you come here?
Nsereko:	Ah, me, I come here....Mercy, I beg mercy.
Kirabira:	(*releases him to take another drink*)
Nsereko:	(*surprised at this weakness, gains a little courage*) *Mimi nataka mvuwa*, Kirabira, my friend...
Kirabira:	(*swaying*) This....this is no place for you. This is God's Sanctuary.
Nsereko:	*Nataka mvuwa....mvuwa* (*searching desperately for the English word*) Rain! Ah, Kirabira, *rafiki yan*gu; my brother, my brother, I want RAIN. (*He throws up his arms and goes down on his knees, suddenly remembers something and begins to search his pockets, nodding at Kirabira*) I come here, I say, my father, my friend, to ask for a little rain on my *shamba*.
Kirabira:	Ah, rain? (*laughs, takes a drink*) Hey rain. You get, you don't get.

(*When the Hunchback Made Rain*, pp. 25-26)

The following pun on drunkenness illustrates Elvania Zirimu's attitude to power and its corrosive elements.

Nsereko:	No. Not any more. It is Kirabira. (*For response Kaboggoza hits him.*) Please, why do you hit me now? It is Kirabira who keeps the rain.
Kaboggoza:	The Hunchback!
Nsereko:	Yes, yes, the Hunchback.
Kaboggoza:	Tell me again.
Nsereko:	If you can touch him on the hump, and wake him from his drunkenness.
Kaboggoza:	He's drunk, eh?
Nsereko:	Soaked!
Kaboggoza:	Drunk, yes, with power, no doubt.
Nsereko:	No, with drink; with ordinary human drink.
Kaboggoza:	Power is ordinary human drink, and men do get drunk on it.

(*When the Hunchback Made Rain*, pp. 30-31)

The Hunchback favours Nsereko with rain sheet. However, Kaboggoza, desperate and humiliated by the drunken Hunchback, murders the latter and hides the body among the branches of the mango tree. He then tricks Nsereko into climbing the tree only for the latter to push an already dead Hunchback to the ground. Nsereko has to disentangle himself from the Hunchback's murder and, similar to

Hare in Baganda folktales, concocts and intelligently narrates a story to disentangle himself. He claims that he overheard a benevolent soldier stating that God was about to award a prize to the person who murdered the Hunchback. At this point, Zirimu injects the story with a political sub-text, satirizing a soldier turned honest and considerate to the point of aiding Nsereko. Kaboggoza is so taken up by the story that he wonders how a 'big man' (p. 44) could apologize to a peasant. Nsereko's reply, 'He did, I tell you; which shows you there are some big men who are made with hearts' (p. 44)' is double-edged, for, the audience understands the implied sarcasm about big men. It is interesting to watch two people representing an economically desperate community each justifying his claim for being the true murderer of the Hunchback, in order to get a reward. The scene becomes grotesque when Kaboggoza talks to the Hunchback's corpse while Nsereko frantically blames himself for Kaboggoza's apparent madness. What makes us laugh at this point is the combination of watching a desperate Kaboggoza (representing the community) misjudge God's moods and proudly suggesting to Him that the 'reward will be given in a more public place' (p. 55). Kabogozza voices the feelings of the community on injustices - in economic, judicial and moral issues - being practiced by the state: 'When a poor man kills, let him be killed. When a big man kills, let him be richly rewarded. And when God kills, that is the law' (p. 56).

When you read Elvania Zirimu's *When the Hunchback Made Rain* it is difficult to ignore either the political content of *katemba* - its critique of post-colonial authoritarianism and greed in the guise of nationalism - or the underlying poverty, universal hardship and exploitation that marks the Obote and Amin years. And yet, the play is self-consciously theatrical and humorous and by this means more entertaining. As in *The Burdens*, so also in this play, the insufferable is rendered endurable, and even enjoyable, by means of a striking theatrical presentation of what we can or cannot be visualised or felt at a particular moment.

Kaboggoza: We have toiled and tilled the land. But to what purpose? (*He staresbefore him as if actually seeing pitiful fate of his shamba right there.*) The price of ground nuts went up a shilling last year. Seeing this I prepared a big field. When the planting season came I filled it with seed I had bought with

> borrowed money. I wanted the rain to find my seed already in the ground, but the sun has roasted that seed to nothing. No shoot came out. My peas and beans met with the same fate. Every peasant in my village has the same story to tell. [....] The earth is like hot ashes. (*He's no longer are of where he is. He had stood up unconsciously and now kneels down.*) God, God, how could poor creatures like us incite you to such cruelty? [....] Does human misery amuse the Almighty?
>
> (*When the Hunchback Made Rain*, p. 12)

At this moment, when Kaboggoza confronts God, his feelings of apprehension as well as the expression of the general anguish enveloping the community gives way to silent reflections on the continued relevance of God in their community. Thus, similar to her contemporaries, Elvania Zirimu does not give up hope of presenting a critical reflection, political protest and transgression on stage. This play reflects Elvania Zirimu's search for ways in which to revolutionize the content and form of Ugandan theatre to voice the silenced tales of the people. Politics and theatre cannot be separated from one another here, any more than God's refusal to make rain can be separated from the government's failure to protect ordinary people from armed robbers or government sponsored campaigns that would alienate people from their land. Thus, just like the other works of Elvania Zirimu, this play demonstrates that the only hope for the reinstatement of moral sanity depends on a few brave individuals who will be able to lead the communal voice against retrogressive customs and tyranny.

Chapter 7

THEMES AND TRENDS IN URBAN PERFORMANCE PRACTICES

This chapter examines the various ways through which, once again, performing artists, by adapting and re-creating indigenous theatrical elements, responded to the changing political landscape. The high concentration of people in the urban areas, attracted by employment opportunities, wealth and education, that gave rise to the development of slums such as Kivvulu and Kisenyi soon after independence helped all the varied cultures of Uganda to come into close contact where previously they had lived apart. The 'new urban realities' of the 1960s and 1970s 'allowed for new cultural exchanges' (Lipsitz, 2001: 117) which were not possible in colonial times. This relationship between urbanisation and the transformation of theatrical elements resonates with the discussion in this chapter, which shows how artists have capitalised on the opportunities afforded by a developing interest in hybrid musical performance expression and changing socio-political and economic environments. These 'emerging patterns of urban social organisation and signification', as David Coplan reminds us, 'may determine the selection, rejection or transformation' of 'musical [or theatrical] elements' (Coplan, 1982:112-119). In effect, the implication here is that in the latter Amin's military regime years, migrations to the urban areas were to have deep cultural influences on drama, song, instrumental music and dance whose configuration reflected Ugandan indigenous influences much more than before. The changes in the theatrical landscape, arguably, happened because audiences changed as well.

In discussing theatre performance in Uganda in this chapter, one is reminded of other practices it inscribes, bringing together alternative performances such as *endongo* and *tabbulu*, which deviate from the established interpretation of *katemba* as dramatic performance. When the Western country guitar was introduced in Uganda, it was called *endongo*/pl. *ebidongo* and the popular musicians, *omudongo* (singular) or (plural) *abadongo*[1] (see Nannyonga-Tamusuza, 2006). A night out in the nightclub, described as *kuzina ndongo* or *kugenda mu mazina* literarily means to dance (the jazz or highlife), or, to go to the nightclub, was associated with immoral behaviour. Moreover, as discussed earlier in this book, *kuzina*, means either to dance or to have sex. Colonial administrators and missionaries castigated these activities; while, for instance, John Roscoe, commented, 'The mixed dances ended frequently in immoral conduct' (1965: 24). His compatriots, the missionaries, labelled such popular music activities, including nightclub music and Congolese jazz music, *taboo*. The journalist Drake Ssekeba, in a 2010 interview, confirmed that the Baganda Lugandanised the word, hence, labelling such nocturnal club activities *ttabulu*[2] - immoral, corrupting behaviour alluding to the lifestyle of *abadongo*.[3] Unsurprisingly, respectable members of the community were not expected to engage in this activity. Notably, while there were strong links between popular musical groups of the *abadongo* type and other theatre groups in the Amin and immediate post-Amin period, there were differences in the content of their programmes and limitations in stage dramatisations of the former. Initially, dramatic skits were incorporated into musical performances largely because audiences demanded long four to five hour performances; crucially, the performers' use of the familiar allowed for a broader based appreciation and understanding of the message. Later this led to large-scale dramatisation by groups such as Jimmy Katumba and The Ebonies, Peterson Mutebi and The Thames, and Kadongo Kamu Super Singers.

Today, the liberalisation of the economy that led to the enactment of the 1997 Uganda Communications Act has not only allowed the emergence of privately owned FM radio stations but the expansion of activities by multinational companies. This in turn has influenced changes in the relationship between drama and theatre festivals, particularly the sizable sponsorship deals for large festivals staged by a variety of artists. One of the older generation of artists and theatre administrators (Alice Lwanga the former House Manager of the National Theatre), noted that these *theeta bufffe*, 'theatre buffets' (or ensembles) as they are locally known, have destroyed scripted theatre.[4] They assert that multinationals such as the South African mobile telecommunications company, MTN, or, East African Breweries, are not interested in promoting drama groups but *ba star* (individual actors), who are mostly identified because they anchor popular FM radio programmes. Nevertheless, *ebivvulu* or *ebinyumu* depict intersecting concepts and practices of performance; thus, offering alternative views about corporate sponsorship of festivals. Arguably, the public perceives the development as a revival of the traditional musical beer parties.

Ugandan theatre did not prepare for the period of peace - that has followed decades of conflict - particularly in relation to audience demography and reception. In my 2010 interview with Kalundi Serumaga, a journalist and theatre critic, he remarked that while society concentrated on getting rid of the tyrannical regimes, theatre did not prepare for the post-conflict times, therefore, when peace came, practising artists were not ready to adjust with the times. As a result, very few pre-1986 performing artists or playhouses established since the days when Idi Amin and his cronies closed down football activities and other forms of entertainment, are still active. In an anti-climactic way, Senkubuge remarked that while 'UPC and the military eras produced hate in you, which made you write against them, there is no visible hate figure in the post-1986 period' (Senkubuge, 2010). However, the problem of personalising politics evident in that statement is that one is not obliged to interrogate the system itself. It is therefore problematic for someone who considers theatre as a multi-purpose space.

Shared Laughter: Katemba and Jimmy Katumba's Theatre

The Ebonies' performances are the narratives of 1970s, 1980s and 1990s Uganda, representing socio-political issues. A close examination of this theatre shows that by the 1971 military *coup d'etat* (1971), the content derived from random juxtaposition of music and dramatic skits had already led to the transposition of the popular into protest theatre mediated by music, dance, movement and recitation. Not surprisingly, similar to literary theatre and radio drama, popular music theatre promoted dissent, among other things, especially through its creation of a sense of a dynamic process of representation and reinterpretation of various indigenous genres, forms and styles. Indeed, fractured texts that are products of this experimentation combine to produce codes and symbols, which generate texts that talk directly to the audiences. To defy the terror linked to the disappearances, the artists, as Tricia Rose (1994) has commented elsewhere, 'use[d] language, dance, and music to mock those in power, express rage, and produce fantasies of subversion', and in addition, folk forms 'where oppositional transcripts, or the "unofficial truths" [were] developed, refined, and rehearsed' (1994: 99-100). Thus, the performances included comedic drama skits, dramatisations of syncretic songs and dances, dramatised songs by contemporary Ugandan composers. Unsurprisingly, some literary critics often derided these musical performances as either cheap hybrid entertainment or the visible sign of a faltering culture.

To examine a specific kind of popular music theatre the discussion will concentrate on Jimmy Katumba and The Ebonies, a group that, working in partnership with another drama group, The Theatrikos,[5] jointly owned Theatre Excelsior, a space converted from a disused school hall into an eight hundred-seat playhouse.[6] After the merger, The Ebonies established JK Ebonita, a subsidiary company that focused on plays, which incorporated limited dramatised music and dance elements using urban speech, *Olungeswaganda*.[7] Arguably, both groups presented *katemba* and *bannakatemba* as complex entities not dichotomies of drama and music as some contemporary performers try to differentiate them. They staged a variety of performances composed of full-length dramas with music, musical shows with drama skits, and other dramatised song narratives that, when delineated, engage us with social and political issues of concern. In this way, Katumba, as a performer working between and across musical and dramatic forms, linked indigenous and Western styles, showing how, through hybridised performances, theatre can address present issues and concerns. He presented a model for a new type of *katemba* that through shared laughter, framed a new theatre, which addresses itself to all problems. More interesting for this discussion is that although people may have viewed the musical extravaganzas as the equivalent of *ebinyumu*, the choice of different terms, *ebizibya* or *ebikeesa* (twilight or trans-night dance/musical gatherings), to describe the performances, at different historical moments introduces new meanings to this theatre practice. For, the hybrid nature of the aesthetics, ambiance, form and style is reflected in these new concepts (*ebizibya* or *ebikeesa*) that the group evolved to describe them. Most notably, the usage of *ebikeesa/ebizibya* allude to the 1970s and 1980s hostile political environment and tell the history of a people creating a free performance space (to dance and sing) within the confinement of a militarised state characterised by army brutality, rape, disappearances, internal displacement and murder.[8] In all the above developments, one can see the transformation of *katemba*, within which we have to examine and locate theatre as it changes and transgresses its known boundaries.

Significantly, *katemba* was transformed into a multi-generic, dialogic and hybridised form, which with all the possibilities it suggests, exists alongside other indigenous theatrical expressions (and discourses) which it disrupts. As a 'generic mutation', it used the frame of oral performance (dance, instrumental music, the folk song and solo) 'as a source of new possibilities and connections beyond itself' and as a post-independent form, aiming to 'jolt the audience beyond the values defined by the traditions' (Campbell, 2010: 162) of their respective ethnic cultures into the present reality. A key concern of the artists was the development of a set of artistic practices informed by indigenous and Western forms that would enable people to sustain their identity and sanity in a period of social and political upheavals. Nonetheless, much as artists projected it as a respectable field with a positive role in society, as suggested in the previous chapters, on the streets and in market places, theatre acquired a different meaning whereby performing artists were perceived as tricksters or jokers, people who projected utopian ideals. This may also allude to a lack of seriousness and professionalism among the popular actors, therefore, presenting them as *bakazanyirizi* (comedians).[9] Through shared laughter, *katemba*, it was assumed, would serve as a medium of discourse about the lived experiences and a (comic) relief for the audience. Thus, once again, artists transformed *katemba* to shape society's discourse on oppression, immorality and excessive consumption. In this context, the embedding of hybrid theatrical expressions and farce into theatre alludes to the changes across Ugandan society during this period. The performances discussed below allow us to trace and understand some of the foregoing developments.

'Kakinda Show' and *The Dollar*

Katumba and Katende created dramatic narratives that represented the real and imagined urban life of the 1980s. In this way, they outlined the breakdown of cultural values while, on the other hand, at the risk of alienating the conservative section of the audience, their hybrid folk forms brought into perspective the impact of Western performance styles on indigenous theatre expressions.[10] Working with Baganda and other Ugandan indigenous performers, and operating within a socio-political environment influenced by the existing socio-political upheaval, they sought to turn their actors, who possibly might have come to the city as refugees from conflict zones, labourers, market traders, junior civil servants or students, into professional performers. The transformation of a formerly marginalised people into a professional group is evident in the development of disparate theatrical elements and performance practices into a cohesive theatre expression evident in the musical performances and dramas such as the 'Kakinda Show' (Katende and Katumba, 1988), *The Dollar* (Katende, 1989) and *The Inspector* (Katende, 1989). Katumba's group did not perform traditional music per se, but influenced by the varied indigenous membership of his team, their most popular songs were those rooted in tradition. Musical shows alternated with dramatic productions, giving the producer and stage designer just a fortnight to mount a new show. Most of the plots were topical, discussing social issues in the language of the street, office, market place or *bufunda* (shop-*cum*-bars). Nonetheless, by the end of a twelve-week run, up to ninety thousand people, then a figure unequalled anywhere before in Ugandan theatre would have watched approximately sixty performances.

Songs were initially linked by stand-up comedians who, in semi-traditional style, amused the audiences using pantomime, mimicry of various dialects, and impersonation of members of Amin's military regime. With time, thematic segments connected satirical dialogue (sometimes *ad libbed*) and/or video pictures on a screen.[11] What Karin Barber (1987) has noted about the way people's 'resentment is expressed in a more subterranean manner, in the form of jokes, catchphrases, and anecdotes' (1987: 2) in popular arts in Africa is recognisable in the impersonations, pantomime and linguistic ethnic jokes which are the main sources of farce and comedy in post-Amin military Uganda theatre. Perhaps encouraged by the events in Amin's regime or his character itself - his clowning, demagoguery and megalomania - theatre was dominated by farce. The helmet, the gun, and the Swahili language, which, as Ali Mazrui suggests, are identified with the armed forces, became metonyms for military rule. A typical example is the dramatisation of Peter Clever Lwanga's (1979) 'Give me back my Freedom' and 'Days of the Gun rule' (1979), which, composed and performed soon after the fall of Amin's government in 1979, allude to the monstrosities of Idi Amin's regime, specifically, the activities at the military's 'Go-down'. Many people 'taken' or 'disappeared' by the military forces were dumped in Makindye Military Barracks where, as Kasozi (1994: 220) explains, they were locked up in different rooms "one of which was the 'Go-down', a former storeroom with iron doors, no windows, and little ventilation". According to witness accounts, 'About a hundred prisoners were held [in the Go-down] but the turnover was rapid'. While 'some prisoners living in a cubicle [were] killed off in the Go-down', the other killing room was the 'death cell' that 'was about 20 yards behind the Go-down' (p. 218). Hence, the subject of the songs (rape, torture, imprisonment, and murder) was within the communal experiences of the audiences. As well as narrating the murder of Archbishop Janani Luwum, 'Days of the Gun Rule' describes the brutal punishments meted to the general population by the army. 'Give me back my Freedom' is a confrontation between an unidentified prisoner and Mr. Guard, his captor. It is set against the background of simulated sounds of gunfire and wailing, often related by survivors of torture houses, the State Research Bureau Headquarters and the notorious 'Go-down'. In the dramatised sketch developed from the lyrics, the prisoner speaks to the fierce guard who responds to the cross-examination with brutality expressed with violent gestures. However, the prisoner insists, 'Between you and me Mr. Guard/How many people have you seen/Going in and then going out/Feeling free,/You shake your head Mr. Guard/You seem to know my fate' ('Days of the Gun Rule', 1979). The instrumentation of the songs marries European and Ugandan music aesthetics, a welcome change from the Zairean Rumba rhythms used widely by jazz bands.

Since many of the original performances of The Ebonies in the open air (beaches and football stadiums) used the popular folk rhythms, the audience, basking in their newfound freedom, either joined the performers on the stage or danced in the available space. Popular dramatised dance-songs reworked from folk music that have survived from this period include Sam Kagoda's *Nfiire*, a Soga song depicting a wealthy man about to die, distributing his wealth; and *Sheeta Omwana Afanye Baba We* (the child has behaved bravely like his father), adapted from the song repertoire of the Gishu circumcision rite. Other dramatised songs include 'Njabala' (Lwanga, 1988), a folksong from the Kiganda folktale about a spoilt girl, in which the ghost of her dead mother helps her to dig the garden; and '*Ma* Abong' (Kagoda, 1988), again a modernised Bwola dance song from Acholi praising Abong, a beautiful girl. Thus, action songs like these encouraged the trend towards widespread dramatised musical shows.

After 1986, the group staged the 'Luwero Show' (Katende and Katumba), drawing on the tyrannised experiences of Ugandan society over the fifteen years (1971-1985) of Amin through to ex-President Okello Lutwa regimes. The show attempted to analyse and identify the root of violence that had led to the genocide and massacres in, Acholi, Lango, the Luwero Triangle[12] and West Nile. Uganda's ethnic diversity is surveyed in an improvised dance circle which starts with *Ekitaaguriro* (a cattle dance) from Ankole, moves to *Runyege*, a Banyoro courtship dance, and ends with a hybrid Ebonies' song-dance. Notably, within the performances, themes of love, war, violence, retribution, personal sacrifice, liberation were highly interrelated. Modernized Uganda folk dances advance the plot without restricting it to a traditional context or orchestration. For instance, a courtship folk song-dance from Tooro, *Muhara wa Nyamaizi* (Nyamaizi's daughter) allows the development of the story line, and uses dances from various indigenous groups. The stylised presentation of the NRA guerrillas' wartime experiences in this song reminds the audience of some of the fighting tactics favoured by Museveni's *bukadogo* (child soldiers). Lwanga's *Nnyonta Nsaba ku Mazzi* (I thirst, please give me some water) and the NRA war songs, *Tusonge paka Kampala* (Our destination is Kampala) and *Moto na Waka* (The battle/fire is hot) that formed the core of the dramatised skits linked reality and fiction, by recalling the shared communal experiences.

In a separate show, nicknamed the 'Kakinda Show' (Katende and Katumba, 1988) by the audience, dances, movement and songs intersect with the main themes of betrayal, gender, corruption and violence. Live performance alternates with screened video or both are transmitted simultaneously.[13] In one scene, Milly (Jamila Nalubega), an unscrupulous, undignified and promiscuous woman celebrates when Kyambadde's wife dies. Ambitious and determined to capture his love, she uses expressive body language and practises witchcraft, even visiting Kunjani (Fred Kuunya), the self-styled traditional doctor *cum* herbalist whose services she enlists. She pleads with him to influence 'her boy' to give her some attention.

> Doctor problem *endeese ya nnaku nnyo*
> *Ssaba kyoyagala,* please (*pause) nja kukikuwa*
> *Buli kalina njagala nkeddize, ensimbi zonna ozinfunire,*
> *Ezo emmotoka, amayumba, n'essente byonna obicangaanye*
> Doctor *obinfunire.*
> *Kyenvudde nsalawo nzijje gyoli, olabe mu bintu byo,*
> [Please (*pause*) *tufune* solution.
> Doctor, I have come with a grave problem
> Name your price, please (*pause*) I will give you anything you want
> I want to possess him and all his property, all his money, his cars, his houses,
> Doctor, help me to gain access to all his property.
> That is why I have come to you,
> Consult the stuff (spirits),
> Please, (*pause*) let us find a solution...]
>
> ('Kakinda Show', 1988)

Milly and Kunjani are extortionists; while she confesses that she does not love Kyambadde, her aim is to prove that she can hook any man of her choice. Her resolute determination was typical of a class of people, *banamagendo*, who would risk everything to become rich. While their common expression was, '*nfa essasi ne sifa bwavu* (I would rather die of gun wounds than of poverty)', Kunjani's prescription of *mukooza*, a fetish which must be inserted into her private parts, demonstrates both Milly and Kunjani's uncouth methods. Kakinda, Kunjani's disabled assistant, anxious to take a graduate and 'been-to' to bed, begs Kunjani to allow him to accompany Milly to the '*acuti uniti* (acute unit)', which in reality is the room where they sleep with their patients[14] ('Kakinda Show', 1989). Apart from Kyambadde, whom Milly eventually marries, she flirts with other men including a '*kamanda*' (a National Resistance

Army commander) who eventually murders another of her boyfriends blaming the murder on Kyambadde.[15] The breakdown of values is underlined by the manner in which Kunjani, a quack doctor, for material gain, cheats clients with pseudo-ritual, hence, appearing to manipulate humanity as well as ancestral spirits. Nevertheless, he is also one victim of an immoral society who, forced to live off his wits, emulates the cheating tricks of the powerful people within his immediate experience. Because Kunjani personifies the educated corrupt members of his society (for example, lawyers and architects), some of his statements sound incongruous in a shrine. Indigenous music and dance develop the plot without restricting it to a traditional context or orchestration; only the basic movements are retained. This is a point underlined by Olu Obafemi quoting Akin Euba writing about Hubert Ogunde's theatre, "'the musical idiom is still African, but the composition could fall into Akin Euba's classification of the 'neo-traditional music'" in which 'traditional elements with little stylistic influence from European music are used in new contexts' (Obafemi, 1994: 39). To further their selfish ambitions, Kunjani and Kakinda manipulate language and ritual costume according to the tribal origin of the client or the degree of sophistication. Kunjani, excited by Milly's social status, breaks into a song-dance bragging about his reputation. In addition, supported by a group of dancers, Kunjani vaingloriously leads 'Nyabingi', the praise song and dance to the goddess of fertility, which he has re-worked to include his self-praises.

> *Mwe abaana muimuke tuzaane*
> Kunjani *noho, banga* Kampala, *banga* Jinja, *banga ensi yoona*
> *ebintu ne ngaba.*
>
> [You children stand up let us dance
> Kunjani, the great one
> he is great in Kampala, he is great in Jinja
> he is the greatest across the whole world
> Kunjani, the fountain of wealth.']
>
> ('Kakinda Show', 1988)

By 'alternating dialogue with music, song with action', Katumba and Katende, in the same manner as Ogunde, '[tax] both the audience's visual and aural senses in order to arrest their attention and maximise [their perception of the] message' (Obafemi, 19994: 50).

Whereas these modern adaptations of the Ebonies were opposed by people who disapprove of artistic inventiveness that reworks folk songs for electronic instruments, the dance movements are authentic, the instrumental accompaniment is original, and the producers break rules to insert tradition on modern techniques; hence, the drama is not only didactic but also an aesthetically dynamic performance. Short plays within an extended musical performance illustrate how a new kind of theatre entertains and educates its audience.[16] For instance, the shrine scene is not in the traditional setting of a grass-thatched hut located in a banana grove, rather it takes place in a modern setting represented by a brick house; further, the mediums' and dancers' costumes, hybrid dances and worship music is performed with a mixture of indigenous African and Western instruments. Therefore, if Serumaga's *Majangwa* represents a culture relocated in an urban setting, 'Kakinda Show' is a visual presentation of transformed cultural and performance practices, and signals the performers' relationship with the (new) materialistic culture. The presentation of scenes symbolising indigenous worship echo Guy Debord's assertion concerning spectacle: 'the spectacle's job is to cause a world that is no longer directly perceptible to be *seen* via different specialized mediations' (quoted in Gikandi, 2011: 263). In this way, *Majangwa*, 'Kakinda Show' and *The Dollar* represent the process of developing a response to the postcolonial transformations brought about by acts of vandalism, tyranny and political liberation. 'Kakinda Show', in particular, marks the first stages in re-creating and reconstituting *katemba* into a performance genre that relates to post-Amin generations.

In *The Inspector*, police officers are shown assaulting a prisoner; allegedly for urinating on a car wheel, while bigger criminals such as Kihuguru, a city advocate, insults police officers with impunity.[17] The most violent police officer at the station is the officer-in-charge, Nalongo (a character based on a notorious female police constable in the city), who kicks and slaps the prisoner. Her sadistic attitude is underlined soon after when, switching languages from Luganda to Swahili, she warns the prisoner not to address her as '*Maama*' (Maam or Madam): '*Maama... Maama, we apana jjuwa Maama yaako. Na nani nasema nyinyi Maama yaako*? [Don't you know your mother? Who of us has said that I am your mother?]' (*The Inspector*, 1989).

The sudden switch of language to a rude Swahili dialogue is typical of members of the security forces, army and police alike. In the same scene, Kutte's response to a telephone call from a family trapped by armed robbers is farcical.

Kutte: *Allo*, this is police, can we help you? *Allo, wewe nani, aa, onasema nini*? What? *Babbi? Babbi bali ludda ki*? Ee? *Allo, waizi wuko faasi gaani. Yi - ee*, Nkrumah Road, *apa apa kwa* Kampala *apa.*
[Allo, who are you, *aa*, what did you say? Thieves? Which side are they? Ee? Allo, where are the thieves? Yi - ee, Nkrumah Road, right here in Kampala?]
Allo - eh, yes, tell me, what are they doing? Yes...*aa aa, ee ee, kyogamba nti mwe muli mu dduuka munda ababbi babeetolodde wabweru*? You are inside the shop, and the thieves have surrounded you? *Aa, allo*, tell me, how many are they?
Bangi nnyo nnyo? *Ee, allo, ha yiko nani*? *Bunduki*? *Bunduki naani*? *Mmundu nyingi nnyo nnyo*? *Ee, kati mwagala ffe tukole ki*? *Ee. Ee. Aa*. Ok. *Allo, sijjuyi kidogo.*
[How many are there? Very many. What's that? Guns? Ee, allo, what do they have? Guns? What type of guns? Very many guns? What do you want us to do? Ee. Ee. Aa. Allo, Wait a minute.]
(*Pause. Consults fellow officers.*) *Wajjama, yiko gari apa yingye tunaweyiwa wantu yii*?
[My friends, is there a free vehicle so that we go to help these people?]

All Officers: (*Refusing.*) *Aa aa.*

Kutte: Ok. (*To the people under attack.*) *Allo, sasa nyinyi hakuna* transport, *lakini munawezi kutowa sisi apa*?
Can you come and pick us so that we can help you... You can't. Now what can we do? (*Pause*) Yees. *Ee*...the...they are breaking inside...they are breaking the door? And you're inside the shop. Ok. Now you listen to me. Just listen to my advice. *Aa, aa, gwe tolaga kutya, temutya, temufaayo. Wulira...gwe kati wuliriza, nze kye nkugamba...baleke bamenye... Allo...aa, sasa ni natowa* order *kutoka apa, allo, mugumbe gani kwa dduukani...*
[Don't panic. Don't worry. Listen...leave them to break in...Allo...Listen to my orders...You just stay inside the shop and don't panic.]
(*Replaces receiver*)

(*The Inspector*, 1988)

Crucial in all these performances is the dynamic nature of language, which evolves and changes, much as people are still entrenched in their ethnicity. This is more evident as Katende exploits language to create character, comedy, and bridge the gap between the audience and the performers, therefore, suggesting that spontaneity and creativity arise from traditional folk dance and music. Significantly, this development not only questioned the perception of a Lugandanised theatre that had dominated the debates in the 1970s, it also underscored the image of an emerging inter-ethnic, multilingual theatre (also see Mbowa, 1999). While, as I noted in Chapter 4, Kiyingi's theatre, blending Swahili, English and Luganda, was relatively associated with the notion of strangers, he did not explore the use of multiple ethnic languages as much as Katende and Katumba do in their theatre. A blend of English, Luganda, Swahili, and the major Ugandan vernacular languages or what one newspaper columnist termed *Olungeswaganda*,[18] was frequently used both to reach a wider audience and for dramatic purposes.

While to many critics the play was a typical example of *katemba*, which in this context could refer to cheap drama, Katende exploited this slapstick entertainment, similar to what Obafemi has described as the '*Yeye*' tradition in Nigeria, to examine serious issues through shared laughter. Drawing from the work of George Kernodle and J. E Adedeji, Obafemi applies what Adedeji calls '*Yeye*' to Moses Olaiya's theatre style. According to Obafemi, its 'main function is the provision of laughter in the midst of self and public ridicule'; thus the artist who takes a break from serious theatre to create these dramas 'points the way, mostly unobtrusively, to improvement and takes stock of social satire' (Obafemi, 1994; 56). *Katemba* or '*Yeye*' theatre styles, therefore, '[provide] public entertainment and relaxation for the audience while satirizing what is wrong in society' (Obafemi, 1994: 56). Although *The Dollar* represents one of the many plays in Katende and Katumba's repertoire, it demonstrates all the characteristics that Obafemi notes, which are typical in the work of popular dramatists such as Olaiya in Nigeria or Gibson Kente in South Africa.

Kadongo Kamu

When Amin 'disappeared' theatre artists and forced others into exile the quality of staged dramas declined. Interestingly, this trend coincided with an expanded interest in popular musical theatre, a subgenre mainly popular because it merged shared theatrical expressions (dance, song, instrumental music) and other forms including Western and Zairean (Congolese) music. Some of the songs and dramatisations are about the social and political realities, specifically, politics, the critical silence, conflicts and violence, betrayals as well as the conditions that have brought about the moral breakdown within Ugandan society. *Kadongo Kamu* (one guitar solo performer), which appropriated the indigenous travelling music forms as well as other folk forms and styles to create an alternative musical genre, is a good example of performance as a form of resistance. Given its artistic origin, *Kadongo Kamu* genre is recognised more for its musical excellence than for its dramatic quality and narratives of resistance. Started by Christopher Sebadduka in the 1960s, *Kadongo Kamu* became very popular in the 1970s and 1980s. Like his predecessors, the *abadongo*, *abadingidi*, and *abagoma*, Sebadduka, accompanying his one-man performance with a single box guitar, played in market places, trading centres, and various spots in Kampala city. The crowd's responses were spontaneous - laughing, clapping, commenting on the performance and rewarding him with money.[19]

The ability to perform in any available space - on the streets, in the slums, in school halls, even in market places - made his Kadongo Kamu Super Singers the first group to both, transform *abadongo* music and disused bars into playhouses. Nonetheless, incorporating dramatic elements 'conceived and acted by the cast within the song' (Mugambi, 1994: 5), the form emerged as a hybrid of indigenous music that responded to social issues; both, the musical and the dramatic elements interacted practically and ideologically. Similar to oral performances, both songs and drama skits were not based on a fixed written text; therefore, they did not lend themselves to state censorship. But in a context in which 'every word carried an innuendo' and 'every gesture was a sign', the audience '[became] good "interpreters" or readers of the sign' and discourse of resistance (Taylor, 1997: 237). In a way, *Kadongo Kamu* prompted enthusiastic responses from audiences and became popular because artists were aware that censors could not control it as much as they did scripted drama. Notably, throughout this period, living in the shadow of institutional oppression, the idea that attending a performance signified an act of resistance theatre increased people's participation in artistic activities and influenced the emergence of small town playhouses. Society did not achieve its liberation through theatre but the emergence and performance of hybrid musical dramas was critical to the transformation of people from oppressed citizens to conscientised individuals.

As an art form, *Kadongo Kamu* was exceptional, mainly because of the manner in which it appropriated other aesthetic and stylistic forms. It draws on indigenous performance forms and other old oral forms and meaning to create new meanings that allow it to make subtle statements on the political status quo, mock and satirise real life characters, and focus on the absurd and grotesque. *Kadongo Kamu* instrumental accompaniment is rudimentary, the main instrument being the country guitar, although today amplified electric guitars are used as well. That they imitate *baakisimba* drum rhythms on the guitars makes their music accessible and appealing to the ordinary audience. Willy Mukaabya, in his interview with Nannyonga-Tamusuza, explains that in writing his hit song, *Kayanda Oliira Otya mu Sowani Yange*? [Kayanda, How dare you eat off my plate?] (1988), 'he intended that each instrument should imitate a *Kiganda* instrument'. Hence, 'the rhythm guitar imitates the *ndongo* (bowl lyre), which takes an accompanying role to the voice, while the bass guitar simulates the Ngoma (drums) and the keyboard imitates the *madinda* (a log xylophone)' (Nannyonga-Tamusuza, 2002: 137). Significantly, although the original groups had no accompanying mime and dance troupes, three key additions to the form have been a repertoire of *baakisimba nankasa* and *mbaga* (wedding) dancers; mime and improvised dialogue act as connectives. In Uganda, the ordinary person likes a voice produced traditionally and so the coarse traditional tone of these musicians is a key asset. Through improvisation, the lead performer, usually the owner of the group accentuates the narrative with exaggerated gestures and clowning, in the manner of the traditional solo performer. The atmosphere is that of an indigenous interactive performance; audiences walk on and off stage tipping performers and participating in the dance skits.

By the 1980s, *Kadongo Kamu* was not just another music genre but it embedded dramatic skits, and today, its dramatised narrative (performances) are electronically recorded and marketed as part of the *KinaUganda* films. Thus, 'the difference between the song texts in this genre and other songs' performed by groups such as The Ebonies and

The Afrigo Band, as Mugambi explains, 'lies not only in the manner of their circulation, by radio, cassette and video', and I would add, staged performance, 'but also in the style and content'. For, overall, 'these songs dramatize events and lives of fictional or real people; they incorporate discourses on family, community and the nation at large' (1994: 1). Mugambi further asserts that 'the oral narrative tradition that traverses the traditional narrative story, the radio song, the public performance' involve a migratory process where 'new meanings are constructed by the transitions between one medium and another, and/or at the points where media converge or intersect'. Therefore, 'within these transitions or "moments of transition"' the 'transformative reconstructions occur' (1994b: 14). She adds most significantly, 'New meanings thus reconfigure and transcend original meanings to produce new codes of signification. In essence, newly created forms become metaphorical or rhetorical strategies that transform song performance into an arena for contemporary ideological and political discourses' (Mugambi 1994b: 14-15). In this sense, it is not different but rather, it reflects the extraordinary changes taking place elsewhere in theatre.

Kadongo Kamu is a theatre that enjoyed popular support and commercial success, and yet, at the same time, it also courted controversy as the two significant critical studies by Nannyonga-Tamusuza and Mugambi, which have focused on the negative gender discourse, embedded in songs, specifically by male artists, that silences women, demonstrate. On the other hand, Mugambi, maintains that the songs, 'intrinsically constituted by migratory elements derived from the traditional oral narrative' (1994b: 1) underline the practice of analyzing and contemplating the cultural representation of woman in folksongs/tales by contemporary female performers. Nannyonga-Tamusuza, in a similar vein as Mugambi, as well as underlining that the genre is typified by negative representations of women, locates her analysis in the post-colonial context hence, highlighting its hybrid nature. Both scholars argue that *Kadongo Kamu* male artists practice the elision of female subjugation in their recreation of the postcolonial socio-political experiences. Interestingly, Mugambi reminds us that *Kadongo Kamu* theatre forms part of the 'traditional narrative' that 'essentially functions as a migratory unit, binding story' both, to song and dramatic skits, but whose function is similar to storytelling performances. Whether performing on radio or any other public space, the artists, self-consciously 'declare themselves critics, teachers, or embodiments of the moral conscience of the community/nation' (Mugambi, 1994: 1). In this way, therefore, '[t]hey define themselves as the acknowledged authors of contemporary morality, inheriting the function from anonymous communal authorship of traditional moral codes' (Mugambi, 1994: 1).

As previously stated, there has been a debate concerning the categorisation of music theatre artists as *bannakatemba* (theatre artists/stage artists) or *abayimbi* (musicians); however, *Kadongo Kamu*'s performance practice is ambiguous, meeting the criteria for both, the musical and the dramatic, to demonstrate its connectedness to the folk and the modern. For Nannyonga-Tamusuza, the critical element in the development of *Kadongo Kamu* has been the merging of the 'musical and dramatic aspects' of performance, 'a style' which was 'spearheaded by Matiya Luyima' (Nannyonga-Tamusuza, 2002: 135). Similar to the re-created *katemba*, in staged dramas, *Kadongo Kamu* builds upon the definitions of *abadongo*, which links individual performers not only to the instrument but also to the aesthetics, style and form of performance, aspects of cultural history and politics. In this way, it allows us to appreciate the intersection between artists and the audience and the complex web of discourses embedded in the performance. The power and novelty of the *Kadongo Kamu* genre lies in the wittiness and passion with which it transforms the travelling musician and other artistic traditions into a dynamic theatre expression. For instance, Sebadduka's song, *Enkomerero eri Kumpi Mwenenye* [Repent, for [political] life is ending] (1969), which made the form even better known, was a response to the political crisis of the late 1960s. It alludes to the Biblical doomsday, which warns irreverent leaders that political power backed by the gun must end someday. As forms of expression, *Kadongo Kamu* and other musical theatres are complex and more difficult for the government to suppress than formal theatre; tyrannical institutions have often relied on paid informers to interpret it, as was the case when Obote's government forced Sebadduka into exile. Groups such as Dan Mugula & Filida Namuddu, Lukwata Guitar Singers, Matia Luyima and Group, and Fred and Pross Sebatta Singers continued to develop the form in the theatre, which they used to 'clear or create a social space where new connections could be made and rehearsed in public' and articulate voices of resistance (Gikandi, 2011: 265). Indeed, because of *Kadongo Kamu*'s 'sense of deviance' and the political discourse it generated, specifically through the lyrics, it 'became a source of anxiety and fear across' the state institutions (Gikandi, 2011: 264).

Participating artists are from the labourers or unemployed young men/women, who share the plight of a large section of society struggling to find their *voice*. Since they live with the people in villages and urban slums, they know the language of the street and the phrases in common currency. Most notably, the language is vivid: pure Luganda and all kinds of Luganda clichés, Ugandanised Swahili catchphrases and slang are used to deride the singer's targets. All classes of people are criticised, including *abasoma*, *ba enewe* or *ba maayika* - these phrases, meaning either the said literate ones, 'anyways, or 'my car', ridicule people who mix English and Ugandan vernaculars and selfish wealthy car owners. The lyrics, often sung with a touch of satire, are truthful. Social deprivation[20] is a major topic. Thus, Sebadduka's '*Ensi Ekyuuka* (The world/country is changing)' (1980), for example, draws our attention to the changing prices of goods before and after the Amin coup. On the other hand, criticising the political classes preoccupies Fred Kigozi in Owino *Yafuuka Muzadde* [Owino suckles us all] (1990). He describes himself as '*eriiso lya gavumenti mbadde neebase nendoota* (the government's eye rising from a stupor)' in praise of the ordinary man's market, Owino.

Luyima's *Olugendo lwe Masaka*, [The trip to Masaka] (1986), a collective plea to the security forces to stop terrorising innocent civilians and Dan Mugula's *Ebikolobero by'Abanyanya* [*Abanyanya* mercenaries' atrocious behaviour] (1986) are some of the most fascinating examples of this hybrid genre. They demonstrate the creative 'subterranean manner' in which popular theatre is used to express people's resentment of the oppressor (Karin Barber, 1987). Although the songs represent a small part of their corpus and performances, both, *Olugendo lwe Masaka* and *Ebikolobero by'Abanyanya*, show all the features that Mugambi and Nannyonga-Tamusuza note as being characteristic of *Kadongo Kamu* songs and theatre, which allow it to disrupt the official narratives (Mugambi, 1994; Nannyonga-Tamusuza, 2002). Luyima and the chorus attempt to depict acts of torture and banditry through impersonation, parody and mimicry. It can be argued that Luyima and Mugula's performances point towards the re-creation of the traditional folktale. Indeed, as Mugambi suggests, in post-conflict contexts, 'the traditional folktale, in its original from, has no place during … tragic phases in people's lives' (Mugambi, 1994: 6). Thus, instead, narratives of violent deaths and confrontations with military personnel that are similar to what Luyima self-consciously reconstructs and re-enacts in *Olugendo lwe Masaka*, provide a clear vision of a people besieged by terror and divided by indigenous differences. Luyima narrates his experience of the journey concluding with the plea: *Apaana wuwa sasi, apana wuwa muntu* [Please don't shoot me, don't kill the poor human being].'

Lakini watu gani nyinyi?
Netubaddamu.
Caca munatooka wapi?
Netusirika.
Aya nyinyi mulale chini.
Netweyala.
Wewe nafanya wapi?
Ne mbaddamu.
Wonesa kadi yako.
Ne njijjayo.
Aya niwe ludi zenyu.
Ne neyala.
Sasa towa pesa yote?
Ne tuzigyayo.

[What kind of people are you?
We answered them.
Where are you coming from?
We kept quiet.
Lie down all of you.
We lay down.
You, where do you work?
I answered them.
Show your [identity] card.
I pulled it out.
You move aside.
I lay down.
Give us all your money.
We did].

(*Olugendo lwe Masaka*, 1986)

The audience, for whom brutality has become a norm, appreciates the irony; especially drawing parallels between Luyima's light tone to that used by survivors to report the military's gruesome acts of torture. This style makes a realistic presentation of people's daily experience; juxtaposing the Swahili-speaking soldiers' dialogue with passengers' responses in Luganda. Most people are non-literate in Swahili; although it is the official national language in Uganda, it personifies the callous, brutish, soldiers. Originally, Swahili was used to recruit non-English speakers into the army, police and prison services during colonial times. Hence, while he uses Swahili to give his performance credibility, Luyima has to perform 'his eyewitness account of the event in the audience's primary language' (Mugambi, 1994: 3).[21] Ali Mazrui (1980: 52) draws parallels between the association of Swahili with 'militarism' in Uganda and apartheid Afrikaans within South Africa. 'The children of Soweto in South Africa refused to learn Afrikaans because it was the voice of apartheid', he states, 'will Ugandan kids now refuse to learn Swahili because it was once the language of the Barracks? The analogy [is] not entirely far-fetched.' Other writers, particularly readers publishing their views in the vernacular newspapers, continue to indict Swahili as *OluSwahili olutulabizza ennaku* [Swahili the oppressor's language of choice], unfit to be a national language.

In *Ebikolobero by'Abanyanya* composed after the 1986 guerrilla war, Mugula reworked *Moto na Waka* [The battle/fire is hot], the NRA's war song, for the stage. Mugula, the narrator, relates his experiences to his friend Muzeeyi Zedde, a pseudonym for the people's voice, and ubiquitous columnist, who presented the shared communal concerns in the Luganda daily newspaper, *Ngabo*. Between Amin and Obote 1's time, this unrelenting, non-apologetic criticism of society made Muzeeyi Zedde the most popular, albeit, anonymous character, presented in various dramatic sketches. Muzeeyi Zedde narrates the experiences of war from the ordinary people's perspective. He uses his own war experience signalled by the reference to the military roadblocks and the agents of death, Colinayo Aladipo and the *abanyanya*, to rework the song, while also using idioms from old folk songs and cultural practices to develop the triumphant theme. Throughout the performance, while addressing the audience as *bakawonawo* (war veterans) Mzeeyi Zedde celebrates the defeat of the Anyanya. He refers to familiar and iconic landmarks such as the solar power clock at Wandegeya trading centre, Kololo Summit that not only hosted the first television mast in Uganda but also safe houses for the military intelligence, and Katonga River which witnessed the most intense battles between government forces and the guerrilla army, to add verisimilitude.

Mugula presents Uganda as place scarred by the battle between the combined Uganda Armed Forces and Anyanya mercenaries and a grassroots guerrilla force. His position of participation without becoming an active combatant allows his outsider's perspective to emerge; this is underscored by the dialogue with his friend, Muzeeyi Zedde, who, 'inject[ing] humor in the song' (Mugambi, 1994: 3), dramatises his witness account of the battle for Kampala. Muzeeyi Zedde, in one of the best demonstrations of the Kadongo Kamu opening formula, adopts the Baganda recitative style (*okuttontoma*), personifying the battle-hardened Ugandans who had acquired a flair for identifying guns, mortars and small fire-arms by their explosive sounds, describes the gun duel in a call and response style. The clearest evidence of the people's defiance occurs when they stage a passive resistance through their submission to the soldier's demands for identity and money. At the end of the performance, Mugula creates a counterpoint to the soldiers' ugly brutish behaviour; faced with a disciplined opposition, they abandon their loot and escape from the city. The audience would be familiar with the absurd and comic scenes that followed the routing of the Anyanya mercenaries together with the Ugandan Army. The audience's perspective when juxtaposed with that of the vanquished army reveals the depth of hatred between the two parties. In one scene, Zedde's stylised performance underlined by heavy drumming and the random plucking of guitar strings recapitulates the audience's fear and hatred for the Anyanya.

Bayimbula emisinde eyo netubasaasira.
Nendyoka nkulabira
Abanyanya abaali batutta
Abanyanya abaali balatta
Abanyanya abaali babadala
Abanyanya abaali badigidda.
Abamannyo amawagale
Abamannyo agasasamala
Nebatandika okuwanjaga!

Abamu ne besisiwala
Abamu ne bajjugumira
Nenkulabira bwe badduka!
Amaziga ne gabayitamu,
'*Batuleeteranga mu nnyonyi...*
Bazilio ye ali ludda wa?
Kama Muceveni na yingiya!'
Kwata kitaawo, kwata nnyoko.
Pereketya mpa ku nswa.
Tito Tito, Toko, Toko, Bazilio, Bazilio
Tito Tito, Toko, Toko, Bazilio, Bazilio.

[They run like mad. We pitied them.
Words aren't enough to describe the sight.
The Anyanya who butchered people
Arrogant and inflated
Those with sharpened teeth
Those with dented teeth
Suddenly they started pleading.
They were in shock.
They started running!
They pleaded to their warlord, - Bazilio
Who had airlifted them (from Sudan)
'Where is Bazilio (Okello)
We came to protect his government.
Now, Museveni has broken through the barricades!
Help'.]
(*Imitating sounds of Museveni's* small military mortar and small arms sounds):[That is for your mother. That is your father.]
(*Imitating Anyanyas machine gun sounds*) [Tito Tito, Toko, Toko, Bazilio Bazilio
Tito Tito, Toko, Toko, Bazilio, Bazilio.][22]

(*Ebikolobero by'Abanyanya*, 1986)

Mugula's creation of an intertextual dialogue with *Mwoto na Waka* and other folk songs signify on the NRA's idea of friend and fiend war song, and *Pereketya*, a folksong from an oral tale of the same title. The intertextual connections result from the shared experiences of oral performance and post-colonial political violence. By highlighting *Pereketya*, Mugula creates a resonance with the Baganda indigenous practice of trapping *ennaka*, a type of white ant that is a delicacy in this part of Buganda, during which the trapper appeals to Pereketya, the god of *ennaka*, to bless his harvest. This is further underlined through the song lyrics, '*Pereketya mpa ku nswa, akajja nkabojja*, -

Pereketya, bless by harvest, I shall catch [and eat] whatever ant appears from the anthill' - ('*Ebikolobero by'abanyanya*', 1986) that allude to the skilful snipers of the NRA guerrilla force. Hence, the thematic interrelationship with *Pereketya* underscores the successful conclusion of the war. The introduction of an alternative multi-layered perspective that represents the reality of the non-combatants, such as Muzeeyi Zedde's narrative, suggests that the work of Mugula and other contemporary performers encourages the use of 'migratory' elements that allow the performer (narrator) to assume the role of a witness and comment on the events. (See Mugambi, 1994) Significantly, the song draws on shared historical and performance experiences, which allows the interaction between the initiate audience and the performers.

Apart from urbanisation, a number of significant points led to the emergence of *katemba* and its irruption throughout the country: first, the spread of indigenous performances (dance, song and instrumental music) throughout the schools; second, the celebration of the Roman Catholic and Church of Uganda centenaries between 1977 and 1979; third, the victimisation of various ethnic groups such as the Acholis and the Baganda that later led the people to join the opposition to tyranny; and lastly, the search by the younger generations for performance forms that related to international contemporary popular styles. As most performances from this period demonstrate, just as the governments staged farce, for example, in expelling and confiscating Ugandan Asian's properties or hunting for invisible bandits, artists, through *katemba*, staged farce to resist oppressive practices. Indeed, as noted earlier, *katemba* is as much concerned with the use of farce in times of political crisis as with the radical transformation of performance to develop hybrid theatrical expressions, stage *lingua franca* that mixes Ugandan languages with Swahili and English.

However, sometimes the process of merging folk theatrical expressions and modern Western styles and forms created concerns. For, the transformation in performance styles brought about by the use of electronic equipment such as electric guitars, synthesisers and video technology as well as amplifiers modernised staged performances. Despite the inherent aesthetic quality of these developments, some people felt this theatre disrespected cultural traditions and disrupted conventional theatre styles.

Nevertheless, as Gikandi suggests, in his discussion 'regarding the emergence of a space of cultural expression outside the hermeneutics of modernity' during slavery, 'forms of cultural expression that were the most likely to be dismissed as meaningless spectacle' by slave masters in America or colonial rulers in Africa were also the most valued by the people. Thus, it is not surprising that despite the opposition, they were valued by the people 'as they sought to produce a counterculture, including one that went against the grain of sense and sensibility' (Gikandi, 2011: 262-3). Europeans could categorise rituals and other modern artistic forms as *taboo*, since, although they 'could discern the significance of what they saw', they 'were not sure what it meant and were then left pondering the meaning of a spectacle that was disharmonious and at odds with European aesthetic practices' (Gikandi, 263). Gikandi's comments have a pertinent meaning to theatre and performance in Uganda: during the post-colonial era, the artists' 'performance' may comprise 'an assemblage of values', including cultural expressions/forms, which are inaccessible or incomprehensible to the oppressive institutions and dissociated from the accepted social order, the realm of surveillance' (Gikandi, 2011: 263). Hence, given its 'sense of deviance' (Gikandi 264) *katemba* (performance) becomes the focal point of expressing resistance among the oppressed communities. In this way, while music helps to 'spread the language of insurgency', ritual festivals and cultural practices, funerals and final funeral rites ceremonies, for instance, give people opportunities to congregate.

Radio and Theatre: Kibuuka and Senkubuge's *Ebimeeza*

FM radios has not only given artists an alternative performance space but also expanded their capacity to create and perform subversive and other messages to a wider audience. Indeed, today popular artists who anchor popular FM radio programmes, develop concepts that they transfer from theatre to radio, and vice versa - such as Radio Simba's *Simbawo Akati* (literally meaning, 'pause and plant a twig to mark the spot'), hosted by Kibuuka and Senkubuge, which borrows a peasant farmers' metaphor, that defines shared experiences. Both artists present the most popular FM Radio programme on Radio Simba which, in the manner of the banned *ebimeeza* and 'phone-in talk shows' (broadcasts that aired public debates and opinions relating to current events), debate issues of public concern. In reality, these discourses are extensions of the practices that took place in the then *bufunda* or *binywero*, illegal but safe drinking places that mushroomed during the second UPC government. This radio programme dramatises lived experiences and political conflicts in the manner of staged performances, through satire and subversive humour. It challenges listeners to witness, practise remembrance, mark and record milestones in politics; as well as inviting them to, literally, plant a twig (which may sprout!), it hails them to stop, think, listen, witness, and archive.[23] Senkubuge and Kibuuka who also stage performances such as the television serial *Dube Atasasula Boda* [Dube the Fare Dodger] (2011 -), have become more satirical. In a statement that draws our attention to the thematic characteristics of their theatre they have asserted, 'FM radios, *oba* theatre, *ye parliament yaffe* -Our [the people's] parliament is either the FM radio or the theatre stage-' (Senkubuge and Kibuuka, 2010). In this way, the focus of these performances is to give witness accounts and engage in an open debate of issues sidelined by the executive and the legislature. As a concept, *simbawo akati* significantly relates to current performance practices and resonates with Copland's comments on the interrelationship between urbanisation and the transformation of performance expressions, a process that critical artists understand and refer to in their discourse of post-conflict political systems. Significantly, similar to Kiyingi, when performers such as Senkubuge and Kibuuka deliberately use the expression in the radio point of view and talk show programmes they consciously create a dialogical space between radio and theatre in which audience and performers bear witness. Thus, the performance of apparently routine roles that aim to broadcast news as well as harmless entertainment can have alternative critical effects by publicising and communicating subversive messages and gathering collective points of view.

Chapter 8

RECONSTRUCTING CONTEMPORARY EXPERIENCES IN *KINAUGANDA*: MARIAM NDAGIRE AND ASHRAF SIMWOGERERE

The major aesthetic, forms and stylistic elements discussed in the earlier chapters of this book on contemporary Ugandan theatre have remained invariable since 1960. However, there is a constant contact and interchange between local and international theatre scenes, which are encouraged by the search for innovative ways to address new socio-political experiences. As discussed in Chapter 7, since the National Resistance Movement came into power, non-scripted theatre invariably supported by developments of new media has taken prominence over scripted drama. Noticeably, since a younger generation of Ugandans who never experienced the 1970s and 1980s violent conflicts has since matured and is willing to engage with issues relevant to their communities, the Ugandan scripted theatre has largely been transferred to dvds/videos. Additionally, older dramatists have abandoned theatre and active performance and moved to FM radios and/or filmic activities, locally known as *KinaUganda*. *KinaUganda* means, of Ugandan origin. It refers to that which is typically Uganda - bearing indigenous cultural characteristics and articulating a Ugandan point of view. It is the prefix *kina*- (of), that invokes the question of cultural identity in the word; and expresses the meaning of home movies.[1] The genre rejects the division between indigenous and Western, local languages and English, to create hierarchies of audiences and complexities in its reception. It has emerged as a performance space, benefiting from the National Resistance Movement government's peace and economic growth. The openness of this form means that artists can engage with the thematic as well as artistic elements discussed in previous chapters, while engaging and subverting social, political and economic realities.

Since the major practitioners of *KinaUganda* were also the supporters and stars of scripted theatre, for this chapter, interviews with two home movie directors, Mariam Ndagire working in English, and Ashraf Simwogerere working in Luganda and other Bantu languages were transcribed and translated.

A Conversation with Mariam Ndagire

Mariam Ndagire has been producing films since *Down This Road I Walk* (2007). She is the only successful young female director ever to work in kinaUganda. Because she has been able to attract sponsorships, thanks to her success in the popular music theatre - her films have been successful and have made money. The interview took place in her office at Bat Valley Theatre (formerly Theatre Exclesior), a converted school hall, in Kampala City. Her favourite film, she said, was *Down This Road I Walk* because it 'was my first movie so I love it'.

The questions covered issues such as her initial work in theatre, representation of women in her scripts, and the future of *KinaUganda.*

MN: I can't put a finger on anything because it was a calling for me. I found a passion for theatre.

SK: What brought you into the area of video?

MN: As an amateur, I was working with Omugave Ndugwa in the Black Pearls. From there, a few of us including Kato Lubwama, Ashraf Simwogerere, John Segawa, Abby Mukiibi formed our own group, the Afri Diamonds. After a few years, we thought we had done everything so we decided to try film.

However, I must say that all along I had a crush on the screen, particularly when I was watching movies on the screen. I am a fan of movies. Since I used to do many stage plays, I thought I could give it a go. Before I started, I read a lot of literature about filming.

SK: When did you start video filming?

MN: My first movie, *Down This Road I Walk*, was in 2007. I spent a whole year between 2006 and 2007 writing the script. In 2007, I decided to try it out and called the auditions but of course, until then I wasn't sure whether Ugandan actors were interested in filming. An overwhelming number of people came so I auditioned, cast and started shooting. I got somebody, Chris, who I had met at Wavah Broadcasting Service (WBS) while shooting *Ensitaano*[2] who was a good cameraman (cinematographer). I told him that I had a script I intended to direct, 'could he do the shooting?' I have been with him ever since.

SK: Under what circumstances did the video film industry start in Uganda?

MN: I think people who first made movies saw a gap because there were many Nigerian films in circulation and our audiences seemed interested in them. Therefore, they asked, 'what if our own people acted something like that?' Remember, what made the Nigerian stories so interesting were stories that were close to our hearts.

SK: Ordinary stories…

MN: Yes. The audience would say, 'I think I have seen that before… I have seen that happen at my neighbour's home'. Therefore, those people who started thought they could have Nigerian movies done in a Ugandan way.

SK: So, is that is how they started?

MN: That is how they started. They were emulating the Nigerians. Basically that is what happened. However, I for one when I came in I didn't want to emulate the Nigerians, I wanted to make films telling our Ugandan stories. I wanted to have a Ugandan style of movie making, telling our Ugandan stories in a better way, better than the Nigerians do.

SK: How do you distribute and market your movies to the public?

MN: Initially when I was writing the script, I got the Nile Breweries to sponsor me. Up to now, they still give me some sponsorship. They introduced me to DSTV, the cable network that shows in several African countries…so that is one of my outlets. A month after the movie premier I distribute it on DVD. I negotiate with businesspersons with retail/wholesale outlets who sell the movies in their shops in the City and upcountry towns. In addition, I distribute outside the country.

SK: Some Ugandans have said that home videos/DVDs lack artistic merit, that this is a moneymaking industry that peddles special effects, witchcraft and magic. What are your comments on this?

MN: I would say that there are varieties of filmmakers in the industry … with several intentions. Each person comes in with different aims. Those who first started in the industry looked at making money because they were seeing a gap … there was that demand for movies. They were not looking at the quality of the movie, the stories and all those basics of making a good film, but they were just looking at the [finished] product and getting money out of it. Then there are some others who take their time, put in a lot effort, do the homework and release very good movies.

SK: Would you say that that there have been phases in the development of *KinaUganda*?

MN: There was a phase when they were in it for money although now they are more professional. Nevertheless, I think both, professionals and profiteers are here. The good thing is that the modern day Ugandans are getting to know the difference; they appreciate good movies. People in the second category … the mediocre… are starting to fade out.

SK: How would you describe your work? Is it as video film, home video or home movie?

MN: I wouldn't say it is home video [or video film] because it wouldn't be taken to cable television. There are several Ugandan moviemakers who would like their products to be bought [or sponsored] by these multinational companies but they are struggling because their films are of a basic nature; they are so 'home' ... not for the diverse audience. I wouldn't say that mine are very good but they are ok.

SK: Would you categorise yours as home movies?

MN: Yes.

MN: Ok.

SK: How do you go about developing film scripts, shooting scenes and bringing the complete work to the consumer's screens?

MN: I first prepare myself. I first come up with the story ... what I want to talk about, the log line...

SK: What do you mean by log line?

MN: I don't know what you would call it in UK...but it is the line that governs the story ... what the movie is going to be about. Then I come up with my characters, how I want the plot to move; and I come up with the treatment. By this I mean, how the story is going to move...which scene comes after the other and how the story develops. Then I put the flesh on the skeleton... At times, I have a scene breakdown; at other times, I don't because when you are writing the story just flows... I just write the script then I go back and look at what I have....

SK: How long does it take you to write a script?

MN: Aaa, I wouldn't say...it depends on the strength of the script...the story... *Down this Road I Walk* took me a long time because I didn't know what I was doing. I was transforming from stage to screen so I didn't know the basics; I didn't know anything. *Hearts in Pieces* took me one month to write the draft; one month to come up with the draft; and after that, it took me up to the audition time to make it right. Sometimes you may look at what you have written only to discover that there are not enough conflicts or there isn't enough suspense...

SK: Why did you kill off your characters?

MN: [*Laughter*] Ha ha ha... do you mean in *Down This Road I Walk*? [*Laughter*] I didn't want a Part 2 [a sequel].

SK: You don't have to have a Part 2.

MN: I didn't want a Part 2 so I had to solve the conflict. I had to resolve everything...all the conflicts...

SK: By killing...

MN: [*Laughter*] Haa. Haa. No, that is how it was flowing in my head. Because if this man stayed around the movie would have ended on a cliff-hanger, he wouldn't have anywhere to go.

SK: Do your actors experience (emotional) reactions from the audience when they walk on the street?

MN: Yes they do.

SK: In the past people wanted to relate to us on the street as if we are the stage characters…

MN: This is happening more in the TV series, *Tendo Sisters.*[3] In that script, there is a wicked girl studying at the University who is always disorganising her friends. When the public meets her, they call her names. It doesn't happen to me because I play many roles in various performance events, for instance, I am a musician, film director, and actress so it is very hard to pin me on [identify me with] any character. However, for others they have not seen before they think that the movie character and the individual are the same, therefore, they are treated differently.

SK: Filmmaking is expensive, how you do finance your projects?

MN: As I told you before, I have Nile Breweries who have supported me since I launched my film career. At first they didn't trust the [home movie] industry they said, 'how are we sure we are going to benefit out of it?' However, with time they started to believe in me and offered me sponsorship. I get some money out of product placement from *The Weekly Observer* [News Co-corporation], and other companies. I also get money when I sell the DVDs of my movies and television serials of my other plays. Finally, my singing [musical performances], an area that is already established earns me a reasonable income. That is how I finance my film projects.

SK: What are the sources of your stories?

MN: It is just what is around me at the time. They are not from what I have read, heard or recollections of folk stories. Maybe one time I will write a play on [the Baganda myth of] Kintu and Nambi. I am so much into fiction…I love creating stuff. I am not like Ashraf [Simwogerere] who is very good at adapting contemporary events for film. The problem with that style is that people will say, 'That is not how it happened'. I am not good at that.

SK: So, you love fiction not faction.

MN: I love fiction.

SK: Why don't you work with oral tales or folk narratives?

MN: I haven't looked at that angle. It hasn't inspired me yet because I think I still have some good stories in my head.

SK: But you don't travel in commuter taxis so you don't know the stories people tell.

MN: I speak to people who use them and others who leave in *mizigos*, two roomed houses.

SK: Have you ever thought of adapting Ugandan literary work?

MN: Yes. It is just that I don't have a lot of time on me to adapt them. I only do one movie a year. For instance, I would like to adapt Omugave Ndugwa's plays…that would be my starting point.

SK: What about other works, for example, Kawere's *Zinnunula Omunaku*[4] or Kiyingi's *Lozio Bba Ssesiriya*[5]?

MN: Well, because I was in Black Pearls I know Ndugwa's plays on my fingertips; therefore, it would be easier to work on them.

SK: Why don't you do two movies a year?

MN: Because I have several projects, for example, I have a television serial that runs for two seasons a year. I have another reality show - a talent search show for young musicians - so I don't have a lot of time. On top of that, I have the singing, ha ha [*Laughter*]. When I was doing *Hearts in Pieces,* I wrote two scripts and I thought I would be able to produce them but I didn't get the time; therefore, I shall work on the second script this year.

SK: Is that as depressing as *Hearts in Pieces*?

MN: [*Laughter*] Ha ha, I don't know.

SK: What kind of stories do you tell?

MN: [*Silence*]

SK: Have I asked a difficult question?

MN: [*Laughter*] Ha ha ha, kind of. I am told that my movies demonstrate that I am fighting for women's rights - that struggling woman. [*Laughter*]

SK: What you have said brings me to the next point. Certain scenes seem to be stable in *KinaUganda* home movies. There are domestic scenes in which cameras zoom on the interior decorations of the houses or on beautiful girls or cars. However, the real people are not there.

MN: It is because Ugandans love beautiful things such as women, property and cars. They aspire to possess them. When they see something beautiful they ask, 'Where did you get that from?' So, the more you put these in your movies the more they watch them.

SK: What you have said brings us to that crucial question concerning your work and women. You have stated that you are committed to women but from your work and that of other artists, women are presented from a male perspective. In addition, they are not assigned leading roles. Is this a fair observation?

MN: Yes, that is a fair comment but this is how we as Ugandans, whether male or female, see women.

SK: Is that how you see the woman?

MN: It is not just me but other Ugandan directors as well. That is why I start by presenting the woman as they see her. Nevertheless, I also try to bring her out, as she would like to be seen.

SK: But the role you play in *Down This Road I Walk* is the role of a woman who is malevolent, an evil mother-in-law. No woman is positively portrayed in that movie.

MN: There is. The mother to the young woman is portrayed very positively.

SK: But she is a minor character.

MN: True. Because we want to show these evil women so that people see that, these types of women should be eliminated from society.

SK: But there are many strong women in Uganda....

MN: There are very many women who are oppressed. Many of these can't stand up to talk about their problems. Domestic violence is rampant and it directly affects around seventy-eight per cent of the women's population.

SK: But in your film, the mother-in-law inflicts torture on her daughter-in-law and in the end, she does not learn from her mistakes.

MN: She does. She is taken to jail.

SK: But she is removed from the scene of her atrocities...

MN: That is why I didn't want Part 2 because then I would have to show the details. However, since she goes to jail, she learns that if you behave like that [in that manner] your end is not going to be very good.

SK: In future, do you intend to portray stronger women on stage?

MN: It is unfortunate you did not watch *Strength of a Stranger* because there is a widow oppressed by the sister-in-law but in the end, she wins.

SK: Which of your films is your favourite?

MN: That is a hard question. I have a passion for each of them; *Down This Road* was my first movie so I love it. *Strength of a Stranger* has its own style...it has a strong woman who wins. *Hearts in Pieces* is different because it represents culture in a variety of ways.

SK: Do you get a lot of media reviews or feedback from people?

MN: Yes I do. When I wrote *Down This Road,* I had a screen bash where I invited the cast, well-wishers and the media. At the end, everyone had to write their comments on the back of the invitation.

SK: What do you think about theatre reviewers in Uganda?

MN: Some good ones give you a genuine opinion. The genuine ones don't write it for money whereas others demand money before they publish the reviews. So, the latter write impressive reviews for monetary gain. These always come to you asking your opinion about the review even before it is published. I don't like that category of reviewers. I don't want to hear the praises but critical evaluations.

SK: Do your films address themselves to any specific audience?

MN: I am targeting that woman between the ages of 15 - 55. Their response is good.

SK: What is the age group of your audience?

MN: Fifteen to sixty.

SK: Is the reception the same across the age range?

MN: I think so.

SK: When you observe audiences watching films in *bibanda*[6] or makeshift cinema halls, they tend to interact with the films. Sometimes they denounce actions that they see as unacceptable or confirm actions. Is such audience interaction what *KinaUganda* directors aim for? Is that what you aim for?

MN: I do to a limited extent because it is part of the Ugandan popular culture. That aspect is there because it is the traditional Ugandan way of engaging with a performance. When they watch a play/film, they interact with the actors. Nevertheless, I would like my movie to be screened in a cinema where people will watch quietly just like what happens in modern movie halls. I would like them to receive my films the same way they would receive any other.

SK: What languages do you use?

MN: I use English in the movies but sometimes I drop in some few lines of Luganda that I have to translate. I use subtitles because I am not aiming exclusively at local Ugandan audiences but I want to tell the story to the rest of the world.

SK: So, is the language aspect important?

MN: It wouldn't be very important but the reason why I didn't want to use Luganda was because I was moving from stage to film which meant using the same actors that performed in stage productions. Hence, using the same language [Luganda] would mean having actors who adlib or replicate live stage styles on screen, which is wrong. You have to remember that actors have been exposed to theatre for a long time and they know how that medium works; so even if they have not learnt their lines they adlib.

SK: When one watches your movies, there are three variations of English, Ugandan, West African and 'British' English. Do you deliberately use Ugandan English?

MN: Yes because I wouldn't want the story to get lost. In Uganda there are people who 'translate' the movies; I mean they do live voice-over translations. I don't know whether you have watched a Ugandan translation of a foreign movie because there are people in makeshift cinema halls whose occupation is to make these translations. It sounds like a running commentary. Some of my movies are translated as well. However, my aim is to enable people outside Uganda to watch, understand and enjoy the movie.

SK: Does this influence the casting process?

MN: Yes, because in the Ugandan context people will not understand the performer who speaks posh English, moreover, he will appear 'foreign' to the rest of the cast. I have a Nigerian performer in one of my movies who speaks English with a heavy accent that is different from Ugandan English. I intentionally gave her a character that is foreign to the community so that people notice her indigenous or (African) regional origin. Because there is an international Luganda speaking audience in the diaspora who I would want to watch my films in the movies I include some few lines of Luganda.

SK: What do you think about the comment that home movies use stage scripts not filmic scripts?

MN: It is because we don't have film schools, and people have no reading culture. I have a large library but when I invite people to borrow books on film no one bothers to come. With theatre, they know how it works so they tend do what they want.

SK: Is the home movie just a phenomenon or does it have a future?

MN: It will fade into television soaps and serials.

SK: Why?

MN: Because I don't think it has a sense of direction. I don't think home movies will survive.

SK: Won't they fade into full-blown films?

MN: May be if they change the way they are made.

SK: Do you think you will come to a point when you remake your movies into full films?

MN: I don't think so. Maybe directors will do if they want to remake them.

SK: Have you been in touch with the so-called serious committed Ugandan writers from the 70s and 80s?

MN: Not really...I think it is because I don't know where to find them. Mind you, a few of them are outside the country.

SK: Tell me something about your own work as a writer or a director.

MN: I like making quality movies, scriptwriting and casting. I like focusing on the best product; something better than what came before.

SK: What do you see as the important themes that you may pursue in the future especially if you are to reflect on Uganda after the 1986 grassroots struggle?

MN: I grew up after the Milton Obote regime of the early 1980s. This is the time when ethnic discrimination was widespread particularly concerning people from Northern Uganda. I would like to work on this theme. Another area I want to explore concerns the growing up experience of King Oyo of Toro Kingdom [in Western Uganda]. We don't know what happened during the sixteen-year period from when he was crowned aged three years until his eighteenth birthday when he took charge of the kingdom. Finally, I would like to work on a script exploring the world of night dancers (wizards) because I believe that practice or cult only exists in Uganda.

SK: Have you read Nuwa Sentongo's play, *The Invisible Bond*[7]?

MN: No. When I was at Kampala High School, my colleagues, [Benoni] Kibuuka and [Charles] Senkubuge, told me that they had taken part in the production. I may make a filmic adaptation of the play.

SK: Apart from the adaptation of *Tendo Sisters* to a home movie, what else are you working on now?

MN: I am working on a movie about a childless couple.

SK: Why?

MN: Just as I told you, I see these things happening around me; stuff we don't talk about, so if we bring them into the open we may be more accepting about people's situations. If we expose the issues, the process may provide answers or solutions and give the audience a different perspective of the problem.

SK: I have known of people who have had no children but have adapted by adopting children.

MN: But have they been successful in their venture?

SK: I think they have but I know that in Uganda, people will blame...

MN: Blame the woman.

SK: In that case, do you see *KinaUganda* as an instrument to address the problems of modern Uganda?

MN: I look at it as a medium for telling our stories and definitely, when you tell a story you have to have a solution to the problem. To me storytelling is about identifying a problem, telling a story about the problem and finding a solution to the problem. Therefore, I look at *KinaUganda* as a form that is trying to tell our stories.

SK: Is there anything you would like to say?

MN: Making a movie in Uganda is very expensive although making money out of it is much more expensive. The government is not helping so much but I wouldn't say they are the problem, so I would just love to call upon filmmakers to get together and try to work to uplift the industry.

SK: Is it possible to work as a cooperative?

MN: May be...if we reach some form of agreement. However, because you are a director in your own entity when you meet with your colleagues you find it difficult to blend. I am not worried whether the government knows that we exist or not but I just want filmmakers to come together.

SK: Do Western film artists inform your work?

MN: Somehow.

SK: How?

MN: I am fond of Tyler Perry. I like the way he tells the story of how black Americans can live better. Just like him, I am trying to tell Ugandan stories which demonstrate that people can change their lives.

SK: Thank very much.[8]

An Interview with Ashraf Simwogerere

It is evident from his filmography that Simwogerere, reputed to be the most successful *KinaUganda* director, has expanded his movie portfolio since *Feelings of Struggle*. For this interview, I wanted to underline key aspects of his career in film. In particular, I wanted to explore the socio-political context informing his work, including movies such as *Murder in the City* and *Mukajanga*. And in addition, I wanted to discuss the absence of strong women characters in his movies. We talked in the Green Room at the Uganda National Theatre, Kampala, which is the meeting point for many Ugandan artists. At the start of our conversation I asked him which language he would prefer for the interview; not surprisingly, while he indicated that he was comfortable speaking in English and Luganda, most of his responses were in the latter.

SK: How did you start in theatre and *KinaUganda*?

IS: I spent twenty-four years working in theatre as a playwright, actor and director. I started acting in dramas when I was in primary school but when I joined Kampala High School I met Joy Matovu who introduced me to Kampala Dramactors. This group later broke up and they formed the present day Bakayimbira Dramactors. During that period we staged Shaw's *Androcles and the Lion* [1946], Soyinka's *The Lion and the Jewel* [1963] and *The Road* [1965]. However, at that time I was acting like a parrot because I did not even understand the plays. Although I went to Makerere University to study dentistry, I continued acting with another group, The Black Pearls. In 1994, I wrote my first play, *Omuyaga mu Makoola* that won the prize for the best production. In 1994, we formed our performance company, The Diamond Ensemble. Our most successful project was *London Shock*, staged both in Kampala and in London, in 1999. The implication in the play is refugees should not look at London as a solution for all their problems. Following the live productions, we filmed the selected scenes on locations in London and Kampala. Uganda Television (UTV) serialised the play but it only lasted six weeks, therefore, they asked us to make more episodes. This was very demanding especially because we were filming on location every week. UTV would give us a camera for three hours, which meant we would shoot on Tuesdays, edit on Thursdays and these would air on the weekend. The play became very popular with the audience and within four years, we aired thirty eight episodes. Nevertheless, local productions were not popular with sponsors so we were always competing with these for up to four years. When Nigerian films came on the scene in 2004 it gave me an idea to make my own full-length movie. I bought my own camera, a Sony DSR-PD170. I had a young man, Kimera, who had trained in Nairobi, Kenya. I know how to tell a story, so I was determined to venture into the industry. We filmed, edited, and premiered a movie on a young man's struggle through life. The story was *Feelings Struggle*. Some professional cameramen, for example, Faustin Misanvu and George Sengendo, formerly of Uganda Television (UTV), who attended the premier screening of the movie were impressed. Some other people had started making local movies but they had problems marketing and distributing them; however, our marketing was effective. The film craft was not the best but the audience liked the story, and I have never looked back. The movie premiered in Britain where it was a hit with the African diaspora community. A company called Urban bought the distribution rights. Up to now, this film has been the most profitable. My other profitable film is *Mukajanga.*

SK: Say something about your work.

AS: First of all, my work is affected by the shortage of money to fund large projects. Secondly, I experience problems with the professional attitude of people working in the industry. Ugandan performers lack professionalism and this is affected by the culture's attitude to theatre. They use the concept, '*ngenda kuzanya'*, which loosely translated means, 'I am going to play'. This connoted a lack of seriousness or commitment, for instance, they don't always keep time. It is disappointing that the good ones do not keep time. For this reason, I always kick them off the production. Cinematographers do not always do that and worst of all, they hate directors who impose their authority. Even though we don't have movie stars (only stage stars), there are no stars cast in major roles in my films because they give me headaches. When I am casting I avoid them unless that person gives me the commitment. If you dock their pay, because of undisciplined behaviour, they don't turn up; a situation that may arise after you have shot half of the script.

SK: Under what circumstances did *KinaUganda* start?

AS: To begin with Ugandans had started making films on a small scale, but the arrival of *EkiNigeriya* (Nollywood) on the scene demonstrated that our stories were similar to the Nigerians so they expanded their activities. I realised that if people like Nigerian stories they will be more excited by well-made local movies. The key issue is that all of us have learnt through experience, by trial and error. The truth is, *KinaUganda* is very popular with Ugandans in the diaspora.

During the initial period, there were many writers, producers and stage scripts but very few screenplay scriptwriters and actors; hence, people who formerly worked in theatre joined film production. As a result, when popular theatre actors, for instance, Kato Lubwama and Abby Mukiibi, are in a movie, it sells a lot. Most Ugandans buy the movies because 'their' favourite actors are the stars of the show. Nevertheless, there are people such as Maisha (a training organisation for filmmaking) who, apart from training people, bring into the country professional directors and producers to conduct workshops. That said, we are still in a transition stage moving from stage to screen.

SK: How has the transition from stage to screen impacted the way you make films?

AS: Stories are the same but the delivery differs. The way you present a play on stage is different to the way you produce it for the screen. Mind you, my initial training was rooted in live theatre performances and on stage, you engage with eyes and ears but for the screen, you are solely focusing on the visual. You have to imagine that you are producing a movie for the Chinese to watch and understand. For example, we buy Chinese films in which characters speak Mandarin, but the housemaid (semi-literate in English) at home will watch it and narrate the story. Now there lies the difference; before venturing into movie making, we were focusing on the dialogue at the expense of the visual images but now we are trying to strike a balance.

SK: Some people say home movies lack artistic merit, and that the industry is just moneymaking, merely showing effects, magic or witchcraft….

AS: The percentage of *KinaUganda* films that focus on magic is very small. However, in Nigeria, the situation may be different, because from my experience - I have been to the country several times - witchcraft is common and acceptable in some indigenous groups. I disagree with the allegation that there is plenty of witchcraft in our movies. Nevertheless, while there will be a few producers who want to copy *EkiNigeriya* styles, most of us have made a conscious effort to avoid presenting scenes of magic and witchcraft. On the issue of labelling home movie producers as money-makers one has to draw a line between stage and filmic productions. In the Ugandan theatre context, if you have a working script, you may gather some people together, cast, rehearse, advertise and stage the play. In fact, you may premier your play without investing any money. However, in filmmaking you need a lot of capital before you start. When I started I thought I would mint money but I realised that it would be difficult therefore, after filming the movie I had to hawk it, screening it in small places around the country; for instance, in Jinja, Mbarara, Masaka and Entebbe. Surprisingly, most people thought I had made a lot of money so they jumped on the bandwagon. However, as I said earlier, there are few scriptwriters and skilled directors of photography, therefore, their film scripts were underdeveloped; in addition, their artistic work and photography were poor. Unlike Kenya where there are many film schools, Uganda has none. Nevertheless, I don't discourage anyone from venturing into the industry, all I say is that we should get together and start training. Although the university has a section in the literature department that focuses on critical cinematography there are hardly any local films to critique.

SK: There was a German national who ran a film school during the early eighties…

AS: Those were Germans who came in during Obote's political regime but they left soon after his government was overthrown. Our colonisers (the British) did not encourage this craft, whereas if you look at Kenya where they developed the industry, the local people are skilled. In the current economic climate, you can start to make a film on a limited budget. People with limited funds come to me wanting to start filming a movie. Maybe this is better because my view is that artistic content will follow after we have launched ourselves into the trade.

SK: How do you go about developing your scripts? How long does it take you?

AS: It depends on the project. I got training at the Makerere University Department of Music, Dance and Drama. I also attended a summer residence at the Royal Court [in Britain]. Therefore, I have developed script-writing skills. I have learnt other skills through correspondence studies or e-materials downloaded from the internet. It [the script] takes me up to a month to write the draft, but if it needs researching, it may take longer. My handicap is English. If I am working on a commissioned project where the person wants it in English I have to look for a translator. After writing the script, I give it to various people to read it, both ordinary people and academics at the Makerere University. After their feedback, I write the final scripts. Nevertheless, if it is in Luganda, it takes a short time. For instance, since *Mukajanga* was a historical play, I did not want to write it in foreign languages other than Luganda, so it took a short time. The only other languages were Runyankore and Rutooro because I wanted characters from other indigenous groups to speak in their languages.

SK: How long did you take to write *Mukajanga*?

AS: It took six months to research. The advantage was that everything was in Buganda, the central region, and I did not need to go up country.

SK: Did you interview many people?

AS: Wakayima, my grandfather who died in 1979, was a great resource. At the time, he was over one hundred years of age. When they killed the martyrs, he was about six years old. He lived in Kira village, a suburb of Namugongo one of the main sites of the massacres. One day in 1977, when he was hospitalised in Mengo Hospital, they played *Bewaayo*, the Church of Uganda martyrs' anthem. However, when he heard the chorus, 'bewaayo... *battibwa nga bayimba*' (they died singing...) his response was that those reports had been falsified. He said that they cried a lot. In addition, he told me about Kyaliwajjala, which is on the outskirts of Namugongo.

SK: Why do they call it Kyaliwajjala?

AS: The boys thought that King Mwanga was joking and he wouldn't massacre them because they were his friends. They expected him to send a messenger to instruct Mukajanga to stay the execution; therefore, they resisted the guards' commands to move them at a fast speed. Unfortunately, the guards in a streak of violence hit them and threw their bodies in the King's gardens, looked after by Kyaliwajjala. Hence the saying, 'What happened at Kyaliwajja's garden's is shocking'.

SK: I want to know about King Mwanga as a young man, what are the possible sources of information?

AS: You may go to Mackay's archives at Mackay's Church in Nateete (five miles from Kampala City Centre) or his contemporary the Roman Catholic Mapera's archives (Fr. Loudel) at Mapera Church Place in Kasubi, just three miles from Kampala. Mackay was the leader of the CMS (Church Missionary Society) missionaries while Mapera (Fr. Loudel) led the White Fathers Missionaries of Africa group[9]. The problem is that their records are biased because the narratives are told from a European perspective. But there is a man called Bulwadda whose archives are kept by his great grandchildren. He used to be Mwanga's Arabic translator. Unfortunately, many of the diaries have not been fully translated, from Arabic into English.

SK: How do you go about shooting the screenplay?

AS: I don't do auditions. Many people who come to auditions are not good actors; they are after jobs. Out of 300 who come, you may only need 20. I like people who have a passion for the acting. Sometimes I approach people who I have seen in films or on stage. It might take me a month before I finalise casting and start filming. I try to change cameramen (cinematographers) or directors of photography (DPO) depending on their work portfolio. I avoid people who film documentaries or news reports. They are not as artistic as those who film music videos. For example, Bashir, the cameraman for *Mukajanga,* had previously worked with music video producers. Because the budgets are limited, I try not to spend a long time shooting; at the same time, I avoid using numerous locations.

SK: How do you finance your productions?

AS: I use my own resources. From the start, I inform the cast that since I have limited resources I will pay them per hour/day spent on location. They are not paid if they don't turn up. Sometimes I make part-payments and the rest is paid following the completion of the project. These days it is easy to talk to distributors because they like my work. They pay you an advance; therefore, they fund part of the projects. Therefore, they have funded all my recent film projects.

SK: How do you distribute the movies?

AS: That is a big challenge. Apart from my first film, I have not distributed any of my movies. We start our distribution at the Kampala movie premier by auctioning the DVDs; but after that, the distributors take over. They usually advertise on radio and television channels. Initially, I give them rights for three years but after that, I regain the copyrights. Although the new establishments of new cable television companies has been an exciting positive development for the movie maker, most of them are more interested in soaps which cost them up to 150 pounds as opposed to films/movies that cost 300 pounds a week in sponsorship.

SK: What are the sources of your stories?

AS: Most of my stories are from local news. I read local newspapers, watch and listen to television news but I do not read (source) stories from books. The last book I read was Apollo Lawoko's *The Dungeons of Nakasero* [2005].

SK: Tell us about your home movies, *Murder in the City*.

AS: *The Daily Monitor* was the first to publish the story. After it was alleged that Dr Kiyingi killed his wife, the ensuing court case was widely reported in the local newspapers. I used the opportunity to write a script with a (fictional) story with characters that had resonant experiences. One journalist who interviewed me asked whether I had based my film on that particular court case but my response was that these were similar not the same characters. At that point, I was already scheduled to attend the London premier of my movie, *Feelings Struggle*; in addition, I had arranged to shoot some scenes in London locations for a new play. The presiding judge's reaction to the movie's reviews was to summon me to court to explain why I was prejudicing the case of the defendant (Dr Kiyingi). I got the court summons and notice of a court date on my return to Kampala. The Ugandan Citizens Rescue Organisation (CITRO) sponsored a lawyer to represent me in court. The judge concluded that although the story was similar there was no evidence that I had based it on the case.

SK: Do you base your narratives on oral folk stories?

AS: Sometimes I do. But apart from the folk stories, I base some on Ugandan contemporary socio-political experiences. My new film is based on the [Yoweri] Museveni's Luweero triangle liberation struggle. I have called it *Museveni the Wild Cat.*[10] When Museveni was in the 'bush' (waging a guerrilla war against the Uganda government) many people, particularly members of the armed forces, believed in the fallacy that he used special powers to turn himself into a cat or other forms of wild animals. For instance, one day a man was travelling along Gayaza Road, northeast of Kampala, when at Magigye 'road block' (an army checkpoint) a cat escaped from his bag. The army men panicked, shot at the cat but it disappeared. The man was accused of collaborating with the 'bandits' (guerrillas) and we all suspected that he was killed afterwards.

Other movies in this category include a movie based on the Baganda myth, *Kintu and Nambi.* However, I use it for demonstrations at film festivals. You know it is impossible to market a fifteen-minute movie DVD in Uganda.

SK: Have you thought about adapting Ugandan literary works?

AS: In Uganda, the reading culture is very poor. A large percentage of Ugandans like watching films but they do not buy or read books. For example, apart from secondary school students how many people have read Soyinka's play, *The Lion and the Jewel.* Alex Mukulu's *Wounds of Africa* [1993] is a published play but I don't know whether many people have read it whereas hundreds watched it at the National Theatre. So, if he made it into a movie it would help him reach a wider audience.

SK: What stories do you tell?

AS: Melodramatic stories especially those that narrate events or reflect on people's urban experiences. However, my interest is in faction.

SK: What is your favourite film?

AS: *Feelings Struggle,* my first film, set me up and gave me a reputation as a good movie director. Because of this film, people call me the pioneer. *Murder in the City* made me a household name; *Honourable* introduced me to multinational sponsors and partnerships work with non-government organisations (NGO), and *Mukajanga* put me on the international market. I like *Mukajanga* because of the professional work I invested in it. However, although people call me the pioneer of Ugandan movies I was not the first one on the scene.

SK: Wasn't Jimmy Katumba, the late popular music theatre artist, the first person to make a local Ugandan movie?

AS: No, it is Ngoma Players when you made *The City Game* television episodes in the late seventies. *The City Game* reminds [one] of Katende Lutwama because he played a key role both as a star and in influencing me to think about the moving image as an option to stage plays. The only problem is that you never marketed your films.

SK: Unlike today, at the time very few people owned TV sets.

AS: In Uganda people who buy films are very few, maybe not more than 10,000, however, in Nigeria there is a large market. In Ugandan village communities there are very few people who own video players but quite a few will have television sets. Those who own DVDs have to hide them because they fear being robbed.

SK: In *KinaUganda* home movies, cameras zoom in on beautiful women, cars, good décor. Why?

AS: That is a Nigerian influence but it is not evident in my films. It is not a Ugandan culture, nevertheless, it is encouraged by the distributors who push this practice, and therefore, cars used in filming may include SUVs or other front-wheel drive vehicles, Mercedes Benz and other expensive cars. Most times, they forget that the story cannot accommodate these things. Concerning houses, I watched a film where someone used a hotel as the main character's home. Nonetheless, this is not true of Ugandan society but the directors are using stereotypes.

SK: Why don't we have strong women in these stories?

AS: Well, if you look at the Holy Scriptures or the Koran, women are the sinners. We tend to present stereotypes of our society that takes women as bad people. Arguably, the directors are men who are products of these ideologies, so they project weak women. However, Mariam Ndagire as a female director is trying to project positive female characters.

SK: How are you going to change these representations of stereotypes?

AS: I have tried in some of my films, for instance, in *Honourable* I have positive female characters. I am aware that films play a role in changing people's attitudes and perceptions but you will note that women, who control homes and make up a large percentage of our audiences, like films with evil women characters. By extension, in Uganda where most people employ house girls to look after their homes and care for the children, surprisingly, what house girls (housemaids) enjoy is what the men enjoy.

SK: In the Luweero triangle movie, are you going to present the strong female liberators (fighters)?

AS: Yes, fighters like Lieutenant Colonel Nalweyiso and Captain Zizinga, but the problem is that the leaders of the uprising also leave them out of the narrative of the struggle. These were the first ever women to join the army in Uganda...

SK: Nobody has told their stories...

AS: Not yet...even in Museveni's *Mustard Seed*, they are not mentioned. But I shall try to project those women who were at the frontline. I shall be exploring Hajati Mukwaya's (another brave female liberator) experiences in the 'bush'.

SK: Do you receive feedback from the audience?

AS: Yes, I try to talk to the audience after the screening of my movies. The problem with Uganda is that because of insecurities during Milton Obote's second presidency (1980 - 1985), live theatre performances would last up to four hours. Contrary to this, movies are two hours in length. Since people remain seated, I take the opportunity to ask them for their views.

Journalists are a problem because they try to compare you with international filmmakers such as Kevin MacDonald, the director of the *Last King of Scotland*; but we try to respond to their interviews by informing them that the *KinaUganda* industry is still in its infancy. There are major problems of sound for our films because on many occasions we use camera mikes [microphones].

SK: Can you comment on the fact that in live performances people tend to talk to the actors and interact with the audience.

AS: I am happy with it because when it happens I know my message has been delivered. My problem is when they react negatively to a sad scene.

SK: Do you have a policy of encouraging upcoming directors?

AS: I am organising a clinic that will last for a month. I will be taking on 20 people. I will not charge them a lot.
SK: When will this film be ready?
AS: June this year.
SK: Thank you[11]

Overview of *KinaUganda*

Following the revolution in video technology in the 1980s, the most significant development in the distribution and presentation of Ugandan home movies has been the technological evolution of digital video discs (DVD), and their proliferation in Uganda in the twenty-first century. The transformation of (indigenous) relationships and the benefits of these technologies have enabled the growth of low-budget *KinaUganda* home movie productions that aim to entertain Ugandans. Since the audience has 'more control over the way that film and television can be watched, consumed and collected' (Paul Grainge, 2003:11), the new media technologies have created a wider market for popular performances albeit at the expense of live theatre where attendance has dwindled. Unlike other African countries, Uganda during Amin's regime (1971 - 1979) imported no Western films, therefore, to generate an income cinema owners converted halls into playhouses. The situation where international distributors dump their films in a country has no bearing on the development or not of a Ugandan local film industry since it is only in the nineteen-nineties that international distributors started coming back into the country. In addition, state bureaucracy does not encumber home movie producers for, apart from the copyright law, no laws regulate this industry. As discussed earlier in this book, an interesting development has been the increase in FM radio and independent television stations, which have multiplied since the 1993 de-regularisation and privatisation of the broadcasting/communications industry.

The problems faced by movie producers are finance and the reluctance by government to regulate the programming of foreign produced films in television media. As in Nigeria, home movies are 'produced on a shoestring', and producers belong to the 'informal sector of the economy' (Jonathan Haynes and Onookome Okome, 2000: 29). In their scramble to share some of the wealth generated from home movies various directors have rehashed television episodes and stage plays into home movies. Not surprisingly, some of the producers have little sense of film production and 'possess a dramatic consciousness that does not extend beyond the parlor audience mentality' (Afolobe Adesanya, 2000: 48). Consciously incorporating traditional and contemporary social and cultural norms, the home movies concentrate on common socio-political themes, for instance, sexuality, violence, corruption, ethnicity, gender and class, which emerge and intersect. Within this emerging space, various practices interact with (new) stories and myths, thereby constructing a dynamic (urban) performance genre.

Linguistically, *KinaUganda* is restricted to Luganda and English and its themes are repetitive. Few producers work exclusively in English but indigenous language movies, either in Luganda, or blending Luganda, Swahili, other Bantu languages and English, dominate the market because of the need for ordinary people to enjoy some form of entertainment (Adesanya, 2000:48). It is easy to recognise the story lines since they are mostly based on print media stories, shared life experiences or social gossip; once reconstituted by the producers and scriptwriters, they form the discourse of the home movie. Some of the movies are 'as naïve and unsophisticated in their 'visual aesthetics' as they are in their 'simple narrative' (Dovey and Impey, 2010: 63), nevertheless, they are popular because the audiences can identify with the performers since, many of them have transferred from stage to movie or are key presenters on FM radios. Comedy, melodrama, farce, and tragedy often overlap in these movies and as Haynes has observed about Nolllywood, 'stimulate conversation and gossip among viewers, preserving and extending forms of sociality' (Haynes, 2000: 27).

The ancient function of indigenous dance, music and song in enacting one's existence has not been transposed to the area of home movies. How far home movie practitioners as opposed to live theatre artists will adopt this in their future productions is debatable. Nevertheless, by using *Kadongo Kamu* (a late twentieth century music genre) in *Mukajanga,* Simwogerere successfully revises the meanings of the songs to present his 'preferred interpretations of lyrics [that] create[s] a stylistic and physical context for reception' (Rose, 1994: 9). This practice of defining twenty-first century Uganda could be described as 're-storying', to borrow a phrase from Campbell, or 'creating new stories to counter and displace the mythic ones that have, for so long, framed the vision' (Campbell, 2000: 94) of Uganda in the imagination of Ugandans and the world. Specifically significant in this process are the voices of women, children and the economically and politically disempowered members of the community. A small selection of home movies presents distinctive performances by women who use specific female interpretations of the key roles, to engage in dialogue with patriarchy and to assert their power. However, generally, popular re-presentations of vengeful, covetous, and self-centred women are common. These representations encode the cultural vision of womanhood and gender specifically more pronounced throughout Amin's reign. During that time, conservative Ugandans used derogative words, for instance, *BanaDubai* (women who transact business in Dubai) or *Ba-Auntie* (elderly women), connoting the new class of enterprising women.

KinaUganda and Nollywood share a common root (form and style) in Africa; specific social/political interests of their respective societies influence the trajectories of style and theme. While there are complex relations between Nollywood and *KinaUganda*, the latter is typified by its tendency to focus on one main narrative - the making of an evil woman. Additionally, the directors and scriptwriters interrogate internalised forms of oppression, conflict and violence of the new rich classes. The new stories and myths, for example, Simwogerere's *Honourable* and *Mukajanga*, or Ndagire's *Hearts in Pieces* and *Strength of a Stranger*, are symptomatic of the wider Ugandan mindset anxious to hold on to old certainties about cultural values, ethnicity, gender, identity, nation, and women's sexual liberation, while embracing post-Idi Amin economic and socio-political changes.

Mukajanga presents a failing state ruled by King Mutesa I's son, Mwanga, whose lieutenants' machinations lead to the murder of innocent boys. Its framing narrative is of the appointment of Mukajanga (Ashraf Simwogerere) as the army commander, one who still believes in the power of the gods. He is delegated to enforce the flailing King's wishes by any means possible. In this context, Mwanga's acts signify the meaning of the Luganda proverb, *ensi egula mirambo* (nationhood comes at the cost of [human] blood), or, you take death flippantly if it is not your own dying.

Although Mukajanga and the foreigners, namely, (Bishop) Hannington and Mackay, the Anglican missionaries, Mapera, the Roman Catholic missionary, and the Arabs, are never seen on stage, their presence in the country is reported to the audience. The movie scenes fall into several groups: those dealing with Mwanga's vitims, the page boys; those centred around King Mwanga; and those which show Mukajjanga and his fellow chiefs' moral conflicts and infightings. The sequence is framed by Mukajanga's discovery that the King has appointed him to replace the army commander, Senkoole. Power, greed, violence and jealousy intersect in these scenes telling a grisly tale of greed and power inherent in contemporary Uganda. What is at stake is the future of the nation tied inevitably to post-colonial ethnic and religious conflicts. As discussed in earlier chapters, the history of Buganda (and Uganda) is characterised by reigns of violence, hence, Simwogerere's portrayal of Mukajanga is brutal, representing the inevitable cyclic violence. In the movie, Mukajanga and his subordinates are colonised by power while the foreigners are shown to use indigenous Ugandans as a blank slate on which to write. In favour of power, the King and his lieutenants murder young boys, and in particular, in an act symbolic of his thirst for power, Senkoole, Mukajanga's assistant, murders his own daughter.

Simwogerere's writing of history evidences his authorisation of a particular colonial moment, specifically illustrated by the manner in which he conflates two important events of massacre that happened in the reigns of both King Mutesa I and Mwanga. Notably, before the arrival of the Christian missionaries in Uganda, Mutesa's name was Mukaabya, a name that resonated with his violent character. This play reminds us of the unavoidability of history in the interrelatedness of the past, present and future for, Mutesa I's murderous trait returns in Mwanga's reign as evidenced in the film by Mukajanga and his lieutenants' behaviour. Moreover, as the audience will know, the past returned in Amin and Obote's regimes.

By putting Mukajanga, indigenous religion and Islam at the centre of the plot, and drawing on oral counter-narratives, Simwogerere manipulates his audience's cultural and religious memory to highlight relevant questions about postcolonial representations of the massacres. In the movie, the struggle of indigenous religions to break away from the grip of the three foreign religions (Protestant, Roman Catholic and Islam), here embodied in Mukajanga and his wife is an attempt to express society's discontent with the status quo. In this way, Simwogerere constructs an affective environment that would encourage his audience to search for explanations for Mukajanga and his lieutenants' behaviour.

Adopting a religious (Islamic) outsider's identity, Simwogerere, in *Mukajanga*, develops the Uganda martyrs' story and allows it to explore new lines of inquiry and creativity. He is able to re-present the tale and thus reframe the sanitised version, which claims that Mwanga's victims sang religious songs as they were massacred (Interview, 9 April 2010). In the process of revising the martyrs' narrative, he reframes the place and roles of religion, power and post-coloniality in order to underline his views on governance and politics in contemporary Uganda.

What, then can we conclude about the connections between socio-political changes and the emergence of *KinaUganda*? In the performing arts, the impact of post-1986 political order, communication, economic and media liberalisation is felt, perhaps most noticeably, in the decline of live theatre and the development of home movies. And more so, in the home movies' exploration of political history, social inequalities and violence. Noticeably, as with Nollywood, home movies are not produced for the elite but are intended for the ordinary person who formerly enjoyed plays at the National Theatre and other numerous playhouses during the nineteen-eighties and nineteen-nineties. These people went to theatre to be entertained and to forget, albeit shortly, the violence in the outside world. *KinaUganda* draws on specific genres such as melodrama and 'cheap' comedy, which are similar to many West African films. Nevertheless, its film language is rooted in traditional folk song and *katemba* performance practice in which farce, tragicomedy, parody and satire are central.

CONCLUSION

In examining Ugandan theatre today and as we contemplate the effect of violence on the dramatic works in this book, we ask ourselves: what options for fairness do ordinary people have when their freedom is threatened? In Lubwa p'Chong's *The Madman*, the Madman reminds Walukagga about the wisdom of staying calm in the face of adversity: 'We laugh to show the whiteness of our teeth. We don't laugh because we are happy' (Lubwa p'Chong, 1989: 57). He continues, 'If it was because of happiness that people laughed, there would be nobody laughing in this chiefdom. Perhaps only Chief' (*The Madman*, p. 57). Had Walukagga's story been transformed from a folktale (whose aim was to check the morals of traditional rulers) to a performance of resistance to modern autocracy? This study began with the question of the existence of a theatre of resistance, its characteristics and functions under oppressive institutions. As *The Madman* (or Lubwa p'Chong) reminds us, theatre and the culture of (passive) resistance had become part of life in Uganda; so, people staged popular dances, folksongs and satirical dramatic skits for entertainment. Laughter was one of their survival strategies since, similar to humour, it is subversive and in theatre, it enables the performers to construct bonds with the audience. This dialogical relationship is underlined in the scene where Walukagga discloses to Madman Chief's demand for a man fabricated from steel. The scene, underlined by rhythm and musicality, ends with the comments that the man should have 'five balls' and the strength to 'pull the balls of Chief Hard!' (p. 57). Just like elsewhere in his writing, in this scene Lubwa p'Chong comes closest to demonstrating the type of theatre discussed in this book: a theatre that is grounded in pre-colonial orature, folkloric texts and other expressive cultural forms, and yet at close examination it intersects with Western and various non-indigenous forms. The theatre of resistance discussed in this book differs from the protracted resistances against oppressive institutions, which mark Uganda's history since colonisation in reflecting on performance in public and private spaces. However, are all performances discussed in this book transgressive? Do all the artists practise resistance in their works?

Since the beginning of the colonial rule in 1890, Uganda has experienced periods of instability and violence, caused by, among other factors, indigenous and ethnic hatred and the military impunity for violence against ordinary people. After Amin's military regime, people had hoped that institutionalised violence had ended, however, yet another circle of violence started with the second UPC government. While performances staged throughout the post-independent period allow the expression of dissident ideas, not all belong to the theatre of resistance. Some artists, such as Sentongo, Mukiibi, Kibuuka, Katumba and even *Kadongo Kamu* groups, blended critical plays with other farcical and comedy performances.

The period between 1969 and 1986 marked changes in the political landscape: these included the militarisation of state institutions, increased surveillance of ordinary people, a declining economy and moral decadence. Moreover, Amin's expulsion of Ugandan Asians on 7 August 1972 had more dramatic consequences than he could have intended since instead of correcting the imbalance of economic power between the indigenous Ugandans and Asians (strangers), it created hatred and precipitated the breakdown of relationships between indigenous groups, individuals, and between individuals and the state. This action inadvertently put the military at the centre of the debate on the state of the nation, its identity and virtues. These factors, reflected in the performance works in this book, influenced the transformation of theatre. As Lubwa p'Chong's Madman states, 'everything has changed and is changing. Everything and everybody' (*The Madman*, p. 61).

How is this close to Senkubuge and Kibuuka's *Ku Ggirikiti: State of the Nation* (2012), which is a new perspective of theatre of protest?[1] In one scene, Kikapu, who comes on stage carrying a sack that he claims to represent Noah's Ark, tells people that his hope is in the new nation:

> *Essuubi lyange oliri mu kyombo kino ... emisota gyo ngifunye ... enfuddu Omwana azireeta. Wiki egya ngenda Kaseese waliwo envubu ezitayaaya ku kyalo, wild life authority tetuuka abantu mu kifo ky'okuzitta ka ngende nzireete...kimu ku kimu ngenda kubifuna olwo ntandike eggwanga eddonde ... lwaki essuubi lyanzigwamu? Noah bamuyita mulalu. Amataba lwegajja lwebakizuula nti ssi mulalu naye nga tebakkyalina kyebazza...lino lyo ligenda....Ndyoke nkole eryange....Nga buli muntu asooka kufa ku gwanga lino nga tanelowoozaako.*
>
> [This boat is my best hope ... I've collected the vipers ... As for the tortoises, the young man will deliver them to me. Next week, I will go to Kaseese where I intend to capture some of those free-range hippopotamuses that roam the villages. You see, the Wild Life department has not yet

> established an office in the area, therefore, instead of the villagers having to kill them, let me go and collect them myself. I will collect the items, one by one after which, I will start a specially modified new nation. Why should I lose hope? They called Noah a madman! It was not until the floods came when they discovered that he was not mad. However, by that time it was too late … they could not save anything. Right now, the floods are coming … this nation is dead… I shall start my own nation … where people have to think about and work for the nation before paying attention to their own needs.]
>
> (*State of the Nation*, p. 9)

In its performance strategies that link the performers and the audience with each other, this play subverts the narratives that have previously secured the reputation of Uganda's post-liberation history.[2] Undeniably, it should be stated that conflict has not ended in the whole of Uganda. Therefore, the reference to reptiles and animals - vipers, hippopotamuses, and tortoises - gives way to nuanced reflections about the state of a nation in paralysis. The state is 'dead', the economy needs cleansing, yet the people who would do it are busy 'paying attention to their own needs' (*State of the Nation*, p. 9) Because the playwrights satirise nepotism, corruption and abuse of power that have haunted Uganda since independence they implicate current leaders as well as the audience. The Media Council and the police found the performance subversive, specifically in its exposure of issues that are uncomfortable with a cross-section of the political elite and the armed forces.

In several important ways, in mimicking the military and political elites, *State of the Nation* has reminded the audience about the vitality of live theatre. It is impossible to watch *State of the Nation* and ignore either the aesthetics of the performance or the exploitation that mark the anguish within Uganda. Yet, the play is self-consciously satirical, and this way, more aesthetically pleasing and entertaining than it would otherwise be. The parliamentary building according to Kikapu, 'used to host the state of the nation's address until the numbers of the nappers *manya* (I mean) those listening while sleeping increased' (*State of the Nation*, p. 1) offers no hope to the people, only a metaphor for institutional degeneration. Throughout the play, the playwrights attempt to reclaim the life stories of the audience, a practice that resonates with Edward Said's view in *Culture and Resistance* (2003). Said argues 'One has to keep telling the story in as many new ways as possible, as insistently as possible, and in as compelling a way as possible, to keep attention on it, because there is a fear that it might disappear' (Barsamanian and Said, 2003: 187). Ngugi, whose ideas have been discussed in the introduction, wrote in 1998 that like mirrors, performances, apart from 'focusi[ng] on the intended object', are likely to 'reflect other objects around, which makes those viewing the scene see more into it than they were intended to do' (Ngugi, 1998, pp. 30-31). He concludes that 'a mirror that did not reflect would be negating itself as a mirror' (p. 128). This relates to the idea of embedding orature in contemporary theatre, revitalising the traditional function of the artist, as the voice of the people and society's 'mirror'. Efforts to separate *katemba* (performance) into categories of *kuzina* (dance), *kuyimba* (music), *kuzannya* (drama or to play) let alone *Kina*Uganda, inevitably simplifies the complexities of performance and may eliminate its ability to transform and reflect events in society. Undeniably, some of the most interesting transformations of stage plays embedded theatrical expressions popular with the audience. However, as old artists retired, died or were 'disappeared', the cycle of conflicts ended, so did the aesthetics of performance shift and embed modern styles and forms. This study has demonstrated how various performances articulated the relationship between ordinary people and oppressive institutions, private and public spaces, and the various oppositional discourses constructed there.

Dramas such as *State of the Nation* expose the crisis in live theatre because in its shift to a commercialised institution it had so far failed to engage critically with the socio-political reality of society. Once again, the Media Council's reaction to the play offers clues to theatre's changing context. My argument here is that whether the dramas are staged in defiance of military or civilian institutions to mock the culture of greed, these works, in theatre or film, allow the artists to redefine the performance space so as to reaffirm people's humanity and identity.

The focus of this book has been on theatre and the conversation between dance, music, drama and resistance inscribed in the notion of performance. Many artists discussed here have explored the borders between (formal) drama(s) and of music, dance, ritual, song and audience participation; additionally, they have borrowed the aesthetics, contents, styles and qualities of these art forms to investigate and expand their practice in a variety of ways.

The descriptions of the work of pioneering theatre artists, for the most part, do not explain the activities, and experiences, of audiences who were already participating in various forms of performance. In the Ugandan experience, the performer has always been an independent-minded individual who travelled across the country entertaining people and making forthright criticisms. He depended on the freedom from communal control and limitations that society offered him. What travelling musicians and contemporary performers have in common, however, is the experience of the audience and the public space, particularly in the post-colonial urban spaces, theatre and play houses, where various ethnicities meet and interact. And in urban areas, people, performance forms and styles underwent changes which mark the transformation of indigenous theatre expression into hybrid performances or *katemba*. Simply put, *katemba* is a performance through which an artist transforms memory and lived experience into entertainment and/or statements of resistance. *Katemba*, then, signals the transgression of public and private spaces. While indigenous religion believers see acts of possession (*kutemba*) and transgression as occurring to people in a shrine within a ritual performance, artists in theatre undertake acts of transformation (and transgression) as they examine socio-political issues on stage; and in addition, they move between various ethnic and western theatrical forms of expression.

Notably, not all performance and theatre was theatre of resistance. Various artists continued to produce theatre (strictly) for entertainment. Some of the latter theatre performances, particularly after 1962, were rooted in indigenous forms and performance traditions. p' Bitek has argued that in indigenous communities, although some artists are 'in one way or another greater than others', 'every individual is an artist' (1986: 35-6). However, in formal theatre, once the boundaries between drama, dance and music are blurred, artists create hybrid performances that appeal to their audiences; from this practice emerges artistic challenges to political oppression. We are reminded that in pre-colonial times there were no theatre houses but performances that sanctioned and criticised people took place. Many performances involved song dances andgenerally they were aimed to sanction behaviuor and to criticise rulers who were disrespecul to the people. p'Bitek's notes the community's practice of extemporising their own tunes while dancing the love dance, *Orak*. He observes that in response to the chief performer's rhythm (song) men sing the praises of their lovers, (p. 31). Similarly, in contemporary performances audiences gripped by the 'beat' or message of the play, participate in a performance. In this context, participation may be artistic or political.

This book has shown that what is important in the performance practice is the embedment of music, song and dance in theatre and (formal) drama), ascribing new meaning to elements of indigenous performance. Within the constrictions of oppressive laws as well as western performance spaces, this practice allows artists to construct critical statements. Beginning with Serumaga's non-verbal *Renga Moi* to Kawadwa's musical plays, which draw on Baganda dance and music, or, Ruganda's *The Burdens* to Lubwa p'Chong's *The Last Safari*, based on Acholi folktales, Bwola dance and ritual respectively these artists suggest significant ways in which indigenous performance can reinvigorate discourses of resistance in the present. In addition, in their performances and writing, the artists transmit the liveliness and quality of performance expressions so that, in spite of state censorship, messages of protest are still conveyed. The most notable outcome of this practice, one that relates to most artists discussed in this study, is the aesthetic quality of their performances, performances in which not only music, song and dance become part of the text but also the audience participation takes a central position. Moving between dialogue and song, (instrumental) music, ritual, and recitation, Serumaga, Kibuuka and Bakayimbira, Kadongo Kamu and The Ebonies, Kiyingi and Sentongo, building on the popular performance traditions, develop new ways of staging protests, challenging audiences to examine critically their lived experiences. Despite the criticisms aimed against the hybridisation of indigenous theatrical expressions, hybridisation and syncretism has always been part of performance practice in Uganda. To view Ugandan theatre as ethnically authentic, unaffected by both inter-ethnic and Western practices is not possible.

Notwithstanding different assumptions about the presentation, representations, and theorisations of performance, that characterise the area of theatre in East Africa, p'Bitek, Ngugi, Nkashama, Pio Zirimu, Elvania Zirimu, Bukenya, Serumaga, and Mugambi show otherwise. As my discussion has indicated, these writers have generated critical and theoretical interpretations of indigenous and contemporary performances that contribute to, and signify, the beginning of a theory of African performance. In Pio Zirimu's 'An Approach to Black Aesthetics' he observes that 'critics who apply aesthetic critical standards enunciated by conventional white critics and theorists are ape-critics' (1971: 5). At the same time, echoing p'Bitek but not dismissing western approaches, he argues for a Ugandan/black-centred critical discourse when he states that 'The authentic critical standards 'must be born from the works of specific societies and their representative creators' (1971:59). This book began with a discussion of the development of a critical framework for Ugandan theatre; and it touched on what aesthetic and critical assumptions characterise performance. As Mugambi (1996) suggests, indigenous elements fundamental to oral narratives (and performance) have 'migrated' and become part of performance and theatre discourse. Yet, as demonstrated in this book, in order to open a dialogue with the contemporary audiences, it is important for individual artists to construct their own aesthetics, styles and forms. To this end, the discursive approaches and strategies presented by artists and critics in this study begin to present the critical framework that Pio Zirimu, p'Bitek and Bukenya, among others, have been looking for. Collectively, the foregoing authors/critics, without imposing Western critical models, and voices, on African theatre and performance, offer new interpretations mainly rooted in indigenous (aesthetic) discourses and frameworks.

Specifically because of the indigenously diverse selection of artists, this book has examined different performance practices and styles located within the foregoing cohesive groups. One of the main purposes has been to highlight the conversations between various ethnic theatrical expressions. Therefore, from within their indigenous locations, the works of Kiyingi, Kawadwa, Kibuuka and Bakayimbira, Katumba and Lubwa p'Chong, among others, self-consciously or not, undeniably cross boundaries even if the political references are intended to reinforce their separateness. African theatre can therefore choose what to use or leave out.

Throughout the process of writing this work, a number of questions have lingered in my mind, specifically, concerning the meaning of the 'theatre of resistance' in the Ugandan context. As I discussed in the introduction, since colonisation, crisis and resistance mark Uganda's history. Theatre does not start a war but it provides information, which playwrights hope, will bring about change. Thus, artists as well as different ethnic communities have staged performances of crisis, protest and resistance, which are inevitably indebted to the economic, and historical social and political conditions. The drama and performances examined in this study reflect these concerns in similar and different ways, always underlining issues of political freedom, peace, identity, corruption, tyranny and ethnic discrimination. In spite of the disparate Ugandan ethnic communities, these shared conditions underscore my decision to speak of this theatre as Ugandan theatre.

Notes

Preface

[1] The language of the Baganda of Buganda is Luganda and their culture is Kiganda. Similarly, for Bunyoro, the people are Banyoro and speak Lunyolo while the Acholi speak Acholi.
[2] Participants in these performances, as noted by Ludoviko Serwanga and Julian Tamusuza, were trained through an apprenticeship scheme.
[3] See Samuel R. Karugire (1980), *A Political History of Buganda*, Nairobi: Heinemann Educational Books, p. 187.
[4] See Ali Mazrui (1975), *Soldiers and Kinsmen in Uganda*, California, Berverly Hills: Sage Publications Inc., p. 43.
[5] Writing in *Buganda in Modern History*, A.D Low quotes one of Obote's Ministers who stated that Obote's attack on Kabaka Mutesa and the Baganda was aimed at eradicating 'Bugandaism', 'tribalism' and 'religionism' (1971: 242).
[6]These groups included the government's UNLA, Isaac Nkwanga's FEDEMU, Andrew Kayiira`s FEDEMU and Moses Ali's FUNA Federal Democratic Movement of Uganda (FEDEMU), Uganda Freedom Movement (UFM), Former Uganda National Army (FUNA) and Uganda National Rescue Front (UNRF).

Chapter 1

[1] Despite the conspicuous absence of women in *formal* theatre, apart from Rose Mbowa and Elvania Zirimu, in pre-colonial and colonial Africa, gendered participation in performances were more complex. Women played prominent roles as storytellers, dancers, folk soloists, and mediums in ritual festivals. Examples of socio-political critical performances of the colonial period, such as the Columbia Company recordings of popular indigenous music, include performances by women. Thus, although women were not allowed to play drums and their participation was restricted to singing and dancing, their evaluation of the music was valued since they would refuse to perform a dance if the instrumentation and choral accompaniment were poor; hence, they wielded artistic and critical influence through indirect means.
[2] Performance as a concept, Taylor and Townsend explain, 'includes practices such as ritual and dance which do not presume the notion of a "stage"' (2008:2).
[3] While Elvania Zirimu remained in the country throughout Amin's dictatorship, Serumaga, Ruganda and p'Chong escaped the dreaded secret State Research Bureau police and joined the dissident opposition movements in Kenya.
[4] According to Nkashama, there can be no essentialised 'African theatre' for it is just another space, an event, a complex mix of performances, evoked through spaces or performances, writing, creative performance, acting or utterances.
[5] Gilles Deleuze (1998), *Essays Critical and Clinical*, London: Verso.

[6] See also Benjamin D. Powell and Tracy Stephenson Shaffer (2009), 'On the Haunting of Performance Studies' in *Liminalities: A Journal of Performance Studies,* Vol. 5, No. 1, pp. 1 - 18 http://liminalities.net/5-1/hauntology.pdf.
[7] See Mahmood Mamdani (2001), 'Beyond Settler and Native as Political Identities: Overcoming the Political Legacy of Colonialism' in *Comparative Studies in Society and History*, Vol. 43, No. 4, pp. 651-664.
[8] See Sylvia Nanyonga-Tamusuza (2005), *Baakisimba: Gender in the Music and Dance of the Baganda People of Uganda*, London and New York: Routledge, p. 77; See James Scott's chapters (1990), 'The Public Transcript as a Respectable Performance' and 'Voices under Domination: The Arts of Political Disguise', *Domination and the Arts of Resistance: Hidden Transcripts*, New Haven and London: Yale University Press, p. 4; and Helen Nabasuta Mugambi, (1994), 'Intersection: Gender, Orality, Text, and Songs', *Research in African Literatures* Vol. 25, No. 3, pp. 47-70.
[9] In Luganda, *-temba*, the root word for *katemba,* signifies possession and trance, or to climb on to the head. See Kasule (1993), *Tradition and Contemporary Influences Upon Ugandan Theatre Between 1960 and 1990*, Leeds University: Unpublished Phd Dissertation.
[10] Similar to other African communities, in the Baganda and Banyoro belief systems, when the spirits manifest themselves on an individual, sometimes during *kusamira*, religious ritual festivals, they transform him to another state of being.
[11] He is popularly known as *Siyasa*, an allusion to his witty character - a contemporary version of the Hare, the trickster character in the Baganda folklore.
[12] Soon after the 1977, Festival of African Arts and Culture (FESTAC) Amin 'disappeared', several artists including Byron Kawadwa and Galabuzi Mukasa.
[13] A lot of these ideas are revealed in the work of other scholars such as Isidero Okpewho, Karin Barber, Sandra Richards, Harry Elam Jr, Kacke Gotrick and Wole Soyinka.

Chapter 2

[1] See Kasule (1993), *Traditional and Contemporary Influences Upon Ugandan Theatre Between 1960 and 1990.*
[2] This paper was presented in 1977 at the Second World Black and African Festival of Arts and Culture (FESTAC '77) held in Lagos, Nigeria.
[3] This was initially brought about by the unfinished colonial administration's attempt to redistribute land, previously captured by Buganda, to Bunyoro Kingdoms.
[4] Ngugi wa Thiongo writes that under colonial rule in Kenya, the government banned the song-poem-dance, '*Kanyegenyuri'*, which the women had devised to mark the killing of, Harry Thuku, a freedom fighter (1998: 64-65).
[5] In Bill Ashcroft *et. al's* (1994) *The Empire Writes Back* they state: 'The crucial function of language as a medium of power demands that postcolonial writing define itself by seizing the language of the centre and re-placing it in a discourse fully adapted to the colonized place' (p 39).

[6] Serumaga's unscripted plays were successful overseas - being performed in England, Kenya, The Philippines, and Poland - but not in Uganda. Few went to see them, but those few learned from his experiments, as did his students.

[7] When Renga Moi's wife delivers twins, he is reminded that custom forbids him to shed blood before he has performed the twin rites. But before he is able to perform the rituals, his village is invaded, therefore, spurred on by a sense of duty and personal bravery, he goes to war to save the village. At home, the village is plagued with problems that are in turn blamed on the 'unpurified' twins. Before he discovers that the village diviner has sacrificed his twins, Renga Moi is forced to undergo purification.

[8] As Serumaga demonstrates, the articulation of resistance and transgression is a central concern in Ugandan drama of this period. Pre-colonial performance forms and cultural expressions have a high artistic and political value; their staging may be acts of defiance challenging a political or social order; it may be a celebration and an affirmation of a community's existence; finally, it may reinforce a *status quo*. Dramas, for instance, *Renga Moi*, *Majangwa* and Kawadwa's *Makula ga Kulabako,* embody the character of post-colonial performance that suggests ways in which, theatre, through the uses of indigenous forms, can allow a resistance to political and social issues.

[9] The perception may be that the first UPC government was unproductive, however, it can be stated that that was the period that introduced several national infrastructures in the areas of economic activities, education, health and roads.

[10] Loosely, bowl lyres players, but in general, stringed instrument musicians.

[11] Drummers or generally groups of drummers and dancers.

[12] Ludoviko Serwanga, an elderly musician in Lutengo, Kyaggwe, in Uganda informed me in an interview that when he started playing, apart from court musicians, most travelling musicians did not have permanent homes.

[13] Although *Majangwa* has Beckettian elements, seen in the context of the Kiganda traditions, this is no absurdist play; there are theatrical borrowings from Kiganda oral and performance traditions, such as the mythic play-in-play, featuring Walumbe's and Kayiikuzi's scenic structures and the trope of resistance to hostile outsiders.

[14] In one interview, quoted in BBC's The Transcription Centre newsletter, *Cultural Events in Africa*, Serumaga states, '*Majangwa* ... is in many ways a synthesis of several strands in my theatrical development... such for example as its use of fact and legend, reality and myth and its exploitation of the subconscious fears within a basically conscious level' (1971: 2).

[15] Nakirijja's infertility is markedly comparable to Majangwa's impotence brought about by the crowds who cheered him to stage public performances of sexual acts with Nakirijja.

[16] It also alludes to post-colonial destruction and the contemporary political crisis.

[17] In another scene, Majangwa, for instance, attempts to explain to Nakirijja, his wife, the 'mysteries of the womb' through the double-coded legend of the two rivers, Mayanja Kato and Mayanja Waswa Mayanja Kato and Mayanja Waswa in Buganda.

[18] An apt example is, for instance, Wankoko's jig in the first scene of Kawadwa's *Oluyimba lwa Wankoko*.
[19] The drum is the symbol of the kingdom of Buganda and the major motif in the play.

Chapter 3

[1] A version of this chapter was originally published in the *African Performance Review* Vol. 3, No., 1, 2009.
[2] Kawadwa practised theatre beginning in the pre-independence period through to the height of Idi Amin's reign when, in 1977, the State Research Bureau agents murdered him. Through his work as playwright, director, actor, administrator - appointed Artistic Director of the National Cultural Centre in 1973 - and co-founder of Kampala City Players, Kawadwa was able to create a distinctive contemporary Ugandan theatre.
[3] This was a private recording company promoting indigenous Ugandan music and commercial broadcasting.
[4] The vernacular theatre, perhaps the only truly Africanised Ugandan institution, has been foremost in identifying society's shared responsibility in promoting tyranny.
[5] See Mbowa (1996), 'Theatre and Political Repression in Uganda' in *Research in African Literatures*, Vol. 27, No. 3, p. 91.
[6] Theatre advertisement and promotion, aided by *mafutamingis* (the new rich), seeking to show off their newly acquired wealth, followed the pattern of football club publicity.
[7] According to Mbowa (1996) the title, *Serwajja Okwota* [He Who Came to Warm Himself at the Fireside], 'is drawn from the proverb that warns of a lean hungry dog that warms itself at the master's bonfire only to drive him away in a bid to have it all to itself'. So, 'in the play, a male character "oils" his way into the life and house of a single woman, only to end up forcing her out of the house'. Mbowa explains that the plot 'echoes Obote's political manoeuvring in striking an alliance with the Kabaka Yekka party during the 1962 election and his banishing it to political limbo four years later in the "pigeon-hole" Constitution' (p. 88).
[8] In addition to this, the casting of already popular radio and popular music performers, added to the play's initial appeal.
[9] In the play's context, '*makula*' is used to describe a handsome man, a beautiful woman, a beautiful / treasured possession, or present.
[10] For instance, when I worked with Sserukenya on the 1989 production, music rehearsals were an opportunity to interrogate indigenous popular performance forms. Although by this time Uganda was experiencing a political transformation from military dictatorships to the National Resistance Movement's grass-root 'no-party' politics, the play's views on politicians were (and are) still relevant. We did not rehearse performance into fixed roles, but had the actors 'harness' their creativity and positive exhibitionism.

[11] In the 1989 production, Wankoko (Stephen Luswata) stuck two thumbs (claws) on either side of an actress to emphasize the character of Wankoko, and the image of the claw.
[12] Macpherson interviewed by the present writer on 9 May 1991 at Windemere, UK.
[13] *Document No. 2* proposed The National Service (1969); *Document No. 3, The Move to the Left* or *The Communication from the Chair* (1970), created a unified Civil Service. *Document No. 4* or *The Nakivubo Pronouncement* (1970) announced the nationalization of all imports and exports, a 60 per cent control of oil companies, banks and mines. *Document No. 5* or *Proposals for New Methods of Election of Representatives of the People to Parliament* (1970) introduced proportional representation or what was called 'three plus one'; a method of election requiring a candidate to stand and win elections in his own constituency, plus three others in the country (see Willets, 1975). At their launch, the government banned all political parties apart from UPC.

Chapter 4

[1] On the controversial role of the Resistance Councils in Uganda also see Mohamood Mamdani, 'Uganda in Transition: Two years of the NRA/NRM', Public lecture delivered at Makerere University, Kampala, 3 March 1988.
[2] See Kasule, 1993.
[3] That the new sub-culture of money, self-reliance and Europeanised behaviour, has affected society's attitude to death, is underlined by Lozio and Girigooli's animated fantasy of being wealthy individuals.
[4] Kiyingi in conversation with Kasule, 2009.
[5] For details of the Ten Point NRA Code of Conduct, see *Uganda Confidential*, Volume 17 May 1992.
[6] According to Robert Nviiri (2009), 'The bus, *Mpaawo Atalikaaba*, Reg. number 01LA06 was brought into operation shortly after the removal of [Godfrey] Binaisa in May 1980, but during that time it was used to ferry UNLA [Uganda National Liberation Army] soldiers (mainly of Acholi and Langi origin - a fact that brought about a Radio Katwe terminology for the LA markings in the number plate to be substituted for Langi-Acholi'. See "Who started 'Panda Gari' and 'Akandoya' in Uganda", http://ugandansatheart.org/2009/02/13/.
[7] Moses Serwadda, Lecturer in Dance and a professional drummer informed me that when he tried to find the whereabouts of Byron Kawadwa, after the latter had been disappeared by Amin, a member of the State Research Bureau told him, '*Ebiryo by'avunda* [The pumpkin is rotten]' (Conversation with Moses Serwadda, 1990).
[8] Ugandans euphemistically refer to the period as '*ebiseera bya dduka dduka* [the run for your life era]', literally, times when people were always on the run.
[9] The Narrator's interpretation of Jesus' reaction to his betrayal by society, reminds us of the betrayal of Professor Lule, the first President of Uganda after Idi Amin in 1979, by the National Consultative Council.

[10] The interim legislative council formed at Moshi, in Tanzania, at the beginning of the war against Amin.
[11] Unemployed tough and rough gangs that became synonymous with Amin's regime.
[12] Andrew M. Bell states that 'With the increased NRA threat, the UNLA changed tactics. Embarking on a massive civilian victimization campaign in the Luwero Triangle known as the "Grand Offensive", whole villages were emptied as the UNLA turned its firepower on local civilians' (Andrew, M. Bell, 2012: 14).

Chapter 5

[1] See Kasozi (1994), The *Social Origins of Violence in Uganda*, p. 84.
[2] Obbo further comments that in Amin's regime, 'Soldiering became a new door to social mobility, rather than the previous vehicles of education and land tenure' (1983: 313).
[3] The style is close to that used by early Uganda writers, p'Bitek and Tom Omara.
[4] Forests, lakes and rivers became dumping [burial] places for victims of institutionalised terrorism. Namanve forest, eight miles from Kampala City, is a forest reserve that was the most favoured dumping spot. In 1979, after the fall of Amin, former President Binaisa declared it a National Cemetery.
[5] See, Sir Apollo Kagwa (1956), *Engero za Baganda* (Baganda Folk Stories), (London: Sheldon Press) pp. 1-7. In his introduction, Lubwa p'Chong quotes Elvania Zirimu's translation, 'The Counsel of a Mad Man' (1980) as the source of his plot.
[6] Paulo Muwanga, a former Vice President and Minister of Defence, made the statement in 1989 before the Uganda Human Rights Commission in the Obote II government.
[7] Here Lubwa p'Chong adapts and directly translates the saying, '*Obusiru bumuzimbyeko akayumba*', which is in popular use at the time of writing *The Madman.*
[8]This is a parody of the unconstitutional laws imposed on Ugandans under the umbrella of 'Presidential Decrees'. We note that whereas Amin ruled by decrees, the post Amin liberation governments used 'Legal Notices' to impose laws outside the rule of parliament.

Chapter 6

[1] Ruganda uses the Banyankore version of the *Olugero lw'Akakookolo* (The Leper's Tale), to highlight the attitude of Tinka to Wamala her husband, and to underline the general disillusion of society towards the oppressive government.
[2] Retold as a story or performed as part of a drama during the Amin and Obote years of turmoil, the story had moral and political significance to parents who were becoming anxious about the increasing numbers of cross-indigenous marriages, mostly propagated by wealth. Additionally, it was one form of ridiculing the rulers

by projecting them as unworthy of the most beautiful girls (one symbol of the most achievable goals).
[3] Mbowa, observes how her 'production of [the play] was interdicted on the eve of the performance in 1978'. She suggests that the action was taken 'because the play makes reference to an "endless search for fat bottomed wives", which Amin's Ministry of Information's Censorship Board interpreted to refer to Amin's many wives and girlfriends' (Mbowa, 1994a: 123).
[4] Taylor herself, writing in *Disappearing Acts*, has questioned her reference to the 'Madres' activism' as performance (1997: 184).
[5] Amin and his military forces were schizophrenic, theatrical and ritualistic in their performance in real life; and so were the colonialists.

Chapter 7

[1] *Endongo/Ebidongo*, which originates from the Kiganda bowl lyre, *endongo*, is used interchangeably to describe guitarists or nightclub band.
[2] From interview with Drake Ssekeba, Uganda, 2007.
[3] By distancing themselves from popular stage performers, as jazz band artist Joanita Kawalya indicated when I interviewed her in 2010, contemporary popular musicians are claiming a space that lies between indigenous music and dramatic stage performances.
[4] Alice Lwanga interviewed by Sam Kasule at the National Theatre on 6 December, 2010.
[5] John W Katende also co-founded Kayaayu Film Players (later The Theatrikos) with Christopher Mukiibi.
[6] Although founded by Jimmy Katumba, Katende, a Kampala advocate, was the Chairman of the group and its most influential producer and playwright whose collaboration with Katumba included, among others, *The Dollar* and *The Inspector*.
[7] The use of a *lingua franca* with Luganda as a base but incorporating English, Swahili, Luo, Runyankore or Luganda is not universally appreciated.
[8] As the political situation deteriorated, night performances and night clubs went out of fashion forcing Zairean musicians to migrate to neighbouring countries and their patrons to go back to *ebinyumu,* the traditional day-time entertainment/festivals, *ekizibya*, trans-day/twilight performances and *ebikeesa*, all night performances.
[9] In the contemporary context, while artists such as Kibuuka and Senkubuge, have become critical of the popular construction of performers that locates a specific perception of dramatic stage performers as cheap comedians, most popular musicians are (ironically) identifying themselves with the a*badongo*, a concept, which describes indigenous travelling musicians and indigenous music ensembles who entertained people on parties and weddings.
[10] Katumba interviewed by the present writer at Theatre Excelsior, Kampala, October 31, 1990.
[11] See, Eckhard Breitinger (1992), 'Popular Urban Theatre in Uganda: between Self-help and Self-Enrichment', in *New Theatre Quarterly* VIII, 31, pp. 270-290.

[12] This is an area approximately thirty miles from Kampala, the capital of Uganda, that served as a base for Museveni's National Resistance Army guerrilla war.

[13] See Eckard Breitinger, 1992.

[14] This is followed by a heated argument, conducted in vulgar language, within which Kakinda ignorantly, albeit for comic reasons, interprets what Kunjani calls his prerogatives but the illiterate Kakinda pronounces as '*poti zo*', which literary interpreted means his potties. The overtones of the word '*poti*' are not lost on the audience who are aware of the way in which witch doctors and high-class women relate to each other. Yet Kakinda makes Milly pay thirty thousand shillings (about two hundred British pounds) before he can accept to sleep with her.

[15] The inefficient Ugandan Judiciary is ridiculed when an apparently senile high court judge, having slept throughout the court session, finds Kyambadde guilty and sentences him to death by hanging.

[16] At first, the Ebonies aimed at commentaries on love, hatred, jealousy and betrayal as the forerunners of war and violence, but in the late 1980s, they were preoccupied with AIDS. Shifting the focus to the role of honest love, marriage, and traditional communal values as vital weapons in the war against pre-marital sex, infidelity, illicit sex and the AIDS epidemic put them at the vanguard of the emerging theatre for conscientisation.

[17] Kihuguru is lawyer who refers to himself as one of the 'most important people in the country' just because he is a brother to the wife of a Deputy Minister of Industry.

[18] Sentamu Makumbi, '*Ddembe lyo: Okudibaga olulimi Oluganda ng'olutabiikirizaamu ennimi endala* (You are free to bastardise Luganda by mixing it with other languages)', *Ngabo* (Kampala), 26 March 1991.

[19] This cultural gesture, known as *okufuuwa* in Luganda, derives from a traditional practice at beer festivals in Buganda where, in order to show their appreciation for an outstanding musical or dance performance, an individual would blow a mouthful of beer at the performer's body.

[20] *Ensi*, in Luganda may be used to refer to either the country or the world.

[21] Mugambi notes a similar process in her discussion of the radio recording of *Imbalu*, Kadongo Kamu songs about the Bagishu circumcision rituals, sung in both Luganda and Lugishu.

[22] At this time, former members of Aim and Obote's armed forces, Tito Okello Bazilio Okello and Gad Wilson Toko were President, Commander of the Ugandan Army, and Minister of Defence, respectively.

[23] Indeed, during the 2009 Buganda Riots, fearing that the FM radios were mobilising people to revolt, the Broadcasting Council officially banned Radio Simba, *Akaboozi ku Bbiri*, Buganda's Central Broadcasting Service (CBS) as well as 'any open-air broadcasting. These were a very popular forum for public debate in local communities, known as *bimeeza* in Luganda [and] n the [whole] country on any topic' (*Human Rights Watch*, 2010: 4).

Chapter 8

[1] Conversely, *EkiNigeriya* is its opposite and describes Nollywood home movies in Uganda.
[2] Afri-Talent's television serial, *Ensitaano* aired on WBS TV (Wavah Broadcasting Services) between 2003 - 2005.
[3] Mariam Ndagire's *Tendo Sisters* (2009) originally run as a television serial but has now been made into a film
[4] Edward Kawere's *Zinnunula Omunaku (*1961) was the first full-length book of fiction written in Luganda.
[5] Wycliff Kiyingi's *Lozio Bba Ssesiriya* (1972) focuses on poverty and political unrest in Amin's Uganda.
[6] Shelters whose walls constructed using bamboo or *mabanda* in Luganda.
[7] Nuwa Sentongo was one of the early Ugandan playwrights writing in English. His play, *The Invisible Bond* (1999) has been widely performed in East and West Africa.
[8] Interview conducted on 7 April 2010.
[9] There was founded in 1898 in Algiers (North Africa) by Cardinal Lavigerie.
[10] In the present writer's recent discussion with the playwright - on 4 November 2010 - he informed me that government agents have ordered him to drop this title and replace it with *A Night in a Day* otherwise they would withdraw their cooperation on the project. He explained that they were concerned that the title would be negatively interpreted.
[11] Interview conducted on 9 April 2010.

Conclusion

[1] The ruling party has been tested by the emergence of a formidable parliamentary opposition, which, since 2010, has consistently won parliamentary by-elections.
[2] Although the Media Council reacted by banning the play however, under pressure from the public, they were forced to retract the decision.

BIBLIOGRAPHY

Primary Texts

Brecht, Bertolt (1975), *Mother Courage and her children : a chronicle of the Thirty Years War* / trans. by Eric Bentley, London: Eyre Methuen.

Eliot, T. S. (1937), *Murder in the Cathedral*, London Faber and Faber.

Gogol, Nikolai (1975) *The Government Inspector*, London: Methuen Publishing Ltd.

Katende, John and Jimmy Katumba (1986), 'Luwero Show', Unpublished.

Katende, John W and Jimmy Katumba (1988), 'Kakinda Show', (Unpublished).

Katende, John W (1989), *The Dollar*, Unpublished.

Katende, John W (1989), *The Inspector*, Unpublished.

Kawadwa, Byron (1965), *Kateyanira*, Unpublished.

Kawadwa, Byron (1966), *Serwajja Okwota*, Unpublished.

Kawadwa, Byron (1969), *St Lwanga*, Unpublished.

Kawadwa, Byron (1970), *Makula ga Kulabako* (Kulabako's Beauty), Unpublished.

Kawadwa, Byron (1971), *Oluyimba lwa Wankoko* (Song of Wankoko), Unpublished.

Kibuuka, Benoni and Charles Senkubuge (2011 -), *Ddube Atasasula Boda*, Unpublished.

Kibuuka, Benoni and Charles Senkubuge (2012), *Ggirikiti: State of the Nation*, Unpublished.

Kiyingi, Wycliff (1954), *Pio Mberenge Kamulali*, Unpublished.

Kiyingi, Wycliff (1960), *Ekiwonvu kye Ssenya,* (The Ssenya Valley), Unpublished.

Kiyingi, Wycliff (1960), *Wokulira*, Unpublished.

Kiyingi, Wycliff (1962), *Buli Enkya, Buli Ekiro* (Day In, Day Out), Unpublished.

Kiyingi, Wycliff (1969), *Omwana w'Omuntu* (The Son of Man), Unpublished.

Kiyingi, Wycliff (1970) *Nebuba Enkya Nebuba Eggulo*, Unpublished.

Kiyingi, Wycliff (1972), *Lozio Bba Ssesiriya*, Kampala: Jesse Development Co.

Kiyingi, Wycliff (1972), *Obwavu Musolo*, Unpublished.
Kiyingi, Wycliff (1972), *Ssempala bba Mukyala Ssempala*, Unpublished.
Kiyingi, Wycliff (1977), *Muduuma kwe Kwaffe*, Unpublished.
Mukulu, Alex (1993), *Wounds of Africa*, Unpublished.
p'Chong Lubwa, Cliff (1975), *Generosity Kills & The Last Safari*, Nairobi: East African Publishing House.
p'Chong Lubwa, Cliff (1983), *The Minister's Wife*, Kampala: New Expression Press.
p'Chong Lubwa, Cliff (1990), *The Madman*, Unpublished.
Ruganda, John (1972), *The Burdens*, Nairobi: Oxford University Press.
Ruganda, John (1973), *Covenant with Death* and *Black Mamba*, Nairobi: East African Publishing House.
Ruganda, John (1980), *The Floods*, Nairobi: East African Publishing House.
Ruganda, John (1982), *Music Without Tears*, Nairobi: Bookwise.
Rwangyezi, Stephen (2000), *Lawino and Ocol*, Unpublished.
Sentongo Nuwa (1999), *The Invisible Bond and Good Servants*, Kampala: MKM Publishers.
Sentongo, Nuwa (1975), *The City Game,* Unpublished.
Shaw, George Bernad (1946), *Androcles and The Lion: An Old Fable Renovated*, Harmondsworth, Penguin.
Simwogerere, Ashraf (1994), *Omuyaga mu Makoola*, Unpublished.
Soyinka, Wole (1963), *The Lion and the Jewel*, Oxford: Oxford University Press.
Soyinka, Wole (1965), *The Road*, Oxford: Oxford University Press.
Soyinka, Wole (1969), *The Trial of Brother Jero*, Oxford: Oxford University Press.
Sserumaga, Robert (1974), *Amayirikiti*, Unpublished.
Sserumaga, Robert (1974), *Majangwa: A Promise of Rains* and *A Play*, Nairobi: East African Literature Bureau.
Sserumaga, Robert (1974), *Renga Moi*, Unpublished.
Zirimu, Elvania Namukwaya (1973), *The Family Spear* in Gwyneth Henderson (ed.), *African Theatre*, London: Heinemann Inc.
Zirimu, Elvania Namukwaya (1975), *When the Hunchback Made Rain and Snoring Strangers*, Nairobi: East African Publishing House.

Zirimu, Elvania Namukwaya (1980), 'The Counsel of a Mad Man' in Elvania N. Zirimu, *Kamasiira and other Stories*, Nairobi: East African Publishing House.

Filmography

Kasujja, A. (2009), (dir.), *Omwoyo Omutono*, Kampala Videoplex.

MacDonald, Kevin (2007), (dr.), *The Last King of Scotland*, 20th Century Fox, 2007.

Ndagire, Mariam (2003), *Ensitaano*, Kampala, AfriTalent: Unpublished.

Ndagire, Mariam (2007), *Down This Road I Walk*, Kampala: Trendz Studios Ltd.

Ndagire, Mariam (2008), *Strength of a Stranger*, Kampala: Trendz Studios Ltd.

Ndagire, Mariam (2009), *Hearts in Pieces*, Kampala: Trendz Studios Ltd.

Simwogerere, Ashraf 1999), (dir.), *London Shock*, Kampala: Twinex Videos

Simwogerere, Ashraf (2005), (dir.), *Feelings Struggle*, Kampala: Twinex Videos.

Simwogerere, Ashraf (2006) (dir.) *Murder in the City*, Kampala: Twinex Videos.

Simwogerere, Ashraf (2006), (dir.), *Honourable*, Kampala: Twinex Videos.

Simwogerere, Ashraf (2009), (dir.), *Hope/Suubi*, Kampala: Twinex Videos.

Simwogerere, Ashraf (2009), (dir.), *Mukajanga*, Kampala: Twinex Videos.

Simwogerere, Ashraf (2009), (dir.), *Voice of Men on Domestic Violence*, Kampala: Twinex Videos.

Simwogerere, Ashraf (2010), *Museveni the Wildcat/A Night in A Day*, Kampala: Twinex.

Secondary Sources

Adesanya, Afolobe (2000), 'From Film to Video', Jonathan Hayes, *Nigerian Video Films*, Athens: Ohio University Press.

Albuquerque, Severino Joao (1991), *Violent Acts: A Study of Contemporary Latin American Theatre*, Detroit: Wayne State University Press, 1991.

Ali, Pincho (1967), 'The 1967 Republican Constitution of Uganda' in *Transition*, Vol. 7, No.111.

Ashcroft, Bill *et al* (1990), *The Empire Writes Back: Theory and Practice in Post-Colonial Literatures*, London: Routledge.

Banham, Martin (1990), 'Initiates and Outsiders: The Theatre of Africa in the Theatres of Europe' in *The University of Leeds Review*, Vol. 33.

Barsamian, D and E. Said (2003), *Culture and Resistance: Conversations with Edward W. Said*, Cambridge: South End Press.

Bell, Andrew M. (2012), 'The Role of Military Culture in Civilian Victimization during Counterinsurgency: Examining the Ugandan Civil Wars', a paper delivered at the 2012 Annual Meeting of the American Political Science Association Available at SSRN: http://ssrn.com/abstract=2106724.

Boan, Devon (1998), 'Call-and-Response: Parallel 'Slave Narrative' in August Wilson's *The Piano Lesson*' in *African American Review*, Vol. 32.

Breitinger, Eckhard (1992), 'Popular Urban Theatre in Uganda: between Self-Help and Self-Enrichment', *New Theatre Quarterly*, Vol. 3, No. 31.

Bukenya, Austin (2000), 'An Idiom of Blood: Pragmatic Interpretation of Terror and Violence in the Modern Ugandan Novel' in *Uganda Journal*, Vol. 46.

Campbell, Neil (2000), *The Cultures of the American New West*, Edinburgh: Edinburgh University Press.

Campbell, Neil (2008), *The Rhizomatic West: Representing the American West in a Transnational, Global, Media Age*, Lincoln and London: University of Nebrasaka Press.

Conteh-Morgan, John (1994), 'African Traditional Drama and Issues in Theatre Performance Criticism' in *Comparative Drama*, Vol. 28.

Coplan, David (2008), *Township Tonight! South Africa's Black City Music and Theatre*, Chicago IL and London: University of Chicago Press.

Davies, Carole Boyce (1996), 'Transformational Discourses, Afro-Diasporic Culture, and the Literary Imagination' in *Macalester International*, Vol. 3.

Deleuze, Gilles (1998), *Essays Critical and Clinical*, London: Verso.

De Graft, Joe (1972), 'Dramatic Questions' in Andrew Gurr and Angus Calder (eds.), *Writers in East Africa*, Nairobi: East African Literature Bureau.

Dovey, Lindiwe and Angela Impey (2010), "African Jim: sound, politics, and pleasure in early 'black' South African cinema" in *Journal of African Cultural Studies*, Vol. 22, No. 1.

Enns, Adolf (1985), 'The Clocks Have Stopped in Uganda' in Cole P. Dodge, Paul D. Wiebe (eds.), *Crisis in Uganda: The Breakdown of Health Services*, Oxford: Pergamon Press.

Fallers, Lloyd A. (1964), 'Social Stratification in Traditional Buganda' in L. A Fallers (ed.), *The Kings Men*, London: Oxford University Press.

Filewood, Alan (1994), 'Receiving Aboriginality: Tomson Highway and the Crisis of Cultural Authenticity' in *Theatre Journal,* Vol. 46, No. 3.

Franco, Jean (1975), 'Dependency Theory and Literary Hitory: The Case of Latin America' in *Minnesota Review*, No. 5.

Gambaro, Griselda (1967), *El Campo* (The Camp), Buenos Aires: Ediciones Insurrexit (Trans. William I. Oliver, *Voices of Change in the Spanish American Theatre*, Austin: University of Texas Press, 1971).

Gambaro, Griselda (1972), *Information para extranjeros* / 'Information for Foreigners', Trans. Marguerute Feitlowitz, (Unpublished), performed in workshop, River Arts Repertory Theatre, New York.

Gambaro, Griselda (1989), *Las paredes* with Eldesatino and Los siameses, Trans. Marguerite Feitlowirz as 'The Walls', (Unpublished), staged at River Arts Repertory, N.Y.

Gikandi, Simon (2000), *Ngugi was Thiongo*, Cambridge: Cambridge University Press.

Gikandi, Simon and Evan Mwangi (2007), *The Columbia Guide to East African Literature in English Since 1945 (Columbia Guides to Literature Since 1945)*, New York, NY: Columbia University Press.

Gilroy, Paul (1993), The *Black Atlantic: Modernity and Double Consciousness*. Cambridge: Harvard University Press.

Grainge, Paul (2003), 'Introduction: Memory and Popular Film' in Paul Grainge (ed.), *Memory and Popular Film*, Manchester: Manchester University Press.

Hamid Naficy, Hamid (2001), *An Accented Cinema: Exilic and. Diasporic Filmmaking*, Princeton and Oxford: Princeton University Press.

Haynes, Jonathan (2000), *Nigerian Video Films*, Athens: Ohio University Press.

Haynes, Jonathan and Okome, Onookome (2000), 'Evolving Popular Media: Nigerian Video Films', Haynes, Jonathan, *Nigerian Video Films*, Athens: Ohio University Press.

Hutchison, Yvette (2005), 'Truth or Bust: Consensualising a Historic Narrative or Provoking through Theatre. The Place of the Personal Narrative in the Truth and Reconciliation Commission' in *Contemporary Theatre Review*, Vol. 15, No. 3.

Iliffe, John (2005), *Honour in African History* Cambridge: Cambridge University Press.

Impey, Angela and Dovey, Lindiwe (2010), "African Jim: Sound, Politics, and Pleasure in Early 'Black' South African Cinema" in *Journal of African Cultural Studies*, Vol. 22, No. 1.

Irele, Abiola (2001), *The African Imagination: Literature in Africa and the Black Diaspora*, Oxford University Press.

Irobi, Esiaba (2009), 'The Persistence of African Performance Aesthetics in the North American Diaspora - August Wilson, Ntozake Shange and DJanet Sears' in Christine Matzke and Osita Okagbue, *African Theatre Diasporas*, Woodbridge: James Currey.

Johnson, Janet and Robert Serumaga (1970), '*Uganda's experimental theatre*' in *African Arts* Vol. 3, No. 3.

Kagwa, Apollo (1934), *The Customs of the Baganda* (Translated by Ernest Balintuma Kalibbala), New York: Columbia University Press.

Karugire, Samuel R. (1980), *A Political History of Buganda*, Nairobi: Heinemann Educational Books.

Kasozi, Abdu B., *et al* (1994), *The Social Origins of Violence in Uganda, 1964-1985*, Ithaca, Ne: McGill Queens University Press.

Kasozi, Abdu B., (1994), *The Social Origins of Violence in Uganda, 1964-1985*, Montreal, McGill: Queen's University Press.

Kassimir, Ronald (1991), 'Complex Martyrs: Symbols of Catholic Church Transformation and Political Differentiation in Uganda' in *African Affairs*, 1991, Vol. 90, No. 360.

Kasule, Sam (1993), *Traditional and Contemporary Influences Upon Ugandan Theatre Between 1960 and 1990*, Leeds University, Unpublished Ph. D Thesis.

Kasule, Sam (2010), 'Don't Talk into my Talk': Oral Narratives, Cultural Identity & Popular Performance in Colonial Uganda' in Yvette Hutchinson (ed.), *African Theatre 9: Histories 1850-1950*, Woodbridge: James Currey.

Kavanagh, Robert Mshengu (1985), *Theatre and Cultural Struggle in South Africa,* London: Zed Press.

Kawadwa, Byron (1973), National Theatre Board of Trustees Minutes.

Kawere, Edward, K N (1961), *Zinnunula Omunaku,* London: Nelson.

Kiwanuka, M.S (1971), *A History of Buganda*, London: Longman Group Ltd.

Kiyimba, Abbasi (2008), 'Male Identity and Female Space in the Fiction of Ugandan Women Writers' in *Journal of International Women's Studies* Vol. 9, No. 3.

Langseth, Petter and Rick Stapenhurst (1997), *National Integrity System: Country Studies EDI Working Papers*, Washington DC: World Bank.

Lawoko, Apollo (2005), *The Dungeons of Nakasero*, Kampala: JANyeko Publishing Centre Ltd.

Lipsitz, George (2001), *Time Passages: Collective Memory and American Popular Culture*, Minneapolis, MN: University of Minnesota Press.

Low, A. D (1971), *Buganda in Modern History*, London: Weidenfeld and Nicolson.

Makumbi, Sentamu (1991), '*Ddembe lyo: Okudibaga olulimi Oluganda ng'olutabiikirizaamu ennimi endala* (You are free to bastardise Luganda by mixing it with other languages)' in *Ngabo* (Kampala), 26 March 1991.

Mamdani, Mahmood (1988), 'Uganda in Transition: Two Years of the NRA/NRM', Public Lecture delivered at Makerere University, Kampala.

Mamdani, Mahmood (2001), 'Beyond Settler and Native as Political Identities: Overcoming the Political Legacy of Colonialism' in *Comparative Studies in Society and History*, Vol. 43, No. 4.

Mazrui, Ali A. (1975*), Soldiers and Kinsmen in Uganda*, California, Beverly Hills: Sage Publications Inc.

Mazrui, Ali (1980), 'Between Development and Decay: Anarchy, Tyranny and Progress under Idi Amin' in *Third World Quarterly*, Vol. 2, No. 1.

Mbowa, Rose (1994), 'Artists under Siege: Theatre and the Dictatorial Regimes in Uganda' in Eckhard Breitinger (ed.), *Theatre and Performance in Africa: Intercultural Perspectives*, Bayreuth African Studies 31.

Mbowa, Rose (1996a), 'Theatre and political repression in Uganda' in *Research in African Literatures*, Vol. 27, No. 3.

Mbowa, Rose (1996b), 'Trends in Ugandan Theatre Since 1965' in Eckhard Breitinger (ed), D*efining New Idioms and Alternative Forms of Expression: Asnel Papers 1*, Amsterdam: Rodopi.

Mbowa, Rose (1999), 'Luganda Theatre and Its Audience' in *Bayreuth African Studies Series*, Issue 39.

McNulty, Eugene (2011), "Before the Law(s): Wole Soyinka's *Death and the King's Horseman* and the Passages of 'bare life' in *Postcolonial Text*, Vol. 6, No. 3.

McPherson, Margaret (1976), 'What happened to Majangwa?' in *Mawazo*, Vol. II, No. 4.

Minority Rights Group Report (1986), *Uganda and Sudan – North and South*, London: Minority Rights Groups Ltd., No. 66.

Moliere, Jean-Baptiste (2004 edition), *The Miser and Other Plays*, (Trans., David Coward), London: Penguin Classics.

Mugambi, Helen Nabasuuta (1994), 'Intersection: Gender, Orality, Text, and Songs' in *Research in African Literatures*, Vol. 25, No. 3.

Mugambi, Helen Nabasuuta (1994), 'From Radio to Video: Migratory Texts in Contemporary Luganda Song Narratives and Performances' in *Institute for Advanced Study and Research in the African Humanities: Media, Popular Culture, and 'the Public'* in *Africa*, No. 8.

Mugambi, Helen Nabasuuta (1997), 'From Story to Song: Gender, Nationhood, and the Migratory Text' in Maria Grosz-Ngate and Omari Kokole (eds.), *Gendered Encounters: Challenging Cultural*

Boundaries and Social Hierarchies in Africa, New York: Routledge Press.

Mugambi, Helen Nabasuuta (2005), 'Speaking in Song: Power, Subversion and the Postcolonial Text' in *Canadian Review of Contemporary Literature*, Vol. 32, No. 3-4.

Mulvey, Laura (1988), "Afterthoughts on 'Visual Pleasure and Narrative Cinema' inspired by Duel in the Sun" in Constance Penley (ed.), *Feminism and Film Theory*, New York: Routledge.

Museveni, Yoweri (1997), *Sowing the Mustard Seed: The Struggle for Freedom and Democracy in Uganda*, London: Macmillan.

Musisi, Nakanyike B. (1991), '"Elite Polygyny" and Buganda State Formation' in *Signs*, Vol. 16, No. 4.

Mutibwa, Phares (1992), *Uganda Since Independence: A Story of Unfulfilled Hopes*, London: Hurst and Company, 1992.

Nanyonga-Tamusuza, Sylvia (2002), 'Gender, Ethnicity and Politics in Kadongo-Kamu Music of Uganda: Analyzing the Song Kayanda' in Mai Palmberg and Annemette Kirkegaard (eds.), *Playing with Identities in Contemporary Music in Africa*, Uppsala: Nordiska Afrikainstitutet.

Nanyonga-Tamusuza, Sylvia (2005), *Baakisimba: Gender in the Music and Dance of the Baganda People of Uganda*, London & New York: Routledge.

Neale, Steve (1998), "Vanishing Americans: racial and Ethnic Issues in the Interpretation and Context of Post-War 'Pro-Indian' Westerns" in Edward Buscombe and Roberta E. Pearson (eds.), *Back in the Saddle Again: New Essays on the Western*, London: British Film Institute.

Ngugi wa Thiong'o (1997), 'Enactments of Power: The Politics of Performance Space' in *TDR* Vol. 41, No. 3.

Ngugi wa Thiong'o (1998), *Penpoints, Gunpoints, and Dreams: Towards a Critical Theory of the Arts and the State in Africa*, Oxford & New York: Oxford University Press, 1998.

Ngugi wa Thiong'o (2007), 'Notes towards a Performance Theory of Orature' in *Performance Research*, Volume 12, No, 3. Available at http://www.ohio.edu/people/hartleyg/ref/NgugiOrature.html.

Nkashama, Pius Ngandu (2004), 'Theatricality and Social Mimodrama' in John Conteh Morgan and Teju- Molan Olaniyan (eds.), *African Drama and Performance*, Bloomington: Indiana University Press.

Nviiri, Robert (2009), "Who started 'Panda Gari' and 'Akandoya' in Uganda", http://ugandansatheart.org/2009/02/13/.

Obbo, Christine (1979), 'Village strangers in Buganda Society' in William A Shack and Elliot Percival Skinner, *Strangers in African Societies*, Berkley: University of California Press.

Obbo, Christine (1983), 'What Went Wrong in Uganda?: Problems and Solutions' in *Canadian Journal of African Studies*, Vol. 17, No 2.

Okagbue, Osita (2009), *Culture and Identity in African and Caribbean Theatre*, London: Adonis & Abbey Publishers Ltd.

Okpewho, Isidore (1983), *Myth in Africa: A Study of Its Aesthetic and Cultural Relevance*, Cambridge: Cambridge University Press.

Okpewho, Isidore (2003), in 'Oral Tradition: Do Storytellers Lie?' in *Journal of Folklore Research*, Vol. 40, No. 3.

p'Bitek, Okot (1986), *Artist, the Ruler: Essays on Art, Culture, and Values, including extracts from Song of soldier* and *White Teeth Make People Laugh on Earth*, Nairobi: Heinemann.

p'Chong Lubwa, Cliff (1985), Interview with Alex Tetteh-Lartey of the BBC Africa Service Programme in *Arts on Africa*, London.

Pelegri, Teresa Requena (2008), 'Translating the African American experience on the stage' in *Transfer*, Vol. III, No. I.

Perham, Margery and Mary Bull (ed.) (1959), *The Diaries of Lord Lugard, Volume Three,* Evanston, Ill: Northwestern University Press.

Powell, Benjamin D. and Tracy Stephenson Shaffer (2009), 'On the Haunting of Performance Studies' in *Liminalities: A Journal of Performance Studies*, Vol. 5, No. 1. http://liminalities.net/5-1/hauntology.pdf.

Preston, J. (1992), 'Weesagechak begins to dance: Native Earth Performing Arts Inc' in *The Drama Review,* Vol. 36, No. 1.

Puga, Elena (2003), 'Carlos Manuel Varela and the Role of Memory in Covert Resistance' in *Latin American Theatre Review*, Vol. 36, No. 2.

Puga, Elena (2008), *Memory, Testimony, and Allegory in South American Theatre: Upstaging Dictatorship*, New York and Abingdon: Routledge 2008.

Pulitano, Elvira (2003), *Toward a Native American Critical Theory*. Lincoln: University of Nebraska Press.

Quigley, Austin E. (1985), *The Modern Stage and Other Worlds*, London: Taylor & Francis.

Ramírez, Elizabeth C. (2000), *Chicanas/Latinas in American Theatre: A History of. Performance*, Bloomington: Indiana University Press, 2000.

Roscoe, John (1965), *The Baganda: An Account of Their Native Customs and Beliefs*, London: F.Cass.

Rose, Tricia (1994), *Black Noise*, Hanover: University Press New England.

Scott, James (1990), *Domination and the Arts of Resistance: Hidden Transcripts*, New Haven and London: Yale University Press.

Sekamwa, John C. (1990), *Enkuluze y'Eddiini y'Abaganda Eye'nnono* (*A Baganda Traditional Religion Dictionary*), Kampala: Wood Printers and Stationers.

Serumaga, Robert (1971), 'A Mirror of Integration' in Cosmo Pieterse and Donald Munro, (eds.), *Protest and Conflict in African Literature*, New York: Africana Publishing.

Serumaga, Robert (1973), 'Interview with Barbara Kimenye' in *Cultural Events in Africa*, Issues 94-105, Cambridge: African Studies Centre, University of Cambridge.

Sontag, Susan (1989), *Under the Sign of Saturn*, New York: Noonday Press.

Soyinka, Wole (1988), 'Language as a Boundary' in *Art, Dialogue, and Outrage: Essays on Art and Literature,* Ibadan: New Horn Press.

Sseremba, George Bwanika (2008), *Robert Serumaga and the Golden Age of Uganda's Theatre*: *Solipsism*, *Activism*, *Innovation* (1969-1979), Trinity College Dublin, Unpublished Ph. D Thesis.

Sserumaga, Robert (1973), 'Interview with Barbara Kimenye', *Cultural Events in Africa*, Issues 94-105, Cambridge: African Studies Centre, University of Cambridge

Tamale, Sylvia (1999), *When Hens Begin to Crow: Gender and Parliamentary Politics in Uganda*, Boulder: Westview Press.

Tamale, Sylvia (2004), 'Gender Trauma in Africa: Enhancing Women's Links to Resources' in *Journal of Africa Law*, Vol. 48, No. 1.

Taylor, Diana and Sarah J. Townsend (2008), *Stages of Conflict: A Critical Anthology of Latin American Theatre and Performance*, Ann Arbor: University of Michigan Press.

Taylor, Diana (1991), *Theatre of Crisis: Drama and Politics in Latin America*. Lexington (KY): University Press of Kentucky.

Taylor, Diana (1997), *Disappearing Acts: Spectacles of Gender and Nationalism in Argentina's "Dirty War"*, Durham, NC: Duke University Press.

Taylor, Diana (1998), 'A Savage Performance: Guillermo Gómez-Peña and Coco Fusco's Couple in the Cage' in *The Drama Review* Vol. 42, No. 2.

Taylor, Diana (2002), '"You Are Here": The DNA of Performance' in *The Drama Review*, Vol. 46 No. 1.

Taylor, Diana (2003), *The Archive and the Repertoire: Performing Cultural Memory in the Americas*. Durham: Duke University Press.

Taylor, Diana (2004), 'Scenes of Cognition: Performance and Conquest' in *Theatre Journal*, Vol. 56, No.

Taylor, Diana (2005), 'Performing the Claim: Cultural Agents Act Out in Tepoztlán', *Review: Literature and Arts of the Americas*,' Vol. 38, No.2.

Taylor, Diana (2011), 'Memory, Trauma, Performance' in *ALETRIA*, Vol. 21, No. 1.

Thomas, H. B. and Robert Scott (1935), *The Story of Uganda*, London: Oxford University Press.

Uganda Confidential, Vol. 17, May 1992.

Washington, Mary Helen (1998), '"Disturbing the Peace: What Happens to American Studies If You Put African American Studies at the Centre?": Presidential Address to the American Studies Association' in *American Quarterly*, Vol. 50, No. 1.

Willets, Peter (1975), 'The Politics of Uganda as a One-Party State' in *African Affairs*, Vol. 74, No. 296.

Wrigley, Christopher (1996), *Kingship and State: The Buganda Dynasty*, Cambridge: Cambridge University Press.

Zirimu, Elvania Namukwaya (1976), 'Your Experience is Your Truth' in *Ngoma Newsletter*, No. 6.

Zirimu, Pio (1969), 'Interview with Dr Pio Zirimu', (interviewed by Heinz Freidberger), *Cultural Events in Africa*, London: The Transcription Centre, No. 52.

Zirimu, Pio (1971), 'An Approach to Black Aesthetics' in Pio Zirimu and Andrew Gurr (eds.), *Black Aesthetics*, Nairobi: East African Literature Bureau.

Zirimu, Pio and Bukenya, Bukenya L (1986), 'Oracy as a Skill and As a Tool for African Development' in Joseph Ohiomogben Okpaku *et al.*, *Black Civilization and African Languages*, Lagos: The Centre for Black and African Arts and Civilization.

Discography

Kagoda, Sam (1978), *Nfiire*.
Kagoda, Sam (1978), *Ma Abong*.
Katumba, Jimmy (1989), *Tusonge paka Kampala*.
Kigozi, Fred (1990), *Owino Yafuuka Muzadde*, Kampala: Kasajja and Sons Studio.
Luyima, Fred (1986), *Apana Wuwa Ssasi*, Kampala: Kasajja and Sons Studio.
Lwanga, Peter (1979), 'Give Me Back My Freedom'.
Lwanga, Peter (1979), 'Days of Gun Rule'.
Lwanga, Peter (1986), *Nnyonta Nsaba ku Mazzi*.
Lwanga, Peter (1988), *Muhara wa Nyamaizi*.
Lwanga, Peter (1988), *Njabala*.
Mugula, Dan (1980), *Ensi Ekyuuka*, Kampala: Kasajja and Sons Studio.
Mukaabya, Willy (1988), *Kayanda Oliila Otya mu Sowani Yange*? Kampala: Kasajja and Sons Studio.
National Resistance Army (1986), *Moto na Waka*.
Ssebadduka, Christopher (1969) *Enkomerero eri Kumpi*, Kampala: Kasajja and Sons Studio.

INDEX

www.ingramcontent.com/pod-product-compliance
Lightning Source LLC
LaVergne TN
LVHW010939100826
845153LV00001B/97

* 9 7 8 1 9 0 9 1 1 2 3 8 4 *